CINNAMON
Kitchen
THE COOKBOOK

CINNAMON
Kitchen
THE COOKBOOK

VIVEK SINGH

A.

First published in Great Britain in
2012 byAbsolute Press, an imprint
of Bloomsbury Publishing Plc

Absolute Press
Scarborough House
29 James Street West
Bath BA1 2BT

Phone 44 (0) 1225 316013
Fax 44 (0) 1225 445836
E-mail info@absolutepress.co.uk
Website www.absolutepress.co.uk

Publisher Jon Croft
Commissioning Editor Meg Avent
Art Direction Matt Inwood
Design Matt Inwood
Editor Lucy Bridgers
Assistant Editor Beverly LeBlanc
Indexer Zoe Ross
Photography Lara Holmes
Food Styling Vivek Singh and
Abdul Yaseen
Props Styling Matt Inwood and
Lara Holmes

ISBN: 9781906650803

Printed and bound in Italy by
Printer Trento

Bloomsbury Publishing Plc
50 Bedford Square
London WC1B 3DP
www.bloomsbury.com

A note about the text
This book is set in Sabon and
Eagle. Sabon was designed by
Jan Tschichold in 1964. The roman
design is based on type by Claude
Garamond, whereas the italic
design is based on types by
Robert Granjon. The Eagle series of
typefaces are based on an original
design of Eagle Bold by Morris
Fuller Benton.

CONTENTS

INTRODUCTION

THE CLUB GOES CASUAL

The historic Western Courtyard in Devonshire Square where Cinnamon Kitchen and Anise is housed today was first acquired by the East India Company back in 1820 and at the time was used to store spices, forming part of a gigantic warehouse complex covering over five acres. I was first shown around the area in 2007 and I just couldn't imagine a better setting for The Cinnamon Club's new and more casual manifestation than a spice warehouse that once stored India's then premier export and that would shortly house India's best known export of modern times – the Indian restaurant!

But the real reason behind the creation of Cinnamon Kitchen and Anise was much more than the chance to offer a dining space in an old spice warehouse once owned by the East India Company. The idea of Cinnamon Kitchen had begun to take root some years before – ironically, at the time when The Cinnamon Club was already creating waves with its fine dining menu and upmarket approach towards Indian food.

The Cinnamon Club serves no fewer than 100,000 guests per year and yet I am still asked if it is an exclusive, members-only destination! Unashamedly luxurious and high-end it might be, but I always intended it to be a welcoming place, open to all, serving extraordinary Indian food in an extraordinary setting. Although The Cinnamon Club is internationally renowned, I did not want my cuisine to become the preserve exclusively of the famous and fortunate. I had begun to realise that it is entirely possible to be as creative and innovative as we are at The Cinnamon Club while managing to appeal to a wider, more diverse clientele. Indeed, food of this calibre certainly doesn't need to be restricted to the confines of an exclusive restaurant. With this in mind,

Cinnamon Kitchen was born, billed as The Cinnamon Club's younger, cooler sister restaurant in the City and housed – rather appropriately – inside the historic East India Company spice warehouse.

Our menu uses the same local, seasonal ingredients and creative, bold cooking techniques as those that feature at The Cinnamon Club but in a far more relaxed, flexible format. Diners at The Cinnamon Club can enjoy anything up to nine courses and beyond, whereas Cinnamon Kitchen is more about the option of dropping by for a light lunch or a couple of smaller, quicker plates for dinner. We decided on adding a glamorous bar space, which we called Anise, adding to the casual feel by serving pre- or post-work drinks and a few small spicy nibbles. And I insisted on access to a gorgeous tandoor grill, where I now host my cooking masterclasses throughout the year.

At Anise we showcase trademark Cinnamon innovation and creativity, only in this case with drinks! Our cocktails reinterpret classic Western cocktails with homemade spice infusions and exotic tropical juices. Sometimes the drinks also draw inspiration from traditional Indian favourites such as lassis and thandhai, combining them with spirits to create drinks that are very new, very now. And once again this makes a nod to the old East Indian spice warehouse where we find ourselves today.

Put simply, my intention for Cinnamon Kitchen has always been to create a space where great food is served in a casual and friendly atmosphere, free of formality and dress codes – a place where the expectations of the Cinnamon dining experience are fully met in a relaxed, informal setting.

FOOD FOR THOUGHT

When I was developing the menu for The Cinnamon Club, there was great emphasis on exclusive, expensive ingredients. I wanted high-end cooking in a high-end environment; my younger self thought the more expensive the dishes, the more expensive the experience and the more seriously people took it. But from the outset I envisaged Cinnamon Kitchen to be quite different. I wanted the menu to be appealing, fresh, and creative – offering the same quality experience diners had come to expect from The Cinnamon Club but not necessarily the most expensive.

As a young chef, I subscribed to the view that the more resources you had, the more creativity you had, but as my thinking evolved and my experience developed I began to believe that creativity is not linked to the depth of your pockets. Some of my best creations recently have come from the simplest, most cost-effective ingredients.

Cinnamon Kitchen gives me the opportunity to be more creative with lesser-known cuts of meat – it pushes my team to think outside the box and to run free with ideas. Good examples are our much-loved vindaloo of ox cheek and our rump of lamb – both

of which have become Cinnamon Kitchen signature dishes, making use of cuts that would never feature on the Cinnamon Club menu.

In terms of simplicity, not everything comes with an accompaniment – for example, many dishes come with simple salads, while some are served straight up. This lighter, streamlined approach also means that we can have more of a focus on the main components of the dish and let them be the star on the plate.

I also decided to feature an open tandoor grill at the Cinnamon Kitchen – helping to simplify the menu, taking it away from a traditional, structured three-course format to one offering a mix of small plates, grills, larger dishes and desserts and bringing with it a great sense of theatricality. This simple pared-down attitude to the menu has resulted in the creation of some of Cinnamon Kitchen's strongest and best-loved plates, such as the bhaditrakha – a simple grilled dish of lamb escalope that dates back to A.D.1127. Traditionally, the escalope is cut very thinly, spiced and cooked on a grill; Cinnamon Kitchen enables us to do just that and present it in its purest form, the way it was intended.

THE MEN BEHIND THE MENU

While our diners and their experience are key to
Cinnamon Kitchen, so is our team of chefs, and I
was fortunate enough to take a very strong core of
people directly from The Cinnamon Club when I
first opened Cinnamon Kitchen. At the helm is head
chef, Abdul Yaseen – renowned among his peers for
brilliantly combining seasonal European produce with
Indian spicing and cooking techniques – while heading
up Anise was Prakash Shetty from The Cinnamon
Club's bar team, an Indian mixologist who really
loved the idea of combining the new with the old.
I believe Cinnamon Kitchen is as much about
recognising the ambition and aspirations of the
kitchen team as it is about its guests. Recognised in
many arenas – three-time winner of the Square Meal
Canapé Cup, two-time winner of the British BBQ
Championships, and winner of the Craft Guild of
Chefs and Best New Restaurant in 2009 awards –
my team really have the talent to take Cinnamon
Kitchen to the next level.

HAVE BOOK, WILL COOK

The dishes at Cinnamon Kitchen and within this book
draw on inspiration from across the Indian subcontinent, with influences from the east, west, north and
south. They are also shaped by Middle Eastern
influences – so the recipes that you will discover
within this book are multicultural, varied, and above
all, modern. With minimum preparation but maximum
impact, these recipes don't call for a special occasion –
they are for every day. Now, go forth and cook!

Anyone who has enjoyed a curry understands that it has an addictive quality. In fact, 'curry cravings' can become quite overpowering. The pleasure sensations associated with eating curry comes from the release of endorphins, thanks to the spices, and it is this buzz that drives many of us to a curry house when we have abstained for any period of time. This is particularly true when returning from a holiday abroad where curries might be off the menu. I still remember when my wife and I arrived back from our first visit to France several years ago – we headed straight to the kitchen and made dozens of poories and a very spicy potato curry to go with it! Little wonder, then, that when British officers returned from the Subcontinent in the days of the East India Company they would bring back sacks of spices, and sometimes even their own cooks, in order to be able to enjoy the thrill of a curry at home.

The art of spicing in India is arguably the most sophisticated and complex in the world. In other cuisines, spices tend to be used in isolation or in simple combinations. But Indian cooking relies on an intimate knowledge of the way spices work together. Aside from the flavour, it's important to consider the texture, the sequence in which the spices are added, and how long they are cooked for. It is an exciting and challenging way of cooking, and one in which there is always something new to learn.

Spices are used in Indian cooking for a variety of reasons. Foremost among these, of course, is flavour, but historically they were just as important for preservation. In the days before refrigeration, spices helped to prolong the shelf life of fresh ingredients and were also used to tenderise meat. Traditional Ayurvedic medicine relies on spices for medicinal and health benefits. Aside from using spices to treat certain ailments, an Ayurvedic practitioner will assess a person's body type and advise what spices and other foods are beneficial for them to consume and which are best avoided. It is common knowledge in India that cumin aids digestion, while coriander is an antipyretic which is often used to reduce fever in children and has a cooling effect on the body. Fennel seeds aid digestion and are used as a mouth freshener. Turmeric is an effective antiseptic and is frequently used to treat minor cuts, burns and wounds, as well as building up the body's resistance to minor ailments.

Each curry is unique, however, and to understand a particular dish you must look beyond the spicing and acknowledge what the French would call the *terroir*. But cuisines merge and develop every day. Very few chefs' larders are restricted to what's local, and in theory anything goes, with creativity encouraged. Curry, like everything else, is subject to a continual process of change, evolving in order to remain accessible, popular and relevant.

It wouldn't be right to associate curry exclusively with Indian food or ingredients; it needs to be viewed in the context of the influences that have shaped it on a global scale. Even though curry has its culinary roots in India, it has travelled across the world and evolved. We Indians should not arrogantly assume that we own curry. Like Indian cuisine as a whole, it has become an international phenomenon that has thrived as a result of interest, interaction and innovation.

BASIC

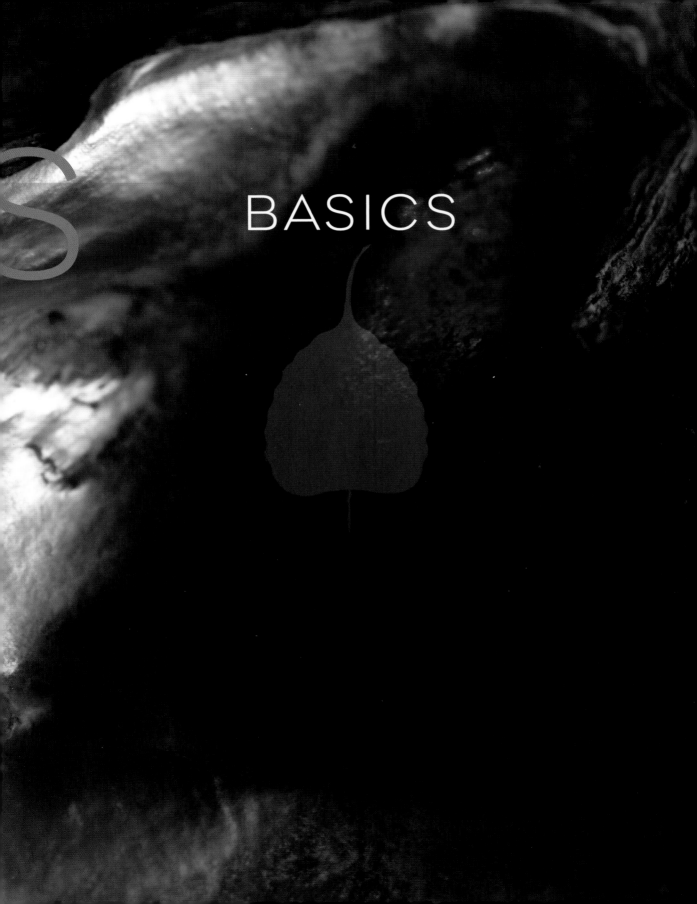

BASICS

BASIC PREPARATIONS

ROASTING AND CRUSHING SEEDS

Put the seeds in a moderately hot frying pan or under the grill and roast for a minute or two, until they are just dried, but not coloured. Remove from the heat and pound together in a mortar and pestle, until the seeds are crushed but still coarse enough to be identified separately. If you want to grind the seeds to a powder, the best way to do this is in a spice grinder.

GINGER PASTE

Makes about 6 tablespoons

175g fresh ginger, peeled
75ml water

Chop up the ginger and process it to a paste with the water in a food processor or blender. The paste will keep for 1 week in the fridge.

GARLIC PASTE

Makes about 6 tablespoons

175g peeled garlic
75ml water

Chop up the garlic and process it to a paste with the water in a food processor or blender. The paste will keep for 1 week in the fridge, but if you substitute oil for water, it should keep for 2 weeks.

GINGER AND GARLIC PASTE

Makes about 8 tablespoons

Almost all recipes require ginger paste and garlic paste. There are certain preparations in which more garlic is required. In that case, the pastes could be made separately as described below.

100g ginger peeled
75g garlic peeled
175ml water

Chop up the ginger and garlic and blend it to a fine, thick paste using water.

FRIED CASHEW PASTE

Makes about 300g

200g cashew nuts
2 tablespoons vegetable oil
200ml water

Fry the cashew nuts in the oil until golden, then remove from the pan with a slotted spoon. Soak the nuts in the water for 20 minutes, then drain. Blend to a smooth paste in a food processor or blender with 5 tablespoons of water. The paste will keep for 4 days in the fridge.

BOILED CASHEW PASTE

Makes about 400g

200g cashew nuts
1 blade of mace
1 green cardamom pod
approximately 500ml water

Soak the cashew nuts in enough water to cover for 10 minutes, then drain. Put them in a pan with the mace, cardamom and water, bring to the boil and simmer for 25 minutes. Remove from the heat and leave to cool. Blend to a smooth paste in a food processor or blender with 100ml water. The paste will keep for 4 days in the fridge.

FRIED ONION PASTE

Makes about 150g

600g whole onions, sliced
oil for frying
200ml water

Deep-fry the onions in medium-hot oil until golden brown, then remove and drain on kitchen paper. Put them in a food processor or blender with the water and process until smooth. The paste will keep for 1 week in the fridge. For additional flavour, the water can be replaced with yoghurt, in which case it will make about 350g paste.

The resultant fried onion paste is used as a base and thickening for various sauces, such as Rajasthani roast venison.

BOILED ONION PASTE

Makes about 300g

1 large onion, finely chopped
250ml water

Put the onion and the water in a small pan and simmer for 15–20 minutes, until the onion is soft. Purée in a food processor or blender until smooth. The paste will keep for 3 days in the fridge.

SPICED CASHEW NUT PASTE

This is a pretty widely used base for lots of Indian sauces which don't use red chillies.
This base is also used as a thickener for lots of sauces cooked in industrial kitchens prepared in bulk. This paste is also referred to as a korma sauce.

150g cashew nuts
2 large onions, diced
2 blades mace
3 green cardamom pods
300ml water
470g plain yoghurt

In a saucepan combine the cashew nuts, diced onions, mace and cardamom and cover with the water. Bring to the boil and cook until the cashew nuts and onions are soft. Strain the mixture and then purée until smooth. Return the sauce to the pan and bring to the boil again, remove from the heat and gradually add the yoghurt, a spoonful at a time, stirring to prevent it from splitting, until all the yoghurt is fully incorporated. Allow the sauce to simmer for a further 5–6 minutes. Remove the pan from the heat, cool, cover and set aside in the fridge until required.

MACE AND CARDAMOM POWDER

½ nutmeg
40g blades of mace
50g green cardamom pods

Grate the nutmeg or pound it with a mortar and pestle to break it up. Dry all the spices in a microwave for 30 seconds, then grind them to a fine powder. Store in an airtight container and use within 3–4 days.

GARAM MASALA (HOT SPICE MIX)

There are many versions of garam masala; this is a good basic one. It is generally added to dishes towards the end of cooking – to impart flavour, not to add heat as its name might suggest ('garam' means hot and 'masala' means mix). I would always recommend making your own garam masala if possible. Commercial blends use a larger proportion of cheaper spices and less of the more expensive aromatic ones, such as cardamom and cinnamon.

50g coriander seeds
50g cumin seeds
20 green cardamom pods
10 cinnamon sticks, about 2.5cm long
2 tablespoons cloves
10 blades of mace
10 black cardamom pods
½ nutmeg
1 tablespoon black peppercorns
4 bay leaves

Put all the ingredients on a baking tray and place in a low oven (about 110°C/Gas Mark ¼) for 3–5 minutes; this intensifies the flavours. You could even dry the spices in a microwave for 20 seconds or so. Grind everything to a fine powder in a spice grinder, then sieve the mixture to remove any husks or large particles. Store in an airtight container and use within 2 weeks.

GARAM MASALA (C.K. MIX)

In the Cinnamon Kitchen's version of garam masala, these extra spices are added to the mixture above to impart a special flavour. We also use rock moss, which, like ajino moto in Chinese cooking, brings out the flavours of other ingredients and is absolutely natural and safe. We fly this special ingredient in from India.

petals from 1 pink rose, dried
5 star anise
1 tablespoon fennel seeds
5g patthar ke phool (rock moss)

SOOLA MASALA (RAJASTHANI SPICE MIX)

3 tablespoons mustard oil or
   sunflower oil
I tablespoon ghee
4 garlic cloves, finely sliced
IO cloves
I teaspoon black peppercorns
I tablespoon cumin seeds
5 green cardamom pods
2 tablespoons coriander seeds
3 tablespoons fennel seeds
4 tablespoons chopped coriander
   stems
4 tablespoons Crisp Fried Onions
   (page 23)

Heat the mustard oil in a heavy-based frying pan to smoking point, then add the ghee to reduce the temperature, then add the sliced garlic and cook until it turns a golden colour, then add the cloves and let them pop. Add peppercorns, cumin seeds and cardamom in that order, then add the coriander seeds, fennel seeds, chopped coriander stems, stir quickly, remove from the heat and leave to cool. Add fried onions and transfer the mixture to a food processor or blender and blend to obtain a fine paste.

KADHAI MASALA

This dry, roasted and coarsely crushed mix of spices can be used in curries for flavour and is equally effective as a crust for steaks and stir-fries giving added texture. A very versatile mix.

Makes about 5 tablespoons
I tablespoon cumin seeds
I tablespoon coriander seeds
I teaspoon chilli flakes
I teaspoon black peppercorns
2 tablespoons fennel seeds

Heat a small heavy-based frying pan on a medium heat, and add the cumin and coriander seeds. Dry-roast for a minute or so until aromatic, then add the chilli flakes, peppercorns and fennel seeds. Stir to mix well for 1 minute or so, remove from the heat and transfer to a different container immediately to cool down. Once cooled, grind coarsely, little by little, in a mortar and pestle to obtain an even texture.

If you end up making more than you need, you can store the leftovers in an airtight container away from direct light and heat, for up to 2 weeks.

BENGALI GARAM MASALA

This is a very simple spice mix used to finish off Bengali style dishes and lends the characteristic fragrant aromas reminiscent of Bengali households.

I teaspoon cumin seeds
I tablespoon coriander seeds
I cinnamon stick
seeds from 4 green cardamom pods

Heat a small heavy-based saucepan on a medium heat and dry-roast the cumin, coriander and cinnamon for a couple of minutes, then add the green cardamom and stir for 30 seconds or so until the aromas of the spices begin to be released. Remove from the heat and allow to cool to room temperature, then grind to a fine powder using either a spice mill or a mortar and pestle.

It's best to grind just what you need, but you can store any leftovers in an airtight container away from direct light for up to 2 weeks.

CHAAT MASALA

Originally devised to give an extra zing and tang to 'chaats' (snacks) in north India, this wonderful finishing spice is something most tandoori chefs can't and won't do without. I noticed there are several mentions of chaat masala in our recipes, so it's worth giving a recipe for it. They're easily available in most good Asian grocery stores and online and go by the name – Chunky Chaat Masala'!

I tablespoon cumin seeds
I teaspoon black peppercorns
¼ teaspoon ajowan seeds
I teaspoon white pepper
¼ teaspoon ground asafoetida
I tablespoon rock salt
2 tablespoons dried mango powder
I teaspoon dried ginger powder

½ teaspoon Garam Masala (page 20)
¼ teaspoon tartaric acid (optional)
½ teaspoon dried mint leaves, crushed
1½ teaspoons dried fenugreek leaves, crushed between your fingertips
1 teaspoon salt
1 tablespoon icing sugar

Heat a small heavy-based saucepan on a medium heat and dry-roast the cumin lightly on medium heat for 2–3 minutes until the flavours just begin to be released. The cumin should not be allowed to change colour or become too roasted. Allow it to cool down and then add all the other ingredients.

Grind in a spice mill and pass through a sieve. Stored in an airtight jar, this can keep for months. Sprinkled on kebabs or on salads, it adds a nice tangy, zingy flavour.

GHEE
MAKES ABOUT 200G

This is clarified butter, the pure butterfat, clear and golden in colour. Traditionally in India, ghee is made from buffalo milk, which is higher in fat than cow's milk, and the process involves souring milk to make yoghurt and then churning this to yield butter. Unsalted butter made from cow's milk can also be used for ghee. Ghee is the purest form of butterfat. In the days when there was no refrigeration, milk was converted to ghee to lengthen the storage life. Clarifying butter stops it from going rancid and it is also able to withstand high temperatures and constant reheating.

250g unsalted butter

Place the butter in a pan to heat. As the butter melts, let the liquid come to the boil. Simmer the melted butter for 20–30 minutes. The froth that appears on the surface should be skimmed off and discarded.

The butter will separate into cooked milk solids, which will settle to the bottom of the pan, and clear, golden ghee at the top. Carefully pour off the ghee into a bowl.

As the liquid ghee cools, it will solidify, but will be creamy, like soft margarine. Ghee can be stored for several years, in a cool dark, place in a tin or glass container, free from any obvious moisture or contact with water.

CORIANDER CHUTNEY

100g fresh coriander, washed thoroughly to remove any grit
3 garlic cloves, peeled
3 green chillies, stalks removed
3 tablespoons vegetable oil
1 teaspoon salt
½ teaspoon sugar
juice of ½ lemon

Put all the ingredients in a blender or food processor and blend to a soft, spoonable consistency. If you cover the surface with a layer of oil the chutney can be stored in a fridge for up to 1 week.

TOMATO AND ONION SEED CHUTNEY

This is my mother's recipe for tomato chutney; I've loved it ever since I was a child. Hot, sweet and complex, this is just the best chutney there is. It works well as a spread in breads too, I've devoured many 'poories' (fried breads) with nothing else but this chutney!

3 tablespoons vegetable oil
1 bay leaf
2 whole dry red chillies
½ teaspoon black onion seeds
500g tomatoes, washed and chopped
1½ teaspoons red chilli powder
1 teaspoon salt
200g sugar
2 tablespoons raisins

Heat the oil in a heavy-based pan to smoking point, add the bay leaf, whole red chillies and the onion seeds. When they crackle add the chopped tomatoes and cook until soft and disintegrated. Stir in the chilli powder, salt, sugar and raisins and cook for 15 minutes until most of the moisture has evaporated and the chutney turns glossy. Remove from the heat and allow to cool. Store in an airtight jar for up to 2 weeks.

CRISP FRIED ONIONS

MAKES ABOUT 110G

600g onions, sliced
at least 600ml
vegetable or corn oil for deep-frying

Deep-fry the onions in medium-hot oil until golden brown, then remove and drain on kitchen paper. Store in an airtight container for up to 1 week.

PICKLED ONIONS

½ teaspoon black onion seeds
2 tablespoons white wine vinegar
100ml water
½ teaspoon salt
1 teaspoon sugar
1cm piece of ginger, peeled and finely chopped
2.5cm piece of beetroot (optional)
250g pearl onions

First make the dressing. Heat a small heavy-based saucepan on a low heat and dry-roast the onion seeds for 30 seconds, then add the vinegar and water and bring to the boil. Reduce the heat and add salt, sugar and ginger and beetroot, if using, and remove from the heat. Add the onions to the liquid and let it cool on its own. Once cooled, pour into a bottle or jar, seal and refrigerate. It will keep for up to 2 weeks.

KADHAI SAUCE

Serves 4-6

This is a concassé-style sauce that is frequently used to stir-fry or cook 'kadhai'-style dishes – hence the name.

3 tablespoons vegetable oil
2 whole dried chillies, broken and seeds discarded
1 teaspoon cumin seeds
1 teaspoon coriander seeds
4 garlic cloves, finely chopped
2 onions, finely chopped
2.5cm piece fresh ginger, peeled and finely chopped
2 green chillies, finely chopped
600g fresh ripe tomatoes, finely chopped
1½ teaspoons salt
1 teaspoon Garam Masala (page 20)
1½ teaspoons dried fenugreek leaves, crushed between your fingertips
1 teaspoon sugar (optional)
1 teaspoon Kadhai Masala (page 21)

Heat the oil in a deep heavy-based pan, add the dried broken chillies and stir, let the colour deepen, then add cumin and coriander seeds and let them crackle for 30 seconds or so. Now add the garlic and let it colour, then add onion and cook for 5–7 minutes until it is translucent and slightly golden at the edges, now add ginger and green chillies and add the chopped tomatoes, reduce the heat and cook until all the moisture has evaporated and the oil begins to separate. Add the salt, garam masala and fenugreek and stir. Add the sugar, if needed, and finish with the kadhai masala.

This sauce can be cooled and stored in the fridge for up to a week.

CURRIED YOGHURT

1 tablespoon vegetable oil
½ teaspoon mustard seeds
4 fresh curry leaves
½ teaspoon ground turmeric
1 teaspoon sugar
½ teaspoon salt
250g Greek yoghurt
2.5cm piece of fresh ginger, peeled and finely chopped
1 green chilli, finely chopped

Heat the oil to smoking point in a heavy-based pan, then add the mustard seeds and curry leaves. When they start to crackle, quickly stir in the turmeric, sugar and salt. Add this tempering to the yoghurt, along with the ginger and chillies, and mix well. Adjust the seasoning before serving. This is particularly good with asparagus (see page 191).

BASIC TECHNIQUES

For the purposes of this book, if I were to mention only cooking techniques that are specific to India or just used in Indian cooking, you would not be able to cook half the recipes here. Quite rightly, as a sign of the times, you will notice that the cooking techniques used for various recipes in the book are not just Indian; some are quite Western or European as well. As we have done with the rest of the concept, even in cooking, we have tried to use the best of both worlds and, hence, you will commonly find Western techniques such as searing, oven roasting, grilling, etc. used in many of our recipes.

We are also aware of the limitations that many recipe books present in terms of availability of equipment and also techniques. Therefore, each and every recipe has been tried in a Western domestic kitchen to ensure that the techniques are easy to follow, and most of them are easy to reproduce with the equipment commonly available in most readers' kitchens.

TANDOOR COOKING

In India, mostly northern India, meats, fish and certain vegetables are marinated and cooked on skewers in clay ovens, which are traditionally coal fired. Skewers rest on the sides of the oven, thereby exposing the meat or vegetables to intense heat from the coal flames. The juices that drip on to the burning coal create a smoke that imparts a characteristic flavour to the meat, fish or vegetable cooked in the tandoor.

MARINADES

Originally used to flavour meats with different spices, marinades are often used as a tenderiser and also to protect the meat from the intense heat, thereby keeping it moist upon cooking. Some people also say marinades preserved the meat for longer, thereby preventing it from going off.

It's difficult to say which was the original reason for people to start marinating meat, but our guess is that initially it was used to preserve and tenderise; and, as people discovered how it enhanced flavour, more and more spices were introduced, creating the broad range of marinades used today.

Some people mix all the spices together and mix in the meat or fish, but I prefer to use the two-marinade method. Initially just salt, ginger and garlic pastes, and sometimes lemon juice, are applied and left until the meat or fish has absorbed their flavours. The second marinade contains a more complex mix of spices, plus yoghurt and sometimes cheese. Because a little moisture has been drawn out during the first marinating period the meat or fish takes to the second marinade much better. This method of double marinating also helps to create complex layers of spices in the final dish.

TENDERISERS IN INDIAN COOKING

In some cases meat is mechanically tenderised – for example, by beating with a mallet or pricking, but in most recipes traditionally certain ingredients are used to tenderise meats.

The most commonly used tenderiser is green (raw) papaya, either grated flesh or as juice. It's simply added to the meat with the marinade and allowed to marinate for 1–4 hours, or even overnight in some cases, depending upon the size and cut of meat. Papaya contains an anzyme called papain which breaks down the meat's tissues, thus making it tender. The advantage of using raw papaya is that it has a neutral taste and does not alter the flavour of the final dish.

The other commonly used tenderiser is unripe pineapple juice. This produces an enzyme reaction similar to that of papaya with a similar result on the meat. The difference is that pineapple juice can be tasted in the final dish and therefore can be used only with dishes that take well to it.

Different regions use different marinade ingredients and the one we use, if we have to, is called 'Kachri'. It's used predominantly in Rajasthan and is a complex fruit. When it's raw, it's used as a vegetable; in dried form, pounded it is a very effective and potent tenderiser for meat. It has an extremely hard exterior with numerous small seeds inside. The whole fruit is pounded to powder and added to meat with the marinade and spices.

The advantage of Kachri is that it does not alter the taste of the dish, although it does contribute a bit to the surface texture of the meat. You will not find mention of tenderisers in any of the recipes in this book, as the quality of meat available here today is very good and less and less tenderising is required. As long as you can ensure high quality and fresh supplies, you can now focus more on enhancing the flavour, rather than improving the texture.

SMOKING

This a technique used in traditional Muslim cooking to impart a smoky flavour. After the meat or fish has been marinated, and just before cooking, it is placed in a large container with a small bowl in the centre. The traditional approach is to place a piece of burning charcoal in the small bowl and sprinkle it with cloves or cardamom or any other spices that you want to flavour the smoke with. Then some ghee or oil is poured over the charcoal to generate plenty of smoke. The large container is quickly covered with either a lid or aluminium foil to prevent the smoke from escaping, and it is left for 20 minutes or so for the smoke to permeate the food. The meat can then be fried, grilled or cooked in a tandoor.

As it may be impractical and dangerous to handle burning charcoal in a domestic kitchen I suggest this process be conducted outdoors and with a lot of care. Another option is to heat ghee or oil to smoking point in a pan and add twice the usual quantity of spice and, as it burns in the pan, discard the spices and add the oil or ghee to the dish. It's not quite the real thing, but provides plenty of flavour and has the advantage of being safe.

SEARING

Although this technique is not commonly used in kitchens in India, at the Cinnamon Club – in our endeavour to use the best of all worlds – we use it quite often.

The process of sealing the juices of the meat by placing the meat or fish on a hot pan or grill is called searing and is quite commonly used in European kitchens. In fact, some dishes, such as scallops, are completely cooked this way, but other dishes, such as venison, require further cooking in an oven or under a grill, or several minutes resting in a warm place.

This technique can also be used to achieve the tandoor effect at home, where a tandoor or maybe even a barbecue, is not available.

COOKING UTENSILS

Most of the recipes in this book do not require any special utensils. Traditionally in India a lot of heavy copper pots and pans are used but they can be quite difficult to maintain. Stainless steel pans with alloy bottoms are easily available nowadays and work well on different heat sources. A good set of pots and pans is always a worthwhile investment for any keen cook.

Cast iron frying pan
When you are searing meat and fish, a large, cast iron frying pan is invaluable, as it can be transferred directly to the oven to complete the cooking.

Mortar and pestle
Either a brass mortar and pestle or a stone one is a good investment. It allows you to grind spices freshly and to exactly the texture required. Freshly roasted and ground spices are always advised in preference to ready-prepared spices, as some of the flavour is lost upon keeping.

Food Processor
A food processor is the most effortless way of making spice pastes. Choose a heavy-duty model with a powerful motor.

Spice Mill
In Indian homes, spice mixes are made into a paste by grinding them on a stone slab with a little water, using another piece of stone. For larger quantities, people use wet stone grinders, which are motorised versions of the same concept. Grinding the spices with water means that the spices contribute to the body of the sauce and the water prevents them burning. With changing times, more and more households have done away with stone grinders and use electric spice mills instead. They save a lot of time and mess.

HANDLING AND STORING SPICES

Most basic spices, such as cumin, coriander, red chilli and turmeric are easily available ready ground. More aromatic spices such as cardamom, cinnamon, cloves, mace and star anise should preferably be bought whole and ground just before use. If stored in ground form, spices should be kept in airtight containers, away from moisture and direct sunlight, and used within two weeks. Whole spices should be kept in the same way and used within six months.

TEMPERING

The Indian word 'tadka', or tempering, refers to the process of adding whole or broken spices to hot oil to release their flavours into it. Sometimes spices are also dry-roasted to release their flavours, and then added to dishes to flavour them, but this is not tempering.

In a lot of north Indian dishes, whole spices are added to hot oil or ghee in the beginning and then followed up with onions, tomatoes, garlic, ginger and other ground spices or spice pastes to complete the final dish.

However, some dishes, such as lentils or beans, are finished by adding hot ghee or oil, which has been tempered with spices such as chillies, cumin and garlic just before serving. This is often referred to as 'baghar'.

Tempering is usually a very fast process, and the sequence and timing of adding the different ingredients is crucial. If the correct sequence is not followed, some ingredients might get burnt, while others might be uncooked. The same would happen if there is too much or too little time between adding one ingredient and another, so it's advisable to first collect all the ingredients in the right quantities before starting the tempering.

The temperature of the medium, i.e. the oil or ghee, is also vital, as the medium needs to be hot for the full flavours to be extracted from the spices. The method of tempering adds flavour and also texture to the finished dish.

NORTH INDIAN TADKA

2 tablespoons ghee or vegetable oil
I dried whole chilli
I teaspoon cumin seeds
I teaspoon chopped garlic

Heat the ghee in a heavy-based pan to smoking point, add the chilli and allow the colour to darken, then add the cumin seeds and, as they crackle and pop, add the garlic and cook until golden and crisp. Immediately pour over your lentils, kadhi or curry and serve immediately.

SOUTH INDIAN TADKA OR TEMPERING

2 tablespoons vegetable oil
I dried whole chilli
pinch fenugreek seeds
I teaspoon mustard seeds
½ teaspoon white urad lentils
IO fresh curry leaves

Heat the oil in a heavy-based pan to smoking point, then add the chilli and allow the colour to darken, then add fenugreek and mustard seeds; let them crackle and pop for a minute or so and add the lentils. As they turn golden, almost immediately add the curry leaves, stir to mix well and pour over rice, vegetables, curries or lentils to finish your south Indian dish.

STAR

STARTERS

This recipe features a mix of cinnamon, cloves, fennel and black pepper all quite strong and almost as robust as the flavours associated with traditional game cooking in Rajasthan. Interestingly, mackerel stands up really well to such powerful spices and works brilliantly with the light salad of thinly sliced apples and shaved fennel, served on a simple yoghurt raita.

SERVES 4

GRILLED MACKEREL FILLETS WITH APPLE AND FENNEL SALAD

4 small mackerel fillets, pin-boned and trimmed
5cm piece of cinnamon stick
I teaspoon cloves
I teaspoon cumin seeds
I teaspoon fennel seeds
I teaspoon salt
½ teaspoon coarsely ground black pepper
I tablespoon vegetable oil
juice of ½ lemon
½ teaspoon Kashmiri red chilli powder for garnishing (or substitute smoked paprika)

For the yoghurt raita
200g plain yoghurt
½ teaspoon cumin seeds
½ teaspoon salt
½ teaspoon sugar
juice of ½ lemon

For the apple and fennel salad
I green apple, cored and thinly sliced
I bulb of fennel, finely shaved using a sharp mandolin or very thin knife, refreshed in iced water
a pinch of Chaat Masala (page 21)
juice of ½ lemon
I tablespoon chopped coriander stalk, washed
a pinch of salt
a pinch of sugar

Start by making the yoghurt raita. Whisk together the yoghurt with the rest of the raita ingredients, then pass through a sieve to lose any lumps. Cover and chill until required.

Wash and pat dry the mackerel fillets. Grind or pound together all the spices and salt to a coarse consistency in mortar and pestle, then sprinkle them over the mackerel on both sides. Mix together the oil and lemon juice and drizzle over the fish.

Place the mackerel under a preheated hot grill, skin side up, and grill for 6–8 minutes, until just cooked through and the flesh flakes.

For the salad, just before serving mix together all the ingredients. Divide the yoghurt raita between 4 plates, then top each with a mackerel and the salad, sprinkle with the chilli powder and serve immediately.

This was originally inspired by seeing tuna with mango on a Mexican restaurant menu and when I tried the dish I felt we could do better. I was quite excited by the idea, but each time I prepared the dish it would be met with the same lukewarm response: is it Indian? The short answer was 'no', but then every time I sat on the sun-washed alfresco terrace at Cinnamon Kitchen in the summer of 2008, I imagined this dish working perfectly in the surroundings. So, that is how it made its way on to the menu, during the summer that followed, and it has returned each year since.

SERVES 4

SCALLOP, TUNA AND SALMON CEVICHE WITH MANGO

8 king scallops, cleaned and thinly sliced horizontally into 2 or 3 slices
115g tuna loin, cut in to 1cm dice
60g salmon fillet, skinned and cut into 1cm dice

For the dressing
½ green chilli, deseeded and finely chopped
½ ripe mango, cut into 1cm dice
½ raw green mango, cut into 5mm dice
1cm piece of fresh ginger, peeled and finely chopped
4 tablespoons canned mango purée
2 tablespoons pomegranate seeds
½ teaspoon black onion seeds
juice of 2 limes
a pinch of salt
a pinch of sugar

Prepare the dressing by mixing together all the ingredients. Check the seasoning; it should taste sweet, sour, sharp and hot all at the same time.

Put the scallops, tuna and salmon in a non-metallic bowl, pour the dressing over, stir lightly and leave to stand for 3–5 minutes, allowing the dressing to cure the seafood. When they are extremely fresh, high-quality scallops, salmon and tuna are good enough to eat raw, but when mixed with the dressing they turn slightly opaque, as if they have been cooked. Serve immediately, with salad leaves of your choice.

Everyone loves a moily, the coconut and turmeric curry from Kerala. While most Indian dishes pride themselves on using scores of ingredients and combinations of spices, the beautiful moily uses merely seven ingredients, plus oil, salt and whatever main ingredient you choose to cook in it. Even after twenty years of cooking, there has not been one instance when people haven't been wowed by its simplicity. You can serve this as a soup or as a main course, using shrimp, just about any seafood, chicken or, as in this instance, mussels. I like to serve this with either fresh naan bread or some rice pancakes (uttapams).

SERVES 4

MUSSEL MOILY SOUP

500g fresh mussels
2 tablespoons coconut or vegetable oil
20 fresh curry leaves
6 green chillies, slit lengthways
I large onion, sliced
2.5cm piece of fresh ginger, peeled and cut into thin strips
½ teaspoon ground turmeric
750ml fish or seafood stock
250ml thick coconut milk (if using canned, separate the thick milk from the thin part)
I teaspoon salt

Wash and scrub the mussels. Discard any open ones that do not close when tapped, then set aside the remainder.

Heat the oil in a large pan and add the curry leaves, chillies, onion and ginger and cook, stirring, for 6–8 minutes. When the onion is translucent, add the turmeric and stir for 30 seconds, then add the fish stock, coconut milk and salt. Bring to a simmer and allow to bubble for a couple of minutes.

Adjust the seasoning, if necessary, then add the mussels, cover the pan and simmer for 3–4 minutes. If all the mussels haven't opened, re-cover the pan and simmer another minute. Remove the pan from the heat and discard any unopened mussels. Serve with plenty of bread.

The explosion of flavours and textures from the roasted rice flakes and kadhai spices makes these seared scallops on a bed of stir-fried mushrooms one of those great dishes that are low in effort and high in impact. Impress your dinner guests with this easy dish!

SERVES 4

SEARED SCALLOPS WITH KADHAI MUSHROOMS AND TOMATO AND LIME LEAF SAUCE

12 fresh king scallops
2 tablespoons vegetable oil
1 teaspoon salt
5g butter
juice of ½ lemon
1 teaspoon coriander seeds, roasted and crushed
½ teaspoon cumin seeds, roasted and crushed
2 dried red chillies, roasted and crushed
1 tablespoon rice flakes (pawa), roasted (optional)

For the tomato and lime leaf sauce
1 tablespoon vegetable oil
1 lime leaf
2 tomatoes blended to a fine purée
¼ teaspoon Kadhai Masala (page 21)
2 tablespoons coconut milk
a pinch of salt
a pinch of sugar

For the mushrooms
2 tablespoons vegetable oil
3 garlic cloves, finely chopped
1 onion, thinly sliced
250g assorted mushrooms, trimmed and sliced
1cm piece of fresh ginger, peeled and finely chopped
2 green chillies, finely chopped
1 teaspoon salt
a pinch of sugar
1 tablespoon chopped fresh coriander
juice of ½ lime

To make the sauce, heat the oil in a heavy-based pan. Add the lime leaf and stir to infuse for about a minute, then add the tomato purée and heat through, stirring. Add the kadhai spices and coconut milk and mix well and bring to a simmer for 3–4 minutes. Correct the seasoning with salt and sugar and remove the pan from the heat.

Clean, wash and pat dry the scallops. Heat the oil in a large non-stick frying pan on a medium-high heat, add the scallops and sear for about 1 minute on each side. Sprinkle the salt on top, add the butter and continue cooking the scallops until they are golden brown. Turn the scallops over and repeat the process.

Take the scallops out of the pan and sprinkle with the lemon juice, crushed spices and rice flakes, if using, to form a crust. Set aside and keep hot.

To stir-fry the mushrooms, heat the oil in the same pan until very hot. Add the garlic and onion and stir-fry. When the onion is translucent, add the mushrooms, ginger and chillies and continue stir-frying. When the mushrooms have softened, add the salt and sugar and finish with the fresh coriander and lime juice.

Divide the mushrooms among 4 plates, top each with 3 scallops and serve with the sauce drizzled around.

Adding a sweet, glossy, jammy purée to sardines and then simply grilling them is a quick and easy way to impress your guests at a party. Simply increase the portion size if you want to serve this as a light main course for lunch. Alternatively, use the glaze to stir-fry shrimp or thinly sliced chicken, both of which make great starters, too.

SERVES 4

SARDINES WITH CHILLI AND APRICOT GLAZE

8 sardines, cleaned
2 tablespoons vegetable oil
1/2 teaspoon red chilli powder
1/2 teaspoon salt

For the spice paste
10 cloves
2.5cm piece of cinnamon stick
1/2 teaspoon black peppercorns
1/2 teaspoon coriander seeds
1/2 teaspoon cumin seeds
1 tablespoon vegetable oil
1/2 onion, finely chopped
2 garlic cloves, finely chopped
1 tablespoon tomato purée
1 1/2 teaspoons red chilli powder
2 ready-to-eat dried apricots, soaked
   and puréed
1 teaspoon salt
1/2 teaspoon sugar

Wash and pat dry the sardines. For the spice paste, roast the cloves, cinnamon stick, peppercorns, and coriander and cumin seeds together in a dry frying pan on a medium heat for 1–2 minutes, until they release their aromas, then quickly remove them from the heat. Grind or pound them to a fine powder in a spice mill or using a mortar and pestle and set aside. Heat the oil in a heavy-based pan, add the onion and sauté on a medium heat. When the onions are golden, add the garlic and cook for another minute. Add the tomato purée, chilli powder, apricot purée, salt and sugar and cook to a glossy, jammy consistency. Add the ground roasted spices, then remove the pan from the heat; set aside to cool.

Put the sardines on a plate and drizzle with the oil. Mix together the chilli powder and salt and sprinkle over the fish. Place the sardines on a ribbed pan or baking tray, skin side up. Using the back of a teaspoon, spread the spice paste evenly over each.

Transfer to an oven preheated to 200°C/Gas Mark 6 and roast for 7 minutes, until cooked through and the flesh flakes easily. Serve hot with a salad of your choice.

Think of this as a Thai-spiced tandoori fish tikka. I know that sounds bizarre, but it actually tastes really good! Nile perch is a rather underused fish in restaurants and in home kitchens, but it's widely available in supermarkets and is a good alternative to the bekti or pomfret used in India.
Nile perch has a particularly meaty texture, making it perfect to make kebabs with and it takes well to spice too. Any good satay-style sauce also makes a good accompaniment.

SERVES 4-6

CHAR-GRILLED NILE PERCH WITH LIME LEAF AND CHILLI

600g Nile perch fillets, or any other freshwater fish, cut into 16 x 4cm chunks
lime wedges, to serve

For the first marinade
1½ teaspoons salt
1 teaspoon Ginger Paste (page 18)
1 teaspoon Garlic Paste (page 18)
juice of ½ lemon
½ teaspoon black onion seeds (optional)

For the second marinade
75g Greek yoghurt
2.5cm piece of fresh ginger, peeled and finely chopped
5 lime leaves, finely chopped
2 green chillies, finely chopped
2 tablespoons chopped fresh coriander
1 tablespoon vegetable oil
1½ teaspoons red chilli powder
½ teaspoon sugar

Mix together all the ingredients for the first marinade, then rub them on to the perch, cover and leave to marinate for 15 minutes.

Mix together all the ingredients for the second marinade in a bowl. Gently fold in the fish and adjust the seasoning. Take care not to break up the fish. Set aside, covered, to marinate for another 30 minutes, or overnight in the fridge of you have time.

Soak 4 bamboo skewers in water for 30 minutes or so.

Thread the perch chunks on to the skewers. Try to get 4 pieces per skewer, but if they aren't the right size, don't worry! Cook the skewers on an oiled baking tray in an oven preheated to 220°C/ Gas Mark 7 for 10–12 minutes, turning them over once if the fish begins to colour too much. Alternatively, place them under a hot grill for about 6 minutes.

Remove the skewers from the oven and serve one skewer per person with lime wedges and salad leaves of your choice.

Vivek's tip
Do not thread the fish pieces too close to each other on the skewers. If there is some space between them the heat can penetrate better.

This is a good way of enjoying oysters with a difference – in other words, as if they had been cooked in a tandoor oven. But a word of warning first – if you're like me and like oysters any way they come, start with forty-eight oysters to get twenty-four cooked ones in the end. I can't resist devouring some of these raw with just the dressing!

SERVES 4

TANDOORI-SPICED OYSTERS

24 large oysters

For the dressing
½ teaspoon black onion seeds
100ml water
2 tablespoons white wine vinegar
1cm piece of fresh ginger, peeled and
    finely chopped
1 teaspoon sugar
½ teaspoon salt
2 red onions, finely chopped

For the marinade
1 tablespoon corn or vegetable oil
1 garlic clove, finely chopped
1 tablespoon gram (chickpea) flour
2 green chillies, finely chopped
1 tablespoon Ginger and Garlic Paste
    (page 18)
12g Greek yoghurt
1½ teaspoons chopped fresh
    coriander
½ teaspoon dried fenugreek leaves,
    crushed between your fingertips
½ teaspoon Garam Masala (page 20)
½ teaspoon ground turmeric
½ teaspoon salt
½ teaspoon sugar

To make the dressing, roast the onion seeds in a small dry saucepan on a medium heat for 30 seconds. Add the water and vinegar and bring to the boil. Reduce the heat and add the ginger, sugar and salt, then remove the pan from the heat. When the liquid stops boiling, add the onions and leave them to soften in the liquid as it cools. Strain and transfer to a bowl, cover and chill until ready to serve.

Meanwhile, remove the oysters from their shells and drain. Reserve the shells if you want to use them for serving or discard. Keep the oysters chilled.

To make the marinade, heat the oil in a small pan and add the garlic. When it turns golden, gradually add the gram flour, stirring on a low heat to prevent lumps from forming. When the flour turns golden brown, acquires a slightly sandy texture and releases a roasted aroma, remove the pan from heat, tip the roasted gram flour into a bowl and set aside to cool.

When the gram flour mixture is cool, combine it with the remaining marinade ingredients.

The marinade should have a thick, paste-like consistency. If it is too runny, refrigerate it for about 15 minutes to make it a bit firmer.

If you are cooking and serving the oysters on soaked bamboo skewers, soak 8 skewers in water for 30 minutes.

Thread 3 oysters with their marinade on each of the skewers, or arrange them on a grill rack. Cook them just for a minute or so under a very hot grill. Serve immediately with the dressing.

This is a very simple, yet effective starter, and I particularly like the way the umami-rich prawn flavour is intensified by the dried shrimp paste. It's a clever piece of traditional cooking, and the addition of red chard at the end adds a fresh touch. This also makes a great filling to use in wraps, and they can be passed around with drinks, so I'm suggesting a shopping list for a larger number.

SERVES 6 AS A STARTER, 10 FOR CANAPÉS WITH DRINKS

STIR-FRIED SHRIMPS WITH RED CHARD

2 tablespoons vegetable oil or ghee
1kg raw deveined and peeled shrimps
    or tiny prawns
300g red-veined chard leaves,
    washed and drained
juice of ½ lemon

For the Bengali shrimp paste
2 tablespoons vegetable oil
1cm piece of cinnamon stick
1 bay leaf
1 green cardamom pod
½ teaspoon cumin seeds
2 onions, finely chopped
1 teaspoon Ginger and Garlic Paste
    (page 18)
1 teaspoon salt
1 teaspoon sugar
50g tiny peeled shrimps, thawed if
    frozen, and finely chopped
2 tablespoons dried shrimps, soaked
    in warm water for 15 minutes and
    drained
2 tomatoes, finely chopped
1 teaspoon red chilli powder
½ teaspoon ground cumin
¼ teaspoon ground turmeric
125ml coconut milk
1 green chilli, slit lengthways
½ teaspoon Bengali Garam Masala
    (page 21)
juice of ½ lemon

For the Bengali shrimp paste, heat the oil in a heavy-based frying pan on a medium heat. Add the cinnamon stick, bay leaf, cardamom pod and cumin seeds and fry for 1 minute. Add the onion, ginger and garlic paste, salt and sugar and continue cooking. When the onion is translucent add the fresh and dried shrimps and cook on a low heat for 15 minutes, stirring occasionally. Add the tomatoes and the chilli powder, ground cumin and turmeric and cook until the tomatoes become soft and oil starts to float on the side.

Add the coconut milk and the green chilli and cook for another 5 minutes, stirring occasionally. Add the Bengali garam masala and the lemon juice. Transfer the contents of the pan to a blender or food processor and blend. Leave to cool, cover, then store in a refrigerator until ready for use.

To finish the dish, heat the oil in a large, heavy-based frying pan or wok until very hot. Add the shrimps and stir-fry for a minute or so. When they turn pink, stir in the Bengali shrimp paste, then correct seasoning, if necessary. Finally, throw in the red chard leaves and continue stirring just until they wilt. Squeeze over the lemon juice and serve immediately in bowls as a starter, or spear them with cocktail sticks and pass around as a snack with drinks.

This curry-leaf-and-coconut-flavoured soup is Kerala's answer to lobster bisque, and it's always been a favourite dish at each of our restaurants during the Christmas holidays. The addition of lobster-chilli toasts to serve with the soup is a Cinnamon Kitchen twist and gives the dish an interesting extra dimension.

SERVES 4

LOBSTER SOUP FROM KERALA

50g butter
I tablespoon vegetable oil
½ teaspoon red chilli powder
2 live lobsters, cut in half lengthways, cleaned, with the shells reserved, and cut into Icm dice (you can ask your fishmonger to do this, as long as you cook the lobster the same day), with the claw meat set aside for the toasts
3 tomatoes, quartered
I teaspoon salt
2 tablespoons coconut milk
I tablespoon single cream
½ teaspoon sugar
juice of I lemon
I tablespoon finely chopped fresh coriander

For the stock
I litre water
the reserved lobster shells (see above)
I onion, finely chopped
½ carrot, finely chopped
½ celery stalk, finely chopped
3 shiitake mushrooms, trimmed and cut in half
3 dried bay leaves
I½ teaspoons coriander seeds
I teaspoon black peppercorns
55g fresh coriander roots, washed
I teaspoon salt

For the spice paste
I0 fresh curry leaves
2 garlic cloves, peeled

I tablespoon coriander seeds
I teaspoon cumin seeds
I teaspoon black peppercorns

For the lobster-chilli toasts
85g lobster claw meat and any trimmings, finely chopped (set aside already)
I red onion, finely chopped
I tablespoon chopped fresh coriander
I green chilli, finely chopped
¼ teaspoon black onion seeds
a pinch of salt
20g Cheddar cheese, grated
4 thin slices of baguette or any other crusty bread

First make the stock. Put all the ingredients in a large, deep saucepan and bring to the boil. Reduce the heat and simmer, covered, for 20 minutes, then strain through a fine sieve and set aside.

To make the spice paste, pound all the ingredients together to a coarse paste using a mortar and pestle or process in a blender or food processor.

For the soup, melt half the butter with the oil in a saucepan. Add all the spice paste ingredients and sauté until the garlic turns golden brown. Add the chilli powder and lobster trimmings and sauté for a further minute.

Add the tomatoes and salt and stir until the tomatoes have softened. Now add the stock and bring to the boil. Reduce the heat and simmer, covered, for 30 minutes. Remove the pan from the heat and leave the soup to cool. Transfer the soup to a blender or food processor and blend, then pass it through a fine sieve.

Melt the remaining butter in a large saucepan on a medium heat. Add the lobster and sauté for 1 minute. Pour the soup into the pan and bring to a simmer. Stir in the coconut milk, cream, sugar, lemon juice and coriander, then remove the pan from the heat, adjust the seasoning, if necessary, and keep hot.

Mix together all the ingredients for the lobster-chilli toasts, except the baguette slices. Divide the mixture between the baguette slices and place them in an oven preheated to 200°C/Gas Mark 6 for a couple of minutes, then finish under the hot grill for a minute or so. Divide the soup and the lobster meat between 4 soup plates and serve straightaway with the lobster-chilli toasts.

These humble Nepalese momos get jazzed up with Scottish lobster meat, but you can use chopped prawns or mixed seafood or even bulk up the mix with some fish trimmings, if you prefer. Making your own momo wrappers has a certain sense of achievement, but feel free to reach for the supermarket version of ready-made dumpling pastry if you're in a rush and don't like the mess! This is easy to find in Asian supermarkets.

SERVES 4-6

SCOTTISH LOBSTER MOMOS AND TOMATO AND CURRY LEAF BROTH

500g uncooked lobster meat, removed from shells, and roughly chopped with 4 pieces of claw meat reserved for garnishing (you can ask your fishmonger to do this, as long as you cook the lobster meat on the same day)

4 green chillies, chopped

2 garlic cloves, finely chopped

2 spring onions, finely chopped

1 lemongrass stalk, outer layer removed and stalk finely chopped

1 red onion, finely chopped

5cm piece of fresh ginger, peeled and finely chopped

50g butter

1 teaspoon peppercorns, crushed

2 tablespoons chopped fresh coriander

1¼ teaspoons salt

juice of 1 lemon

micro herbs, to garnish

For the Tomato and Curry Leaf Broth

2 tablespoons vegetable oil

4 garlic cloves, crushed

2.5cm piece fresh ginger, peeled and crushed

12 fresh curry leaves

12 tomatoes, halved

¼ teaspoon red chilli powder

¼ teaspoon ground turmeric

600ml fish stock or water

1 teaspoon cumin seeds

1 teaspoon black peppercorns

50g fresh coriander roots, washed

1 teaspoon salt

½ teaspoon sugar

1 tomato, deseeded and cut into 1cm dice

1 tablespoon chopped fresh coriander

For the momo wrappers

300g plain white flour, plus 150g for dusting

½ teaspoon baking powder

a good pinch of salt

120ml water

For tempering

1 tablespoon vegetable oil

¼ teaspoon black mustard seeds

2 dried red chillies, each split lengthways

10 fresh curry leaves

a pinch of ground asafoetida (optional)

To make the broth, heat the oil in a large saucepan on a medium heat, add the garlic and ginger and sauté for 1 minute. When they start to colour, add the curry leaves and tomatoes and continue cooking. When the tomatoes have softened, stir in the chilli powder and turmeric and cook, stirring, for 2 minutes. Add the stock and bring to a simmer. Meanwhile, coarsely crush the cumin seeds and peppercorns together in a mortar and pestle. Add them to the simmering stock with the coriander roots and simmer for 20 minutes. Strain the broth through a fine sieve into another pan, pressing down on the mixture to extract all the liquid. Add the salt and sugar. Bring to a boil again and add the diced tomatoes and the chopped coriander.

Meanwhile, to make the momo wrappers, sift the flour, baking powder and salt on to a work surface. Make a well in the centre, add half the water and mix well with your hands. Add the rest of the water and continue to work together until the dough is smooth. Knead well for about 5 minutes. Cover with a damp cloth and set aside for 15 minutes.

Clean the work surface, dust it generously with flour and place the dough on it. Roll the dough with your hands into a long cylindrical shape, about 2.5cm in diameter. Cut into 18 x 2.5cm pieces. Dust each piece with flour and flatten into a circular shape. Roll out each piece with a rolling pin until you have a circle 7.5–8cm in diameter and the thickness of a 10p coin. Layer the circles, dusting with flour between each layer, and cover with a damp cloth to prevent them from drying out.

To make the lobster filling, put the lobster meat in a bowl and mix in the remaining ingredients.

Working with one momo wrapper at a time, wet the inside circular edge with water, then place a heaped teaspoonful of lobster filling in the centre and make small folds, starting from one point on the outer edge of the wrapper and working in a circular motion until you come back to the same point. Now hold all the folds together and twist them slightly to seal the opening. Repeat the same process until all the wrappers and filling are used. Cover with a damp cloth and set aside until you're ready to cook.

Transfer all the momos to a steamer, cover and steam on a high heat for 10–12 minutes, until the filling is well cooked. Make sure the bubbling water doesn't touch the bottom of the momos.

Back to the broth: add the tomatoes and coriander and temper the soup by heating the oil in a heavy-based pan until smoking hot. Add the mustard seeds. When they crackle, add the red chilli, followed by the curry leaves and the asafoetida, then immediately pour the mixture into the hot soup.

Divide the momos between 4 soup plates, ladle in the soup, garnish with extra lobster meat and micro herbs and serve.

We love using these king crabs, from the North Sea off the Norwegian coast, whenever we can for this dish, but you can substitute regular crab pincers if you can't get hold of these real beauties. The meat from king crab legs is sweeter than that of lobster and there is lots more of it, making it worth every penny of the £50-a-kilo price tag that comes attached.

SERVES 4

KING CRAB CLAWS WITH GOAN SPICES AND CRAB MASALA

800g king crab claws, separated at the joints and cut in half lengthways
15g butter, melted
1 teaspoon salt
½ teaspoon sugar
1 tablespoon coconut milk
1 tablespoon chopped fresh coriander
juice of 1 lemon

For the Goan spice mix
6 green cardamom pods
4 dried red chillies
4 cloves
10cm piece of cinnamon stick, broken into 4 equal pieces
1½ teaspoons coriander seeds
1 teaspoon cumin seeds

For the crab masala
3 tablespoons vegetable oil
½ teaspoon cumin seeds
1 large onion, chopped
3 green chillies, chopped
5cm piece of fresh ginger, peeled and finely chopped
1 teaspoon salt
½ teaspoon ground turmeric
1 teaspoon red chilli powder
½ teaspoon ground coriander
350g hand-picked fresh white crab meat
2 tablespoons chopped fresh coriander
juice of 1 lemon

To make the Goan spice mix, roast all the spices individually in a dry frying pan on a medium heat, then mix them together and grind or pound them in a spice mill or mortar and pestle into a smooth powder.

Arrange the prepared crab claws in a baking tray, flesh side up, and brush them with the melted butter. Sprinkle with salt, sugar and the Goan spice mix. Drizzle with the coconut milk and set aside.

Meanwhile, to stir-fry the crab, heat the oil in a heavy-based frying pan or wok until very hot and add the cumin seeds. When they start to crackle, add the onion and sweat on a low heat for 3–4 minutes until translucent. Stir in the remaining ingredients, except the crab meat, fresh coriander and lemon juice, and cook, stirring for 30 seconds. Gently fold in the crab and cook, stirring on a low heat for 2–3 minutes. Finally, add the fresh coriander and lemon juice. Adjust the seasoning.

Place the seasoned claws under a hot grill for 6–8 minutes, until golden. Remove them from the grill and sprinkle with the fresh coriander and lemon juice. Serve immediately with the crab masala.

These chicken wings come out much better when the skins have been removed, as it allows the flavours to really penetrate and the skin doesn't get all soggy and chewy when coated with the spicy sauce. The cracked pepper adds a final kick and bit of texture. I particularly like the delayed heat of cracked pepper in this dish.

SERVES 4

STIR-FRIED CHICKEN WINGS WITH CRACKED PEPPER

600g chicken wings, skin removed
oil for deep-frying

For the marinade
3 tablespoons cornflour
1½ teaspoons red chilli powder
1½ teaspoons salt
I teaspoon Garlic Paste (page 18)
I teaspoon Ginger Paste (page 18)
½ teaspoon black peppercorns,
   coarsely ground
juice of ½ lemon

For the stir-fry sauce
2 tablespoons vegetable oil
I green cardamom pod
2.5cm piece of cinnamon stick
I large onion, finely chopped
I teaspoon salt
I teaspoon red chilli powder
I teaspoon black peppercorns,
   coarsely crushed
2 tomatoes, finely chopped
2.5cm piece of fresh ginger, peeled
   and finely chopped
I green chilli, finely chopped
I tablespoon chopped fresh coriander
juice of ½ lemon

Mix together all the ingredients for the marinade, then rub this over the chicken wings and leave to marinate for 15 minutes.

Meanwhile, make the sauce for the stir-fry. Heat the oil in a pan until smoking, add the cardamom pod and cinnamon stick and fry for about 30 seconds until they release their aromas. Reduce the heat, add the chilli, onion and salt and cook for 5–6 minutes, until the onion is translucent. Add the chilli powder, peppercorns and tomatoes, chopped ginger and green chilli and stir for 3–5 minutes, until the liquid has evaporated. Finish the sauce with fresh coriander and lemon juice.

Now heat enough oil for deep-frying in a deep-fat fryer or a deep, heavy-based saucepan to 190°C. Add the chicken wings and deep-fry for about 4 minutes, until crisp and cooked. Drain them on kitchen paper, then transfer them to a heavy-based wok or frying pan. Add the sauce and stir-fry on a high heat for about 3 minutes, until the chicken pieces are nicely coated in the sauce. Adjust the seasoning and serve immediately.

This is a variation of the ever-popular tandoori 'malai' chicken with extra fennel and coriander for flavour and texture.

TANDOORI CHICKEN WITH FENNEL AND CORIANDER

4 chicken breasts, skin off and
   trimmed and cut into 4 pieces each
1 tablespoon vegetable oil

For the first marinade
1 tablespoon Ginger and Garlic Paste
   (page 18)
1½ teaspoons salt
1 teaspoon red chilli powder
1 teaspoon dried red chilli flakes
juice of 1 lemon

For the second marinade
½ teaspoon powdered allspice
1 teaspoon cracked black
   peppercorns
3 cloves
1 teaspoon fennel seeds
25g plain yoghurt
1 tablespoon finely chopped coriander
   stems
1 teaspoon salt

For the coarsely ground spice crust
1 teaspoons cracked black
   peppercorns
3 cloves
1 teaspoons fennel seeds

Mix together the ginger and garlic paste, salt, chilli powder and flakes and lemon juice. Rub the mixture over the chicken breast pieces, cover and set aside.

Mix together the ingredients for the second marinade. Apply to the pieces of chicken breast to complete the marinading. (In the restaurant, at this point, we skewer and cook the chicken in the tandoor to colour evenly, finishing off in a preheated oven.)

However, if you don't have access to a tandoor, heat the oil in an ovenproof pan and sear the pieces of chicken breasts on both sides for 2 minutes. Mix together the ingredients for the coarsely ground spice crust and sprinkle over the chicken. Place them in an oven preheated to 200°C/Gas Mark 6 and cook for 8–10 minutes, until the meat juices run clear, and serve hot.

This dish works well served with Coriander Chutney (see page 22).

This was one of our first dishes at Cinnamon Kitchen on the original menu, and we chose this deliberately to showcase two very familiar forms of lamb kebab, but highlight the differences by playing about with the quality of the main ingredient and its different textures. Fear not if you dread the thought of having to skewer mince on to metal skewers. You can always shape them as patties or burgers and cook them in the pan.

SERVES 6

AROMATIC SPICED WELSH LAMB KEBABS

2 rumps of lamb, fat trimmed and
  each cut into 3 slices
I tablespoon vegetable oil
¼ teaspoon black cumin seeds
½ tablespoon gram (chickpea) flour
salad leaves, for garnish
Coriander Chutney (page 22)

For the first marinade
I teaspoon Ginger Paste (page 18)
I teaspoon Garlic Paste (page 18)
½ teaspoon salt
juice of ½ lemon

For the second marinade
25g Greek yoghurt
½ teaspoon red chilli powder
¼ teaspoon ground turmeric
2.5cm piece of fresh ginger, peeled
  and finely chopped
2 green chillies, finely chopped
I tablespoon chopped fresh coriander
¼ nutmeg, grated

For the mince kebab
500g minced lamb or diced boneless
  lamb
2 green chillies
I tablespoon chopped fresh coriander
  stems
3 garlic cloves
Icm piece of fresh ginger, peeled
20g Cheddar cheese, grated
½ teaspoon red chilli powder
¼ teaspoon cumin seeds
I teaspoon salt

Heat the oil in a heavy-based pan on a medium-high heat and add the

black cumin seeds. When the cumin seeds start to crackle, reduce the heat to low and gradually add the gram flour, stirring to prevent lumps from forming. When the flour turns golden brown, acquires a slightly sandy texture and releases a roasted aroma, remove the pan from the heat, tip the roasted gram flour into a bowl and set aside to cool.

Pat the lamb dry. Mix all the ingredients for the first marinade in a large, deep bowl and add the lamb. Cover and set aside for 10–15 minutes.

For the second marinade, mix all the ingredients together in a large bowl and add the ginger- and garlic-coated lamb. Now mix in the roasted gram flour thoroughly, cover and set aside for another 15 minutes.

Pierce a metal skewer through the marinated lamb rump slices to hold them firmly. Sear the lamb in a hot pan on a medium-high heat for 1 minute on each side, then place in the oven at 200°/Gas Mark 6 for 6–8 minutes. (In the restaurant, we cook the lamb rump for 8–10 minutes in a slow tandoori oven.)

If you have a mincer, then you can use diced lamb to make your own mince. Mince the lamb and all the

other ingredients, except the salt, coarsely together in a mincer. Finally, add the salt and, using your hands, combine the ingredients well to get an evenly spiced mince.

Alternatively, use minced lamb and make the kebab mix in a food processor. Firstly combine the spices in the food processor before adding the lamb. Do not process for long as you want to maintain the coarse texture of the meat.

To cook this minced lamb kebab you need a barbecue and more metal skewers. Divide the mince into 4 equal parts. Now take a thick skewer and, with wet hands, slowly spread the mince on to the skewer covering it and squeezing it so it sticks. The kebabs need to be about 20–25cm long and quite thick so they stay juicy. Cover and set aside in the fridge for 30 minutes. As long as you have enough skewers, the mince kebabs can be prepared in advance and cooked once the rump slices are in the oven.

Cook the kebabs on the barbecue or under a grill for 6–8 minutes, turning regularly to ensure the meat is cooked evenly. When both sets of kebabs are ready, serve them with the salad leaves and coriander chutney.

Partridges in a pear tree – does this remind you of Christmas? At Cinnamon Kitchen, it certainly does to us. Both partridges and pears are plentiful in November and December and this combination works very well. Do give it a go!

ROASTED PARTRIDGE WITH CURRIED PEARS

8 partridge breasts, boned and skinned

For the first marinade
1 tablespoon Ginger and Garlic Paste (page 18)
1 teaspoon salt
juice of ½ lemon

For the second marinade
250g plain yoghurt
4 green chillies, finely chopped
2 tablespoons chopped coriander stalks
2 tablespoons white vinegar
2 teaspoons dried mango powder
1 teaspoon Garam Masala (page 20)
1 teaspoon salt
1 teaspoon sugar
3 tablespoons peanuts, roasted in a dry frying pan and then coarsely chopped

For the Curried Pears
2 tablespoons vegetable oil
2.5cm piece of fresh ginger, peeled and finely chopped
1 green chilli, finely chopped
½ teaspoon cumin seeds
a pinch of ground asafoetida
2 pears, peeled, cored and quartered
150g plain yoghurt
1 teaspoon ground turmeric
1 tablespoon sugar
½ teaspoon salt

Mix together all the ingredients for the first marinade, then rub them over the partridge breasts, cover and set aside for 10 minutes.

Meanwhile, mix together all the ingredients for the second marinade, except the peanuts, then spread over the partridge breasts. Cover and leave to marinate for 30 minutes.

Meanwhile, prepare the curried pears. Heat the oil in a large frying pan, add ginger, green chilli, cumin seeds and asafoetida and fry, stirring, for about 30 seconds. Add the pears and stir for 1 minute on a high heat. Gradually add the yoghurt, stirring well after each spoonful, and then the turmeric, sugar and salt. Cook on a low heat, stirring constantly, for a minute or so, until the pears are glazed and evenly coated with the sauce. Remove the pan from the heat and keep warm.

Place the partridge breasts on a baking tray, sprinkle with the roasted peanuts and roast in an oven preheated to 200°C/Gas Mark 6 for 6–8 minutes, until the peanuts turn golden brown and crisp and the breasts are medium-well done (when the juices run clear when the breasts are pierced with a skewer). Let the breasts rest for 5 minutes, then serve with the curried pears.

Inspired by the conventional European duck leg confit, this is a Cinnamon Kitchen take on the confit, shredded and transformed into a filling for a pao, a classic Indian light snack (sometimes also referred to as a pav). These are great either as a starter or a filling snack, and I like serving them as 'hand-helds' in the bar, where they are an especially satisfying late night snack.

MAKES 8 BUNS

HYDERABADI DUCK PAO WITH CITRUS-APPLE CHUTNEY

4 duck legs, skin on
1 tablespoon Ginger and Garlic Paste
    (page 18)
2 teaspoons salt
1 tablespoon vegetable oil, plus extra
    for searing
2 dried bay leaves
1 teaspoon black peppercorns, cracked
1 teaspoon rock moss, optional (a type
    of dried moss which enhances the
    flavour of spices and binds flavours)
2 dried red chillies
2.5cm piece of cinnamon stick

For the Citrus-Apple Chutney
2 tablespoons vegetable oil
1 bay leaf
1 green cardamom pod
1 dried red chilli
1 clove
4 green apples, peeled, cored and cut
    into 1cm dice
50g sugar
1 tablespoon malt vinegar
juice of ½ lemon

For the pao
10g fresh yeast
1½ tablespoons caster sugar
100ml lukewarm water
2 tablespoons milk
1 egg, lightly beaten
15g butter, melted
280g plain white flour
1 teaspoon salt
1 teaspoon cumin seeds, plus extra for
    sprinkling
vegetable oil for brushing

For the pao filling
3 tablespoons Crisp Fried Onions
    (page 23)
1 tablespoon chopped mint
1 tablespoon tamarind paste
1.5cm piece of fresh ginger, peeled
    and finely chopped
1 green chilli, finely chopped
½ teaspoon sugar

Rub the duck legs with the garlic and ginger paste and salt and set aside to marinate for at least 30 minutes (the longer, the better – overnight would be ideal).

Meanwhile, make the citrus-apple chutney. Heat the oil in a heavy-based saucepan. Add the bay leaf, cardamom pod, red chilli and clove and stir for 1–2 minutes, until they release their aromas. Add the apples and cook on a medium-low heat for 3–4 minutes, stirring. When the apples start to change colour, add the sugar and cook, stirring constantly, until the sugar has dissolved and started to caramelise. Add the malt vinegar and lemon juice and cook for another minute or so. Remove the pan from the heat and leave the chutney to cool. You can serve it warm or at room temperature, as you like.

After the duck legs have marinated, heat the oil in a flameproof casserole on a high heat, add the duck legs and sear for 3 minutes on both sides until nicely coloured. Add the remaining ingredients and pour over just about enough water to cover them. Cover the casserole and cook on a low heat for about 90 minutes, until tender. Alternatively, place the duck legs in a roasting tray and pour over enough water to cover. Cover the tray tightly with kitchen foil and cook in an oven preheated to 160°C/Gas Mark 3 for 90 minutes. Once cooked, allow the legs to cool down, then remove the skin and bones and finely shred the meat. Set aside.

Meanwhile, make the pao. Put the yeast and sugar in a small bowl, add the water and milk and stir until the yeast has dissolved. Set aside in a warm place for 15 minutes, until frothy. Add half the egg and the melted butter to the yeast mixture and whisk well.

Sift 250g of the flour with the salt into a bowl. Add the cumin seeds and pour in the yeast mixture and mix to make a smooth dough.

Finally mix in the melted butter. Using the remaining flour, knead the dough for 10 minutes, until it becomes smooth and elastic. Cover the bowl with clingfilm or a damp cloth and leave the dough in a warm place for 30 minutes, or until doubled in size.

To make the pao filling, put the duck meat in a bowl and add the fried onions, mint, tamarind, ginger, chilli and sugar. Divide the mixture into 8 equal balls. Set aside while the dough finishes proving.

When the dough has risen, knock it back and divide it into 8 equal balls. Working with one ball at a time, use your thumb to make a hollow in the centre and fill it with the duck mixture. Squeeze the opening closed. Arrange the stuffed dough balls in a well-greased baking tray about 2cm deep, placing them 1cm apart. Press the balls lightly so they just touch each other, then cover again with clingfilm or a damp cloth and leave in a warm place for 30 minutes, or until they have doubled in volume. They will 'merge' together.

When the dough has risen, brush with the remaining beaten egg and sprinkle some more cumin seeds on top. Bake in an oven preheated to 180°C/Gas Mark 4 for 25 minutes, until golden brown.

Remove the pao from the oven and, while the buns are still hot, brush with oil. Tear them apart or cut them to separate and serve with the citrus-apple chutney, and a salad, if you like.

Vivek's tip
Any leftover chutney can be kept in the fridge for up to a week and I recommend also serving it with the Rabbit Terrine on the following page.

We developed this dish as an interesting way of using up leftover rabbit legs, but you can also make it with chicken thighs, if you'd rather. It may read long and appear fiddly, but once it's done, it's done! If you don't want to make the chutney, serve the sliced terrine with a few dressed salad leaves.

SERVES 6–8

RABBIT AND PISTACHIO TERRINE WITH QUINCE CHUTNEY

8 rabbit legs, skinned and boned

1½ teaspoons Ginger and Garlic Paste (page 18)

2 teaspoons salt

2 tablespoons vegetable, plus extra for greasing the terrine

12g plain yoghurt

1½ teaspoons red chilli powder

½ teaspoon dried fenugreek leaves, crushed between your fingertips

1 teaspoon ground turmeric

1 teaspoon kasundi mustard (Bengali mustard) or wholegrain mustard

100g fresh coriander, stalks and leaves, ground into a paste in a mortar and pestle or blender

juice of ½ lemon

½ teaspoon Mace and Cardamom Powder (page 20)

2.5cm piece of fresh ginger, peeled and finely chopped

2 green chillies, finely chopped

1 tablespoon blanched pistachios, thinly sliced

1 tablespoon raisins, soaked in warm water until plump, then drained and thinly sliced

2 teaspoons pitted and thinly sliced black olives

1 teaspoon Activa or 3 eggs, beaten (Activa is a meat bonding protein available online; it helps stick different cuts of meats together)

For the Quince Chutney

2 tablespoons vegetable oil

2 cloves

1 bay leaf

1 green cardamom pod

1 dried red chilli

½ teaspoon black onion seeds

4 quince, peeled, cored and cut into 1cm dice

125g sugar

2 tablespoons malt vinegar

Divide the rabbit legs into pairs. Marinate the first pair with ½ teaspoon ginger and garlic paste, ½ teaspoon salt, 2 teaspoons oil, 1 teaspoon yoghurt, ½ teaspoon chilli powder and the fenugreek leaves. Marinate the second pair with ½ teaspoon ginger and garlic paste, ½ teaspoon salt, 2 teaspoons oil, the turmeric and the mustard. Marinate the third pair with ½ teaspoon ginger and garlic paste, ½ teaspoon salt, 2 teaspoons oil, the coriander paste and the lemon juice. Mince the final pair in a food processor, adding ½ teaspoon salt, the ground mace and cardamom, chopped ginger and chillies. Cover and leave each pair of legs to marinate separately in the refrigerator for 20 minutes.

Meanwhile, grease an 18cm terrine. Spread the first pair of legs over the base of the terrine.

Add one-third of the rabbit mince and use a wet palm to spread out into an even thickness of 5mm. Sprinkle one-third of the pistachios, one-third of the raisins and one-third of the olives on top of the mince. Sprinkle with one-third of the Activa (or brush with the beaten egg). Now, add the second pair of legs, one-third of the mince and add another third of the pistachios, raisins and olives. Sprinkle with Activa (or brush again with the beaten egg). Finally, add the third pair of legs, the remaining mince and the remaining pistachios, raisins and olives and sprinkle with the last of the Activa (or the beaten egg). Top with the last pair of legs.

Cover the terrine tightly with foil and cook in a bain marie in the oven at 130°C/Gas Mark ½ until the juices run clear when the terrine is pierced with a skewer.

Meanwhile, make the chutney. Heat the oil in a heavy-based frying pan and add the cloves, bay leaf, cardamom pod, chilli and mustard seeds. When the seeds crackle, add the quince and cook on a medium-low heat for 3–4 minutes, stirring. When the quince has started to change colour, add the sugar and cook, stirring, until the sugar has dissolved and started to caramelise. Add the malt vinegar and cook for another minute. Remove the pan from the heat and allow the chutney to cool. You can serve it warm or at room temperature, as you like.

Remove the terrine from the steamer and allow it to cool completely, then transfer to the fridge for at least a couple of hours, covered, with a weight to press the terrine into shape. When ready to serve, bring out the terrine and allow it to return to room temperature, then cut the terrine into 1cm slices and serve with quince chutney and a salad of your choice.

Vivek's tip
Keep the seasoning slightly milder than you'd normally use, as the prolonged cooking makes the final flavour very intense.

This is Cinnamon Kitchen's Indian twist on Spanish gazpacho. The addition of green mango gives the soup an extra zing and depth of flavour. Served along with Quinoa Salad (see page 70) it results in a deliciously different summer starter.

SERVES 6

CHILLED GREEN MANGO AND TOMATO SOUP

10 ripe tomatoes, quartered
5 green mangoes
5 red peppers, deseeded and roughly chopped
5cm piece of fresh ginger, peeled and roughly chopped
5 garlic cloves, peeled
1 teaspoon cumin seeds, roasted
1 teaspoon red chilli powder
3 tablespoons extra-virgin olive oil, plus extra for drizzling
1 teaspoon salt
1/2 teaspoon sugar
250ml water
salad leaves or micro cress leaves, to garnish

For the soup, mix together all the ingredients, except the water, in a non-metallic bowl and leave aside to marinate for about 3 hours. Add the water, transfer to a blender or food processor and blend until smooth. Strain the soup into a bowl, pressing down on the vegetables, to extract as much flavour as possible. Cover and refrigerate until chilled.

Pour the tomato soup into the bowls and drizzle with more olive oil just before serving. Garnish with salad leaves or micro cress. Perfect with the Quinoa Salad (see page 70).

This is Cinnamon Kitchen's adaptation of India's favourite street snack, the spiced potato cakes served with a variety of chutneys and dressings. You'll find it sold in most towns and cities. The term 'chowk' refers to a busy intersection, or crossing, in every city, where street vendors and their patrons congregate in the evenings to take in the atmosphere of the town. They share their news and gossip and exchange opinions while consuming the town's favourite 'chaat'.

SERVES 4–6

'CHOWK KI TIKKI' SEARED POTATO CAKES WITH MASALA CHICKPEAS

4 floury potatoes, boiled, peeled and grated
1 green chilli, finely chopped
1cm piece of fresh ginger, peeled and finely chopped
2 tablespoons chopped fresh coriander
1 teaspoon cumin seeds, roasted
1 teaspoon salt
2 tablespoons cornflour
2 tablespoons vegetable
Tomato and Onion Seed Chutney (page 22)

For the masala chickpeas
400g can of chickpeas or black-eyed beans, drained and rinsed
1 tablespoon vegetable or olive oil
1/2 teaspoon cumin seeds, roasted
1 onion, finely chopped
1 green chilli, finely chopped
1 large tomato, deseeded and finely chopped
1/2 teaspoon salt
1 tablespoon finely chopped fresh coriander
juice of 1 lemon
a pinch of Chaat Masala (page 21)

Mix together all of the ingredients for the masala chickpeas. Cover and chill until required.

To make the potato cakes, put the potatoes in a bowl. Add chilli, ginger, coriander, cumin seeds and salt. Finally add the cornflour and mix well. Divide the mixture into 12 equal-sized balls and, with wet hands, flatten slightly.

Heat enough oil for shallow-frying in a large, heavy-based frying pan on a medium-high heat. Add as many potato cakes as will fit and fry for about 3–4 minutes on each side, until crisp and golden. As each batch is fried, remove and drain well on kitchen paper, then keep hot until they are all fried. To serve, spread some chickpea masala on 4 plates and arrange the potato cakes on top. Serve with a chutney of your choice.

In southern India, the Tamils traditionally make this thin soup, which is usually served poured over rice. The British turned this into what has become known as mulligatawny. Elsewhere in India, tomato rasam is often served with lentil fritters, and that is how we have left it at Cinnamon Kitchen.

SERVES 4

TOMATO RASAM WITH SPICED LENTIL FRITTERS

2 tablespoons vegetable oil
4 garlic cloves, crushed
2.5cm piece of fresh ginger, peeled and crushed
12 fresh curry leaves
12 tomatoes, halved
1½ teaspoons tamarind paste
¼ teaspoon red chilli powder
¼ teaspoon ground turmeric
600ml vegetable stock or boiling water
1 teaspoon cumin seeds
1 teaspoon black peppercorns
50g fresh coriander roots, washed
1 teaspoon salt
½ teaspoon sugar
1 tablespoon chopped fresh coriander leaves

For tempering

1 tablespoon vegetable oil
½ teaspoon black mustard seeds
2 dried red chillies, cut in half
10 fresh curry leaves
a large pinch of ground asafoetida (optional)

For the lentil fritters

200g white urad lentils, picked over, rinsed and soaked overnight
2 tablespoons coarse semolina
1½ teaspoons salt
1 teaspoon black peppercorns, coarsely crushed
oil for deep-frying

Heat the oil in a large saucepan on a medium heat, add the garlic and ginger and sauté for 1 minute. When they start to colour, add the curry leaves and tomatoes and continue sautéing until the tomatoes have softened. Stir in the tamarind, chilli powder and turmeric and cook for 2 minutes. Add the stock and bring to a simmer. Meanwhile, coarsely crush the cumin seeds and peppercorns together in a mortar and pestle. Add them to the simmering stock with the coriander roots and leave to simmer for 20 minutes. Strain the broth through a fine sieve into another saucepan, pressing down to extract all the flavours. Add the salt and sugar. Cover and set aside until you are ready to serve.

Now prepare the lentil fritters. Drain the lentils, transfer them to a blender or food processor and blend until smooth, using just enough fresh water to blend. Transfer to a bowl and add the semolina, salt and black peppercorns. Beat with a spoon until the batter is light and fluffy and divide it into 20 equal balls.

Heat enough oil for deep-frying in a deep-fat fryer or a deep, heavy-based saucepan to 180°C. Using

wet hands, as the batter is sticky, add the balls and fry them for about 3–5 minutes, until lightly browned. Drain well on kitchen paper and keep hot.

Just before you're ready to serve, reheat the soup and sprinkle in the coriander. For tempering, heat the oil in a pan until very hot, then add the mustard seeds. When they crackle, add the red chilli, followed by curry leaves and the asafoetida, if you are using. Immediately pour this mixture into the hot soup. Serve with the hot lentil fritters.

This is an incredibly simple, but delicious way to cook broccoli. You can use the purple sprouting variety when it is in season, and you don't need to blanch it in that case.

SERVES 4

CHAR-GRILLED BROCCOLI FLORETS WITH ROSE PETALS AND ALMONDS

For the marinated broccoli

I tablespoon grated Cheddar cheese

25g Greek yoghurt

I tablespoon Ginger and Garlic Paste (page 18)

I teaspoon salt

Icm piece of fresh ginger, peeled and finely chopped

I green chilli, finely chopped

I tablespoon single cream

I teaspoon dried rose petals

½ teaspoon Mace and Cardamom Powder (see 20)

I head of broccoli or two stalks of purple sprouting broccoli, cut into florets, blanched in salted water for 30 seconds, drained and chilled in ice water

2 tablespoons vegetable oil

To serve

I tablespoon flaked almonds

juice of ½ lemon

Garlic Chutney (page 236) or Coriander Chutney (page 22), to serve

In a bowl, rub the cheese with your fingers to break up any lumps. Add the yoghurt and mix until smooth. Add the ginger and garlic paste, salt, chopped ginger and chilli and mix well, then stir in the cream carefully, as the mixture might separate if mixed too vigorously. Finally add the rose petals, mace and cardamom powder, gently fold in the broccoli florets, and drizzle with a tablespoon of oil. Mix and set aside for 20 minutes.

To cook the broccoli, soak 4 bamboo skewers in water for 30 minutes. Thread the broccoli florets on to the skewers, arrange on an oiled baking tray and place under a hot grill for 5–6 minutes, until the broccoli florets are cooked and slightly charred at the edges. Now sprinkle with the almond flakes and toast for another minute or so. Remove from the grill and serve immediately, squeezing over the lemon and accompanying with a chutney of your choice.

CINNAMON KITCHEN CLASSICS:
STEP BY STEP

1. Mixing the marinade ingredients.
2. Adding the rose petals to the marinade.
3. Folding the broccoli florets into the marinade.
4. Threading the florets onto the skewers.
5. The skewers are finished under the grill and served with garlic chutney.

These are inspired by the omnipresent potato 'tikkis' or cakes sold all over the country on the streets. Ours is a poshed up version using spinach and apricots. I find this is a good way to get the kids to eat spinach!

POTATO CAKES STUFFED WITH SPINACH AND DRIED FRUIT

600g floury potatoes, boiled, peeled and grated

1cm piece of fresh ginger, peeled and finely chopped

3 green chillies, deseeded and finely chopped

1 teaspoon cumin seeds, roasted

2 teaspoons salt

30g cornflour

oil for shallow-frying

micro herbs, to garnish

For the filling

4 tablespoons ghee or vegetable oil

1 teaspoon cumin seeds

4 garlic cloves, finely chopped

1 large onion, finely chopped

3 green chillies, finely chopped

2.5cm piece of fresh ginger, peeled and finely chopped

salt, to taste

500g spinach leaves, blanched, squeezed dry and finely chopped

12 ready-to-eat dried apricots, finely diced

12 ready-to-eat dried figs, finely diced

For the filling, heat the ghee or oil in a pan and add the cumin seeds. When they crackle, add the garlic and onion and sauté for 4–6 minutes, until the onion is translucent. Add the chillies, ginger and salt and stir-fry for a minute or so. Add the spinach, apricots and figs and stir-fry until the spinach wilts, then check the seasoning. Remove the stuffing from the pan and leave to cool.

Meanwhile, mix together all the ingredients for the potato cake, then shape into 10 equal balls and set aside.

When the filling is cool, working with one potato ball at a time, make an insertion with your thumb to create a hollow space. Place 1 tablespoon of the filling into the hollow, then mould the potato mixture to seal closed. Use your palm to lightly press the potato ball into a rounded patty shape. Continue until all the potato cakes are stuffed and shaped.

Heat enough oil for shallow-frying in a large, heavy-based frying pan on a medium-high heat. Add as many potato cakes as will fit and fry for about 3–4 minutes on each side, until crisp and golden. As each batch is fried, remove and drain well on kitchen paper, then keep hot until they are all fried. Garnish with micro herbs and serve hot with a chutney of your choice. Add a salad, too, if you like.

This is a variation on the ever-popular vegetable shammi kebabs sold all over northern India on the streets. For a sophisticated touch, ours has dried rose petals and figs in the belly!

MINCED VEGETABLE KEBAB WITH DRIED FIGS AND ROSE PETALS

80g chana dal (split yellow chickpeas), soaked in cold water for I hour
4 tablespoons vegetable oil
4 green cardamom pods
2 black cardamom pods
2.5 cm piece of cinnamon stick
3 cloves
5cm piece of fresh ginger, peeled and chopped
I bay leaf
500ml whole milk
I teaspoon red chilli powder
I teaspoon ground coriander
I teaspoon ground cumin
I teaspoon salt
100g cauliflower florets
85g French beans, cut into 2.5cm pieces
2 carrots, peeled and roughly chopped
oil for shallow-frying

For the filling
250g Greek yoghurt
8 dried rose petals, crushed
4 ready-to-eat dried figs, finely chopped
4 mint sprigs, finely chopped
1/2 teaspoon salt

Drain the chana dal and set aside. Heat the oil in a heavy-based pan on a medium-high heat and add the green and black cardamom pods, cinnamon stick and cloves. When they start to give off their aromas, add the ginger and bay leaf. When the ginger starts to colour, add the chana dal and the milk, bring to the boil, stirring constantly, then boil for 5–8 minutes, until the lentils begin to soften slightly.

Add the chilli powder, ground coriander and cumin and salt. Now add the vegetables and cook on a medium-low heat for 5 minutes, stirring occasionally, or until the vegetables are cooked, but still slightly crunchy and the mixture is just about moist. Remove the pan from the heat and leave the mixture to cool for 30 minutes. Then chill for another 30 minutes or so in the fridge to make them easier to handle.

Ideally you would pass the mixture through a mincer; if you are using a blender, however, take care not to blend it too finely and set some aside to coarsely chop by hand in order to retain some texture. Mix well and correct the seasoning, if necessary. Divide the mixture into 6 equal balls. To prepare the filling, beat the yoghurt in a bowl, then stir in the remaining ingredients.

With wet hands, working with one vegetable ball at a time, make an insertion with your thumb to create a hollow space. Use a teaspoon to fill the hollow with the yoghurt mixture, then mould the mixture to seal closed. Use your palm to lightly press the vegetable ball into a rounded patty shape. Continue until all the kebabs are stuffed and shaped.

Heat enough oil for shallow-frying in a large, heavy-based frying pan on a medium-high heat. Add the kebabs and fry for about 4–5 minutes on each side, until they are crisp and golden. As each batch is fried, remove and drain well on kitchen paper, then keep hot until they are all fried. Serve immediately.

Vivek's tip
Coriander Chutney (see page 22) makes a great accompaniment to this dish.

My inspiration for this recipe came to me on a trip to Bordeaux when ceps were just coming into season. I ordered delicious, crunchy ceps cooked in butter, garlic, parsley and lemon juice. I was reminded of a simple potato dish my mum makes with sliced potatoes, chilli, turmeric and fresh coriander leaves. At our newest restaurant, Cinnamon Soho, I've combined the two different dishes into this dish. We use king oyster, large shiitake or eryngii mushrooms, otherwise known as chicken-feet mushrooms, but you can use any meaty variety you can lay your hands on. Add a fried or poached egg for an interesting brunch idea. SERVES 4

KADHAI-SPICED MUSHROOMS ON TOAST

4 slices of any good bread
butter, olive oil or pesto sauce
I tablespoon vegetable oil
400g chunky mushrooms, cleaned
    and sliced into 5mm slices
I red onion, finely chopped
2 green chillies, finely chopped
2 tomatoes, deseeded and chopped
    into Icm dice
2.5cm piece of fresh ginger, peeled
    and finely chopped
I teaspoon of Kadhai Masala (page 21)
½ teaspoon salt
a pinch of sugar
15g butter
juice of ½ lemon
I tablespoon chopped fresh coriander
    leaves and/or stalks, washed

Toast the bread and spread with butter, olive oil or pesto, whichever you prefer, and keep warm.

Meanwhile, heat the oil in a large frying pan until it is very hot. Spread out the mushrooms in the pan and leave to brown for 60–90 seconds. Do not move the mushrooms too much until they form a crust.

Now stir in the onion and cook for 1 minute, then add the chillies, tomatoes, ginger, kadhai masala, salt and sugar and stir around for another minute on high heat. Finish by stirring in the butter and lemon juice, allowing the butter to melt. Stir in the coriander and serve immediately on the toast.

These spiced chickpea cakes are inspired by falafel. The list of ingredients may appear daunting, but, once you've got them, this is one of the simplest things to make. Quinoa, even though it's been around for centuries, is not generally used in Indian kitchens, I find it works very well if cooked as you would cook a south Indian upma. Although considered 'the mother of all grains' by the Incas, quinoa is not a true grain, but is rich in both fibre and protein, so is a good alternative to wheat for coeliacs and a great substitute for meat protein for vegetarians.

SERVES 4

SPICED CHICKPEA CAKES WITH QUINOA SALAD

oil for deep-frying
Curried Yoghurt (page 23), to serve

For the spiced chickpea cakes
250g boiled chickpeas, drained and
    coarsely blended
2.5cm piece of fresh ginger, peeled
    and finely chopped
5 fresh curry leaves, finely shredded
2 green chillies, finely chopped
2 lime leaves, finely shredded
1/2 large red onion, finely chopped
2 tablespoons peanuts, roasted in a
    dry frying pan and then coarsely
    crushed
1 tablespoon gram (chickpea) flour
1 tablespoon chopped fresh coriander
2 teaspoons fennel seeds
2 teaspoons salt
1 teaspoon ajowan seeds
1 teaspoon cornflour
1 teaspoon cumin seeds
1 teaspoon sesame seeds
1 teaspoon sugar
1 teaspoon tahini (sesame paste)
1/2 teaspoon black onion seeds
juice of 1 lemon

For the Quinoa Salad
2 teaspoons vegetable oil
1/2 teaspoon black mustard seeds
200g quinoa, boiled, drained and left
    to cool
1 green chilli, finely chopped
1/2 large red onion, thinly sliced
1/2 red pepper, thinly sliced
2.5cm piece of fresh ginger, peeled

and finely chopped
1 tablespoon chopped fresh coriander
1 teaspoon salt
juice of 1/2 lemon

Firstly, prepare the quinoa salad. Heat the oil in a frying pan to smoking point and add the mustard seeds. When they crackle, remove the pan from the heat and pour the oil and seeds into the quinoa. Add the remaining ingredients, mix together, adjust the seasoning and set aside.

Combine all the ingredients for the chickpea cakes. With wet hands, divide the mixture into 12 equal balls (they should each weigh about 30g) and flatten slightly. Heat enough oil for deep-frying in a deep-fat fryer or a deep, heavy-based saucepan to 180°C. Add the chickpea cakes and deep-fry for 1–2 minutes, until crisp and golden brown. Drain well on kitchen paper and serve immediately while still hot with the quinoa salad and curried yoghurt.

Our take on the ever-popular steamed pork or chicken momos you find in Nepal and among the Tibetan community in Delhi. For me, no trip to Delhi is complete without stuffing my face with steamed momos in Chanakyapuri. A few years ago, some Nepalese chefs joined our team at Cinnamon Kitchen and they once made these for a staff meal – I immediately got the idea for my new vegetarian starter! Making hundreds of dumplings and filling them by hand can be an effort, but it's worth it. And don't fret if they are a little irregular in shape – they taste every bit as good!

SERVES 4–6

CHILLI AND CORN MOMOS

For the momo wrappers

300g plain flour, plus 150g for dusting
½ teaspoon baking powder
a good pinch of salt
120ml water

For the momos

2 tablespoons vegetable oil
1 teaspoon cumin seeds
3 cloves garlic, finely chopped
1 large onion, sliced
4 sprigs thyme
2.5cm piece of fresh ginger, peeled and finely chopped
2 green chillies, finely chopped
1 teaspoon salt
1 teaspoon ground turmeric
300g sweetcorn kernels, fresh or thawed, half roughly chopped and other half left whole, plus a few to garnish
50g butter
½ teaspoon sugar
juice of ½ a lemon
4 tablespoons chopped fresh spring onions
2 tablespoons chopped fresh coriander
1 red onion, finely chopped
½ teaspoon black peppercorns, crushed

Firstly, make the momo wrappers. Sift the flour, baking powder and salt on to a work surface. Make a well in the centre, add half the water and mix well with your hands. Add the rest of the water and continue to work together until the dough is smooth. Knead well for about 5 minutes. Cover with a damp cloth and set aside for 15 minutes.

Return the dough to the cleaned work surface, generously dusted with flour. Roll the dough with your hands into a long cylindrical shape, about 2.5cm in diameter. Cut into 20 x 2.5cm pieces. Dust each piece with flour and flatten into a circular shape. Roll out each piece with a rolling pin until you have a circle 7.5–8cm in diameter and the thickness of a 10p coin. This will yield about 20 discs. Layer the circles, dusting with flour between each layer, and cover with a damp cloth to prevent them from drying out.

To make the momos, first heat the oil in a pan on a medium-high heat; add the cumin seeds. When they start to crackle, add the garlic, onion and thyme. Cook for 4–6 minutes, until the onion is translucent, then add the ginger, green chillies, salt and ground turmeric and cook for 1 minute. Now add the sweetcorn and cook for 4–5 minutes, until the corn is soft. Finish with the butter, sugar and lemon juice. Remove from the heat and let cool.

Once the mix has cooled, fold in the rest of the ingredients and adjust the seasoning. Shape into small balls (about 4cm diameter) and chill.

Working with one momo wrapper at a time, wet the inside circular edge with water, then place a ball of filling in the centre and make small folds, starting from one point on the outer edge of the wrapper and working in a circular motion until you come back to the same point. Now hold all the folds together and twist them slightly to seal the opening. Repeat the same process until all the wrappers and filling are used. Cover with a damp cloth and set aside until you're ready to cook.

Transfer all the momos to a steamer and steam on a high heat for 6–8 minutes, or until the pastry is soft. Make sure the bubbling water doesn't touch the bottom of the momos.

Serve the steamed momos with a spicy dip of your choice and a few sweetcorn kernels to garnish.

Vivek's tip
If you prefer, you can buy dumpling pastry sheets from any good Oriental supermarket.

This is a cracking little number to impress your guests at the dinner table. Like a lot of our favourite dishes at Cinnamon Kitchen, it's easy to prepare in advance and to serve whenever you're ready.

SERVES 4

SPICED SWEETCORN SOUP WITH MASALA SWEETCORN KEBABS

2 tablespoons vegetable oil

I teaspoon cumin seeds

3 garlic cloves, chopped

I onion, chopped

300g sweetcorn kernels, fresh or thawed

2.5cm piece of fresh ginger, peeled and chopped

2 hot green chillies, slit lengthways

I teaspoon salt

I teaspoon ground turmeric

400ml light vegetable stock or water

100ml whole milk

3 tablespoons single cream

55g butter

juice of ½ lemon

For the masala sweetcorn kebabs

200g sweetcorn kernels, fresh or thawed

100g paneer cheese, grated

2.5cm piece of fresh ginger, peeled and finely chopped

2 green chillies, finely chopped

2 tablespoons cornflour

I teaspoon cumin seeds, roasted and crushed

I teaspoon salt

½ teaspoon red chilli powder

½ teaspoon dried fenugreek leaves, crushed between your fingertips

oil for deep-frying

For the masala sweetcorn kebabs, mix together all the ingredients in a bowl, then set aside for 15 minutes. Next, using wet hands, divide the mixture into 8–10 equal balls, cover and leave them in the fridge for 20 minutes.

To make the soup heat the oil in a heavy-based pan on a medium-high heat and add the cumin seeds. When they crackle, add the garlic and onion and sauté for 3–4 minutes, until the onion is translucent. Add the sweetcorn kernels, ginger, chillies, salt and half the turmeric and cook for a further 3–4 minutes. Now add the vegetable stock and let the soup simmer for about 20 minutes. Adjust the seasoning, if necessary. Transfer the soup to a blender or food processor and blend, then strain back into the pan.

Return the soup to the heat and add the rest of the turmeric, the milk and the cream. Simmer on a medium-low heat for 3–4 minutes. Adjust the seasoning to your liking. Stir in the butter and lemon juice. Set aside and keep hot while you fry the sweetcorn kebabs.

Heat enough oil for deep-frying in a deep-fat fryer set to 190°C, or use a deep, heavy-based saucepan.

Add the sweetcorn kebabs and deep-fry for about 3–4 minutes, until they are crisp and golden. Drain well on kitchen paper. Serve the soup with the kebabs on the side.

Dosa pancakes are served either as a snack or as a main meal any time of the day, all over India, not just in the south. You can find dosa rice in any Asian food shop or deli. This version uses spiced potatoes as a filling, but the pancakes can also be filled with prawns, cooked chicken or lamb mince. The green coconut chutney is a traditional south Indian breakfast accompaniment.

SERVES 4-6

SOUTH INDIAN DOSA PANCAKES WITH SPICED POTATOES AND GREEN COCONUT CHUTNEY

150g basmati or dosa rice
50g black urad lentils
salt, to taste

For the spiced potatoes
2 tablespoons vegetable oil
½ teaspoon black mustard seeds
1 dried red chilli
½ teaspoon chana dal (split yellow chickpeas)
24 fresh curry leaves
2 red onions, chopped
2 green chillies, chopped
1cm piece of fresh ginger, peeled and chopped
½ teaspoon ground turmeric
1 teaspoon salt
2 floury potatoes, boiled, peeled and crushed

For the green coconut chutney
1 coconut, grated (liquid discarded)
50g fresh coriander leaves
20g mint leaves
4 green chillies, chopped
2 tablespoons chana dal (split yellow chickpeas), roasted
1 teaspoon salt

For tempering
1 tablespoon vegetable oil
10 fresh curry leaves
¼ teaspoon black mustard seeds

Start the rice pancakes 1½ days before you plan to serve. In separate bowls, cover the rice and the black urad lentils with cold water and allow to soak for at least for 6 hours. Drain and rinse with luke-warm water. Transfer the rice and lentils to a blender or food processor and blend together to a fine paste, adding fresh water, as necessary. Leave overnight in a warm place, about 45°C, partially covered, to ferment.

The dosa mixture will be ready when fermentation starts and bubbles begin to appear on the surface. Alternatively, use a dosa pancake mix (available in most Asian food shops) and follow the instructions on the packet.

For the spiced potatoes, heat the oil in a pan over a medium-high heat and add the mustard seeds. When they crackle, add the dried red chilli and chana dal and let the dal turn golden, then throw in the curry leaves. When they wrinkle, add the onions and sauté for 4–6 minutes, until the onions are translucent. Now add the green chillies, ginger and turmeric and sauté for 1 minute. Add the salt and grated potatoes and mix well. Set aside and keep hot.

For the green coconut chutney, mix together all the ingredients in a blender or food processor and blend to a soft spooning consistency. To temper the chutney, heat the oil until very hot, then add the curry leaves and mustard seeds. As soon as they crackle, pour them into the chutney, then set aside.

To make dosa pancakes, add salt to taste to the fermented mixture and mix well. Heat a well-seasoned or non-stick frying pan on a medium heat. Smear the surface of the pan with a little oil and use a ladle to pour 2–3 tablespoons of batter into the centre of the pan. Then, using the back of the ladle, spread it out quickly with an outward circular motion to form a thin pancake about 10cm in diameter. This can be tricky for novices, but gets easier the more you make, so persevere.

When the pancake is crisp and golden, flip it on to a plate, spoon the spiced potatoes into the centre and either roll or fold it into a triangle-shaped parcel. Continue until all the dosa mixture and spiced potatoes are used. Serve hot with the chutney and, if you like, sprinkle with a little chilli powder.

MAIN COURSES

If you can't find sea bream, this very simple baked fish recipe works just as well with any flat fish. The spice and herb paste works especially well with the chilled yoghurt rice as an accompaniment. In the summer cook the fish on a barbecue for an added smoky, char-grilled flavour.

SERVES 4

BAKED SEA BREAM IN GREEN SPICE PASTE WITH YOGHURT RICE

4 sea bream, scaled, gutted and butterflied (ask your fishmonger to do this)
½ teaspoon Chaat Masala (page 21)
juice of 1 lemon

For the marinade
1 teaspoon Garlic Paste (page 18)
1 teaspoon Ginger Paste (page 18)
1 teaspoon finely ground white pepper
1 teaspoon salt
½ teaspoon ground turmeric
2 tablespoons vegetable oil

For the Green Spice Paste
100g fresh coriander (roots, stalks and leaves), washed
30g mint leaves
6 green chillies, chopped
1 teaspoon salt
½ teaspoon Garam Masala (page 20)
42g Greek yoghurt

For the Yoghurt Rice
100g Greek yoghurt
70g basmati rice, boiled
1 green chilli, chopped
1cm piece of fresh ginger, peeled and finely chopped
1½ teaspoons chopped fresh coriander leaves and stalks
½ teaspoon salt
½ teaspoon sugar
1 tablespoon vegetable oil
½ teaspoon black mustard seeds
6 fresh curry leaves
a pinch of ground asafoetida

2 tablespoons whole milk
2 tablespoons fresh pomegranate seeds

Wash and pat dry the sea bream. Mix together all the ingredients for the marinade, then rub them all over the sea bream and set aside to marinate for 15 minutes.

For the green spice paste, put all the ingredients except the yoghurt in a blender or food processor and blitz until a smooth paste forms.

After the fish has marinated, mix the green spice paste with the yoghurt and then gently spread on to the marinated fish, taking care not to break it. Leave the fish to marinate for a further 30 minutes.

Place the sea bream on a baking tray and transfer to an oven preheated to 220°C/Gas Mark 7 and roast for 12–15 minutes, turning the fish over once, until the flesh flakes easily.

Meanwhile, make the yoghurt rice. Stir together the yoghurt, rice, chilli, ginger, coriander, salt and sugar in a small bowl. Heat the oil in a pan until smoking point and add the mustard seeds.

When they crackle, add the curry leaves and, once they have wilted, add the asafoetida. Pour this warm tempering into the rice and yoghurt mixture. Add the milk and fold everything together. Sprinkle with the pomegranate seeds. Cover and chill until required.

When the fish are cooked, remove them from the oven, sprinkle with the chaat masala and lemon juice and serve immediately with the yoghurt rice on the side.

Vivek's tip
Having the fish butterflied by the fishmonger gets rid of most bones. And even though there may still be some small bones for you to pick out, you'll still find it much more convenient.

This is a great recipe for roasting a whole fish with spices. It's quite flexible in the sense that you could use a wide variety of fish, as long as it's the right size for each fish to serve one person. The firm texture of sea bream makes it ideal for roasting and works really well with the flavours from the spices.

SERVES 4

SPICE-CRUSTED WHOLE FISH

4 whole fish, such as bass, bream or red snapper, 350–400g each, cleaned, gutted, scaled if necessary and fins and tail trimmed
4 tablespoons melted butter or ghee, to baste

For the marinade
1 tablespoon Ginger and Garlic Paste (page 18)
1 tablespoon salt
2 teaspoons red chilli powder
1 teaspoon ground turmeric
½ teaspoon ajowan seeds
½ teaspoon black onion seeds
juice of 2 lemons

For the spice crust
2 tablespoons vegetable oil
1 tablespoon gram (chickpea) flour
100g chopped fresh coriander leaves and stalks
6 garlic cloves, coarsely chopped
5cm piece of fresh ginger, peeled and coarsely chopped
1½ tablespoons cumin seeds, roasted
1 tablespoon coriander seeds, roasted
1 teaspoon sugar
½ teaspoon dried red chilli flakes
½ teaspoon salt
50g Greek yoghurt

To start the spice crust, heat 1 tablespoon of the oil in a frying pan. Gradually add the gram flour, stirring over a low heat for 2–3 minutes to prevent lumps from forming. When it is blended and smooth, remove the pan from the heat and set aside to cool.

Wash and pat the fish dry with kitchen paper. Slash the fish 2 or 3 times on each side with a sharp knife. Mix together all the ingredients for the marinade and rub them into the fish, then set aside to marinate for 10–15 minutes.

Meanwhile, finish the spice crust. Put all the ingredients, except the remaining oil and the gram flour mixture, in a mortar and pound into a coarse paste, gradually adding the remaining 1 tablespoon of oil. Mix in the gram flour mixture and the yoghurt. Apply the spice crust on both sides of the fish to form an even coating. Fill the belly of the fish with any leftover mixture.

Place the fish on a baking tray and cook in an oven preheated to 200°C/Gas Mark 6 for 15–18 minutes, turning the fish around once for even cooking. Baste regularly with clarified butter or ghee. If the fish start to get too much colour, reduce the temperature to 180°C/Gas Mark 4 after 6–8 minutes; you may need to cover the fish with kitchen foil to prevent the skin from getting too dark and the spice crust from burning.

Serve the fish with pilau rice and /or a green salad, with lemon wedges for squeezing over.

CINNAMON KITCHEN CLASSICS:
STEP BY STEP

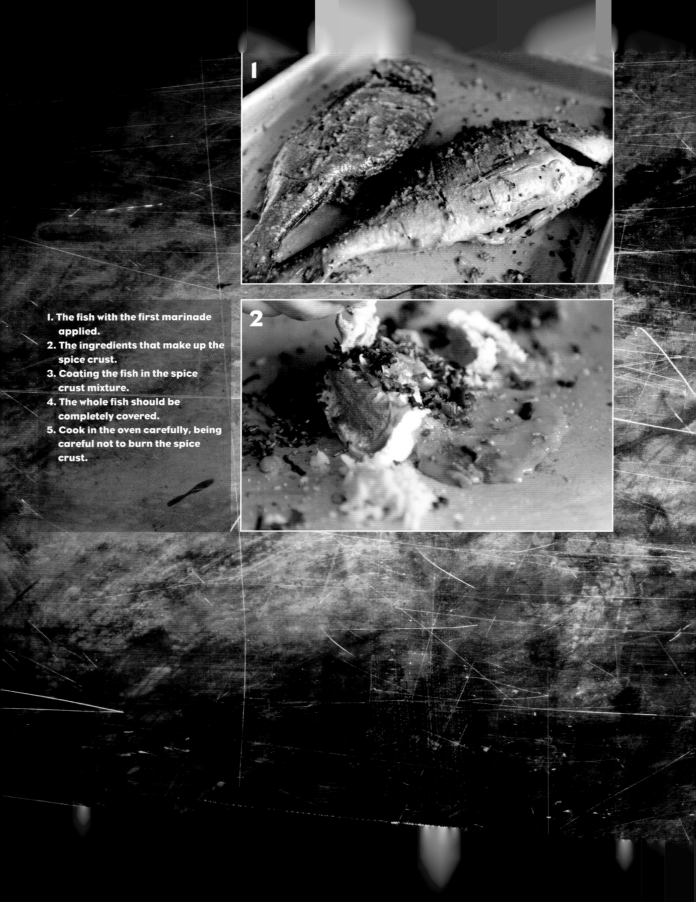

1. The fish with the first marinade applied.
2. The ingredients that make up the spice crust.
3. Coating the fish in the spice crust mixture.
4. The whole fish should be completely covered.
5. Cook in the oven carefully, being careful not to burn the spice crust.

The lime leaves in these fishcakes gives them a fresh zing, which I like a lot, and they complement the acidity in the Goan sauce very well, too. These fishcakes can be seared, as I have suggested below, or steamed if you prefer.

SERVES 4

CRAB AND COD KOFTAS WITH GOAN CURRY SAUCE

500g cod fillet, skinned
300g fresh white crab meat
30g butter, melted
5cm piece of fresh ginger, peeled and finely chopped
4 green chillies, finely chopped
2 fresh lime leaves, finely shredded
2 red onions, finely chopped
2 tablespoons chopped fresh coriander leaves and stalks
1 teaspoon salt
3 tablespoons vegetable oil

For the Goan Spice Mix
10 cloves
1 tablespoon coriander seeds
1½ teaspoons black peppercorns
2 black cardamom pods
3 star anise
5 dried red chillies
4 garlic cloves, chopped
2 tablespoons white vinegar
1 tablespoon sugar
1 teaspoon salt

For the Goan Curry Sauce
3 tablespoons vegetable oil
1 onion, finely chopped
½ teaspoon red chilli powder
2 tomatoes, chopped
125ml fish stock
100ml coconut milk

Wash the cod fillet and dry with kitchen paper. To make the koftas, mince the cod fillet coarsely in a food processor or chop it finely with a large knife. Mix it with the crab, butter, ginger, chillies, lime leaves, onions, coriander and salt, then divide into 8 equal balls and shape them into patties. Cover and chill until required.

For the Goan spice mix, dry-roast the spices individually in a frying pan on a medium heat until they release their aroma. Blend them with the garlic and vinegar in a food processor or a mortar and pestle, gradually adding the sugar and salt.

To make the sauce, heat the oil in a deep pan, add the onion and sauté. When the onion is softened and starts to turn golden, add the chilli powder and cook for 30 seconds. Increase the heat, add the tomatoes and cook for 4–6 minutes, until they have disintegrated and are almost dry. Now lower the heat, add the spice mix and cook for 5–6 minutes, until the oil starts to separate. Add the fish stock and simmer for 3–4 minutes. Increase the heat, add the coconut milk and simmer for about 5 minutes, until the sauce thickens and becomes

glossy. The sauce should now taste hot and sour.

Heat the oil in an ovenproof frying pan on a medium heat, add the koftas and sear for 2–3 minutes on each side until golden brown. Transfer them to an oven preheated to 200°C/Gas Mark 6 and cook for 3–5 minutes.

Pour some sauce on to 4 serving plates and arrange the koftas on top. It is delicious served with Lemon Rice (see page 217) and wilted spinach.

This is one of Cinnamon Kitchen's originals that we had on the menu when we opened back in 2008. The dish received fantastic feedback from critics and customers alike. Feel free to replace the haddock with cod, hake, pollack, plaice or any other white fish of your choice. Hot rice is an ideal accompaniment.

SERVES 4

HADDOCK WITH CRAB AND KOKUM CRUST

4 boneless haddock steaks, about 140g each
2 tablespoons vegetable oil

For the marinade
2 dried whole red chillies, crushed
½ teaspoon salt
½ teaspoon fennel seeds
¼ teaspoon onion seeds

For the Crab and Kokum Crust
80g fresh white crab meat
10g kokum berries, soaked in hot water, then squeezed and chopped
1 tablespoon chopped fresh coriander leaves and stalks
1cm piece of fresh ginger, peeled and finely chopped
1 green chilli, finely chopped
½ red onion, finely chopped
1 teaspoon salt
30g butter
30g breadcrumbs (ideally panko breadcrumbs)

For the Coconut and Ginger Sauce
3 tablespoons vegetable oil
6–8 fresh curry leaves
2 green chillies, slit lengthways
1 onion, sliced
5cm piece of fresh ginger, peeled and cut into fine strips
½ teaspoon ground turmeric
250ml fish stock or water
125ml coconut milk
½ teaspoon salt
a pinch of sugar

Wash the haddock steaks, trim them into square portions and pat dry on kitchen paper. Mix together all the spices for the marinade, then rub them over the fish pieces and leave to marinate for 10 minutes.

For the crab and kokum crust, mix together all the ingredients except the butter and breadcrumbs, then set aside. Heat a pan, add the breadcrumbs and toast on a low heat, gradually adding the butter. Remove from the heat and, when the crumbs are cool, add them to the crab mixture and set aside.

Make the sauce. Heat the oil in a heavy-based pan, add the curry leaves, chillies, onion and ginger and fry them on a medium heat until the onion is softened. Add the turmeric and fry for 1 minute. Add the fish stock, cover and let it simmer for 5 minutes. Add the coconut milk and salt and continue simmering until the sauce thickens. Add the sugar.

Heat the oil in a large ovenproof frying pan on a medium-high heat, add the haddock portions, skin-side down, and sear for 2–3 minutes, until the skin is crisp. Transfer to an oven preheated to 180°C/Gas Mark 4 and cook for about 6 minutes,

until the flesh flakes easily.

Cover the top of the haddock portions evenly with the crust mixture. Place under a hot grill for 1–2 minutes, until golden. To serve, place the fish on 4 serving plates and pour the sauce around. Wilted spinach is a good accompaniment.

In essence, this is a traditional Bengali fish curry, but made more interesting by the addition of shrimps and mussels. Cutting the fish into large chunks allows for better appreciation of the texture of the fish, too. I like barramundi for its meatiness and firm texture. It also reminds me of bekti, a freshwater fish we used to eat all the time in Kolkata, where the Bengalis swear by their fish dishes. Here in the UK, barramundi hasn't been much valued, as some people find it earthy or muddy. Now, however, it seems to be growing in popularity, with barramundi farms established in the New Forest, in Hampshire.

SERVES 4

BARRAMUNDI, MUSSELS AND SHRIMPS, DOI MAACH STYLE

600g barramundi fillets, cut into 8
    equal pieces
150g shrimps or small prawns, peeled
    and deveined
200g live mussels
1 tablespoon chopped fresh coriander
    leaves and stalks

For the marinade
200g plain yoghurt
1½ teaspoons salt
1 teaspoon Garlic Paste (page 18)
1 teaspoon Ginger Paste (page 18)
1 teaspoon red chilli powder
1 teaspoon ground turmeric

For the sauce
4 tablespoons mustard oil (or use 4
    tablespoons vegetable oil mixed
    with 2 teaspoons English mustard),
    plus extra for drizzling
3 cloves
2 green cardamom pods
2.5cm piece of cinnamon stick
1 teaspoon black peppercorns
1 bay leaf
1 teaspoon black mustard seeds
2 onions, finely chopped
1 teaspoon salt
4 green chillies, slit lengthways
200g plain yoghurt

Pat the barramundi pieces and the shrimps dry on kitchen paper, then set aside the shrimps. Mix together all the ingredients for the marinade, then gently rub them over the barramundi pieces and set aside to marinate for 30 minutes. Take care not to break up the fish.

Meanwhile, wash and clean the mussels. Discard any open ones that do not snap shut when tapped, then set aside the remainder.

Heat the mustard oil in a large, heavy-based pan on a medium heat. Add the cloves, cardamom pods, cinnamon, peppercorns and bay leaf and fry for 30 seconds, then add the mustard seeds and let them crackle. Add the onions and sauté for 4–6 minutes, until translucent.

Add the barramundi and its marinade to the pan and mix gently, but thoroughly. Add the salt and cook for 5–6 minutes. Add the shrimps and cook for another 1–2 minutes, stirring occasionally, followed by the green chillies and mussels. Gradually add the yoghurt, stirring well after each spoonful, cover and cook on a low heat for

4–5 minutes, until the fish flakes easily and the mussels open. Discard any mussels that remain closed.

Sprinkle with the coriander and drizzle with the mustard oil. Serve with steamed rice.

When the organisers of a London restaurant festival called upon five chefs from all over the city to give their own 'twist' to quintessential British favourites, this was my interpretation of the ever-popular fish and chips.

SERVES 4

AMRITSAR-SPICED HALIBUT STUFFED WITH MUSTARD MUSHY PEAS WITH CAPER KACHUMBER AND TANDOORI POTATO WEDGES

500g halibut fillets, cut into 4 equal-sized portions
oil for deep-frying

For the Caper Kachumber
½ small cucumber, deseeded and cut into 5mm dice
½ red onion, cut into 5mm dice
2 small tomatoes, deseeded and cut into 5mm dice
3 tablespoons capers
3 tablespoons extra-virgin olive oil
2 teaspoons chopped fresh coriander leaves and stalks
2 teaspoons finely chopped chives
1 teaspoon sugar
1 teaspoon salt
½ teaspoon Chaat Masala (page 21)
juice of ½ lime

For the marinade
1 teaspoon Ginger Paste (page 18)
1 teaspoon Garlic Paste (page 18)
1 teaspoon salt
juice of ½ lime
½ teaspoon red chilli powder

For the Mustard Mushy Peas
300g shelled peas, fresh or thawed (preferably petits pois)
2.5cm piece of fresh ginger, peeled and roughly chopped
3 green chillies
3 garlic cloves, peeled

1½ tablespoons mustard oil (or use 1½ tablespoons vegetable oil mixed with ½ teaspoon English mustard)
½ teaspoon salt
½ teaspoon sugar
juice of ½ lime

For the Tandoori Potato Wedges
4 large Desiree potatoes, peeled and cut in half
1 litre water
3 tablespoons white wine vinegar
2 teaspoons salt

For the potatoes' filling
4 ready-to-eat dried figs, cut into 5mm dice
2 green chillies, finely chopped
2.5cm piece of fresh ginger, peeled and finely chopped
1 tablespoon raisins
1 tablespoon chopped fresh coriander leaves and stalks
1 tablespoon chopped mint
½ tablespoon cashew nuts, fried in a small amount of oil and lightly crushed
½ teaspoon salt
juice of ½ lime

For the batter
2 tablespoons gram (chickpea) flour
1 tablespoon rice flour
½ teaspoon salt

1 teaspoon red chilli powder
juice of 1 lemon
½ teaspoon ajowan seeds
¼ teaspoon Garam Masala (page 20)
1cm piece of fresh ginger, peeled and finely chopped
1 tablespoon chopped fresh coriander leaves and stalks
50ml water

First make the caper kachumber. Place the diced cucumber, red onion, tomato and capers in a non-metallic bowl. Whisk together the olive oil, chives, sugar, salt, chaat masala and lime juice to make a dressing and mix it with the diced vegetables and capers. Check the seasoning, cover, then set aside in the fridge.

Wash and pat dry the halibut fillets on kitchen paper. Mix together all the ingredients for the marinade, rub them over the halibut fillets and leave to marinate for 15 minutes.

To make the mustard mushy peas, put the peas, ginger, chillies, garlic, 1 tablespoon of the mustard oil, salt and sugar in a blender or food processor and blend to make a smooth purée. Check the seasoning and finish with the lime juice, then fold in the rest of the mustard oil. Divide the mixture into 4 equal portions. Place each portion on a sheet of cling film and twist from both ends to make a thin roll, about 1cm in diameter. Put the mushy pea portions in the freezer to set.

Begin the tandoori potato wedges. With an apple corer or a melon baller, carefully scoop out the centre of each potato half to make a hollow shell about 5mm thick, then set aside. Cut the trimmings into 5mm dice and set aside.

Put the water, vinegar and salt in a saucepan and bring to the boil. Add the potato shells and return the water to the boil, then drain. Dry the potatoes on kitchen paper.

Heat enough oil for deep-frying in a deep-fat fryer or a large, deep saucepan to 170°C. Add the potato shells and fry for about 6–7 minutes, until lightly coloured. Remove them and leave to drain on kitchen paper. Now fry the diced potato until crisp and golden and drain on kitchen paper.

Mix together all the ingredients for the potato filling with the fried diced potato and carefully use to stuff the potato shells.

With a filleting knife or a metal skewer, carefully cut a pocket into the centre of each piece of halibut, taking care not to cut through. Remove the mushy pea rods from the freezer and unwrap. Gently press one rod into each pocket.

Transfer the potato shells to a roasting tray, and place in an oven preheated to 180°C/Gas Mark 4 and roast for 10 minutes.

Meanwhile, mix together the ingredients for the batter until smooth and thick. Heat more oil for deep-frying to 190°C. Quickly dip the fish into the batter, letting the excess drip back into the bowl. Fry the fish for 4–5 minutes, until crisp and golden.

Cut each potato shell into 4 wedges and serve with the fried halibut and caper kachumber.

This classic Anglo-Indian dish derives from the popular kichri – rice and lentils cooked together with ginger, chillies and onions. The British adapted the dish by adding eggs and smoked fish and it then made its way back here as a breakfast dish. Often the eggs are just boiled and flaked into the rice, but here we have also poached one and placed it on top. It makes for an excellent brunch dish, too.

SERVES 4

SMOKED HADDOCK KEDGEREE 'KICHRI'

1 tablespoon vegetable oil
1 onion, chopped
2.5cm piece of fresh ginger, peeled and finely chopped
2 green chillies, finely chopped
1 tomato, deseeded and chopped into 1cm dice
1 teaspoon ground turmeric
2 tablespoons fish stock or water
500g basmati rice, boiled
1 teaspoon salt
2 hard-boiled eggs, the whites chopped and yolk discarded
150g undyed smoked haddock, poached in a little milk and flaked
1 tablespoon chopped fresh coriander leaves and stalks
30g butter
2 tablespoons single cream
freshly ground black pepper

For the poached eggs
1 litre water
2 tablespoon white wine vinegar
1 teaspoon salt
4 eggs

Heat the oil in a pan, add the onion and sauté over a medium heat for 4–6 minutes until it is translucent. Add the ginger, chillies and tomato, stirring to mix well. Add the turmeric and cook for a minute and then add the fish stock. Tip in the boiled rice, then add the salt, fold in the chopped egg white and flaked haddock and sprinkle in the coriander. Gently stir in the butter and cream and remove from the heat.

For the poached egg, take a shallow pan and pour in the water, add the vinegar and salt and simmer. Now carefully break the eggs and simmer slowly till the whites coagulate and a thin film is formed on the yolk in the centre. You must take care that, at no stage, the water in the pan comes to boiling point, as it will ruin the eggs.

Divide the kedgeree into bowls, grind a twist or two of freshly milled pepper, top with the poached eggs and serve immediately.

The prawns can be cooked just as well on a barbecue if you happen to have one going, and being served with a simple home-style kedgeree made with rice and lentils completes the dish beautifully. Rather than simply cooking the prawns in the kedgeree, which is traditional but doesn't allow for full appreciation of textures, this version is helped immensely by recreating the tandoori effect, and the spices really bolster the flavours as well as textures.

SERVES 4

TANDOORI-STYLE KING PRAWNS WITH BENGALI KEDGEREE

800g raw, headless king prawns
a few salad leaves or cress to garnish

For the first marinade
I tablespoon Ginger and Garlic Paste
   (page 18)
I teaspoon salt
juice of ½ lemon

For the second marinade
12g Greek yoghurt
½ teaspoon ajowan seeds
½ teaspoon ground turmeric
I teaspoon red chilli powder
2.5cm piece of fresh ginger, finely
   chopped
2 green chillies, finely chopped
I tablespoon vegetable oil

For the Bengali kedgeree
100g split yellow mung beans
500ml water
a pinch of ground turmeric
3 tablespoons ghee or vegetable oil
4 cloves of garlic, finely chopped
½ teaspoon cumin seeds
I large onion, chopped
Icm piece of fresh ginger, peeled and
   finely chopped
2 green chillies, finely chopped
I½ teaspoons salt
75g basmati rice, boiled
I tomato, deseeded and cut into Icm dice
2 tablespoons chopped fresh
   coriander leaves and stalks
juice of I lemon

Peel the prawns and devein them by making a shallow cut along the back and lifting out the dark intestinal vein with the point of a sharp knife. Wash. Put them in a bowl, add the ingredients for the first marinade and mix well. Cover and leave to marinate for 20 minutes. Now combine all the ingredients for the second marinade and coat the prawns well in the mixture. Cover and set aside to marinate for 10 minutes.

To make the kedgeree, wash the mung beans, put them in a pan with the water and turmeric and bring to a boil. Simmer for 25 minutes until the lentils are disintegrated and all the water has evaporated, then remove from the heat and set aside.

Place half a dozen bamboo skewers in a bowl or pan of water and leave them to soak for 30 minutes.

Heat the ghee or oil in a pan to smoking point and add the cumin seeds. When they crackle, add the garlic and onion and cook for 4–6 minutes until translucent. Add the ginger, green chillies and cook for 2 minutes. Stir in the cooked mung beans and salt, and then gently fold in the rice. Mix in

the tomato and stir over a low heat for 3–4 minutes until the tomato has softened. Finish with the coriander and lemon juice. Remove from the heat and keep warm. Now skewer the prawns onto the bamboo skewers and bake in a preheated oven at 200°C/ Gas Mark 6 for 10–12 minutes until cooked. We cook them in a tandoor at 220°C/ Gas Mark 7 for 5–6 minutes.

To serve, divide the kedgeree between 4 serving plates, place the prawns on the kedgeree and garnish with salad leaves.

This recipe for tandoori-style salmon gets an unusual twist from the addition of horseradish in the marinade, a very British combination.

SERVES 4

SALMON WITH DILL AND HORSERADISH

4 salmon fillets, about 150g each, cut
    into 75g chunks

For the first marinade
1 tablespoon Ginger and Garlic Paste
    (page 18)
1 teaspoon salt
juice of 1/2 lemon

For the second marinade
2.5cm piece of fresh ginger, peeled
    and finely chopped
2 green chillies, finely chopped
50g Greek yoghurt
2 tablespoons grated horseradish
2 tablespoons vegetable oil
2 teaspoons chopped dill
1 teaspoon chopped fresh coriander
    leaves and stalks
1 teaspoon finely ground white pepper
1/2 teaspoon sugar

Wash and pat dry the salmon fillets. Mix together all the ingredients for the first marinade, then rub them over the salmon fillets and leave to marinate for 15 minutes.

For the second marinade, mix together all the ingredients, then rub them over the salmon and leave to marinate for an additional 15 minutes.

Use long metal skewers to skewer the fish chunks and place, skin side down, on a baking tray. Roast the salmon in an oven preheated to 200°C/Gas Mark 6 for 7 minutes, then place under a hot grill for 2 minutes.

Alternatively, place the fish skin-side down on a hot barbecue and cook for 10–12 minutes, turning them over every 3–4 minutes, until the skins are crisp and well coloured.

Serve with lemon wedges and chutneys of your choice.

I love southern Indian coconut-based sauces, and sometimes just a little adjustment or shift in the proportions of the spices gives very different results. This recipe gives a little prominence to kokum berries, the astringent, tomato-like fruit so commonly used in Kerala.

SERVES 4

SPICE-CRUSTED TILAPIA WITH KOKUM CURRY

8 tilapia fillets
3 tablespoons vegetable oil
I quantity Citrus Mashed Potatoes
    (page 226)

For the marinade
I teaspoon Ginger Paste (page 18)
½ teaspoon Garlic Paste (page 18)
I teaspoon salt
¾ teaspoon ground turmeric
½ teaspoon red chilli powder
juice of ½ lemon

For the spice crust
I dried red chilli
I teaspoon cumin seeds
I teaspoon coriander seeds

For the kokum curry
3 tablespoons vegetable oil
10 fresh curry leaves
I large onion, chopped
2 teaspoons red chilli powder
I teaspoon salt
2 tomatoes, finely chopped
2 kokum berries, soaked in hot water
    for 20 minutes
3 tablespoons fish stock
250ml coconut milk
juice of ½ lemon

Wash and pat dry the tilapia fillets on kitchen paper. Mix together all the ingredients for the marinade, then rub them over the fish and set aside for 30 minutes.

To make the spice crust, roast the spices together in a dry frying pan on a medium heat for 1–2 minutes, until the aromas are released. Pound together in a mortar and pestle until crushed coarsely. Set aside.

Meanwhile, make the kokum curry. Heat the oil in a heavy-based pan, add the curry leaves and onion and sauté for 6–8 minutes, until the onion is translucent. Add the chilli powder, salt and tomatoes and cook on a high heat until the tomatoes are softened and the liquid has evaporated. Add the kokum berries with the soaking liquid and fish stock and simmer for 2–3 minutes. Stir in the coconut milk and simmer for a further 2–3 minutes, until the sauce is creamy. Finish with a squeeze of lemon.

Heat the remaining 3 tablespoons of oil in an ovenproof frying pan on a medium-low heat, add the tilapia fillets and sear for 2 minutes on each side. Transfer the pan to an oven preheated to 200°C/

Gas Mark 6 and roast for 10 minutes, until the fillets are cooked. Sprinkle the spice crust evenly on the fillets.

Divide the sauce between 4 serving plates, put the fish on top and serve with the citrus mash.

Vivek's tip
You might find kokum berry labelled as black mangosteen in the UK. Look for them in Asian food shops, but if you don't find any, substitute tamarind paste.

The aubergine crush and kachumber are probably two of the most familiar Indian accompaniments and might be considered mundane in most circumstances, but the combination with a simple fried fillet of sea bass is stunning. The sprinkle of stir-fried peas and cumin has a dramatic impact and makes it a great springtime dish. It's also a great dish for entertaining, as much of it can be prepared in advance.

SERVES 4

SEARED SEA BASS WITH ROASTED AUBERGINE CRUSH AND PETITS POIS

4 sea bass fillets (or any white fish), pin-boned, and with skin slashed two or 3 times
1 tablespoon vegetable oil
1 quantity of Aubergine Crush (page 219)
Coriander Chutney (page 22), to serve

For the marinade
1 teaspoon salt
½ teaspoon fennel seeds
½ teaspoon black onion seeds
½ teaspoon red chilli flakes

For the petits pois stir-fry
1 teaspoon vegetable oil
½ teaspoon cumin seeds
1 green chilli, finely chopped
100g shelled petit pois, fresh or thawed
½ teaspoon salt
½ tablespoon chopped mint leaves

First make the marinade by mixing together all the ingredients, then rub them over the fish, cover and set aside for 10 minutes.

Heat the oil in a large, non-stick frying pan, add the fish fillets, skin-side down, and sear on a medium-high heat for 3–4 minutes, until well coloured underneath. Turn and cook for another 2 minutes, or until just cooked through.

To make the petits pois stir-fry, heat the oil in a frying pan to smoking point on a medium-high heat, add the cumin seeds and let them crackle. Then add the green chillies, peas and salt and stir-fry for 2 minutes or so until the peas are cooked but still retain a bright colour. Finish with the chopped mint and remove from the heat.

To serve, place the aubergine crush in the centre of each plate and put the fish on top, then spoon the coriander chutney around. Finish by garnishing with the stir-fried petits pois.

Inspired by a Keralan favourite, moily – a fish curry made with coconut milk, curry leaves, green chillies and ginger – this recipe highlights the beauty of its simplicity. Being so simple, it's also demanding in that the fish must be extremely fresh for the dish to be fully appreciated.

SERVES 4

KERALAN SEAFOOD PIES

500g live mussels, scrubbed and de-
bearded (discard any open ones
that do not snap shut when tapped)
250g peeled and deveined raw
prawns
200g undyed smoked haddock fillet,
cut into 2.5cm dice
200g squid tubes or cuttlefish,
cleaned and scored
2 green chillies, slit lengthways
500g puff pastry, thawed if frozen,
rolled into 4 x 16cm circles, each
about 3mm thick
1 egg, beaten, to glaze
black mustard seeds, to garnish

For the sauce
2 tablespoons coconut oil or
vegetable oil
a sprig of fresh curry leaves (about 20
leaves)
1 large onion, sliced
2.5cm piece of fresh ginger, peeled
and cut into fine strips
6 green chillies, slit lengthways
1/2 teaspoon ground turmeric
1 1/2 teaspoons rice flour
500ml extra-thick coconut milk
(if using canned milk, separate the
thick milk from the thin)
1 teaspoon salt

For the salad
100g sprouted fenugreek seeds
100g sprouted mung beans
1 tomato, deseeded and cut into 5mm
dice

1 green chilli, finely chopped (optional)
1/2 cucumber, deseeded and cut into
5mm dice
2 tablespoons olive oil
juice of 1/2 lemon
1/2 teaspoon salt
1/2 teaspoon sugar

First make the sauce. Heat the oil in a large frying pan, add 12 curry leaves, onion, ginger and green chillies and cook, stirring, for 6–8 minutes, until the onion is translucent. Add the turmeric, followed by the rice flour, stirring to mix in the rice flour evenly. Add the coconut milk and salt.

Add the mussels and simmer for 2–3 minutes, until the mussels open up and sauce begins to turn glossy. Remove the mussels from the pan and discard any mussels that haven't opened. Remove the remainder from their shells and set aside, and discard the shells. Continue simmering the sauce until very thick. Remove from the heat and set aside. When cool, stir in the shelled mussels and remaining seafood.

Divide the mixture among 4 shallow cast-iron skillets or ovenproof dishes and sprinkle each pie with a couple of curry leaves and half a green chilli.

Cover each skillet with a puff pastry circle, brush with the egg glaze and sprinkle with the black onion seeds. Transfer to a fan-assisted oven preheated to 220°C/Gas Mark 7 and bake for 10–12 minutes, until the pastry is crisp and golden. The pies need to be cooked as briefly as possible. In a conventional oven the pies will cook more slowly, so roll the pastry more thinly to help reduce the cooking time (otherwise the fish will overcook).

Meanwhile, make the salad. Place the sprouted seeds and beans, the tomato, green chilli, if using, and cucumber in a mixing bowl. Whisk together the olive oil, lemon juice, salt and sugar to make a dressing and combine it with the diced ingredients. Set aside.

Vivek's tip
It's great if you want to make your own puff pastry, but it's available in supermarkets.
If you are buying, however, go for the all-butter variety. It is by far the best tasting.

A traditional dum-cooked biryani is a classic family dish, suitable for entertaining large numbers. Our Lucknow Biryani is an attempt to simplify this otherwise complex dish. Precooking the chicken and assembling the rice and meat in a casserole pot ensures a quicker, simpler, safer result. Compared to the Hyderabadi version, which uses raw marinated meat, this is easier to master. Remove the lid when all the guests are around, for as the steam escapes the pot, it will fill the surroundings with the aroma of saffron, rose water and spices.

SERVES 4–6

LUCKNOW-STYLE BLACK LEG CHICKEN BIRYANI

250g basmati rice
750g chicken thighs, skin and bones removed and cut in half

For the marinade

2 medium onions, sliced and deep-fried until golden
2 tablespoons Ginger and Garlic Paste (page 18)
1 tablespoon red chilli powder
1 teaspoon turmeric
1 teaspoon Garam Masala (page 20)
1/8 nutmeg grated
6 green chillies, slit lengthways
1 small bunch mint, chopped
1/2 bunch of fresh coriander, chopped
juice of 1 lemon
2 tablespoons vegetable oil
150g plain yoghurt
75ml single cream
1 teaspoon salt
1 teaspoon sugar

Spices for boiling

3 litres water
5 green cardamom pods
2 bay leaves
4 cloves
2 blades of mace
1 tablespoon cumin
3 tablespoons salt

50g ghee or vegetable oil
a few strands saffron, soaked in 1/2 cup warm milk for 5 minutes
1 tablespoon rosewater or screwpine essence

Begin by washing and soaking the rice for 20 minutes in cold water, then allow it to drain in a sieve. Mix all the ingredients for the marinade, add the chicken pieces and set aside for 30 minutes. Meanwhile, mix the saffron and warm milk with the ghee and rosewater or screwpine essence.

In the casserole dish you intend to use for the biryani, bring the chicken and the marinade to a simmer on a low flame and cook for 20 minutes or so until the chicken is tender.

In a large saucepan boil 1.5 litres water with the whole spices and salt, reduce the heat and simmer for 5 minutes. Add the drained, soaked rice and boil for about 8–9 minutes. The rice should be more than three-quarters cooked. Drain and arrange the rice in a layer over the marinated cooked chicken.

Sprinkle some chopped mint over the layer of rice, along with the soaked saffron mix, and cover the casserole with a lid. You may wish to seal the lid using some dough to create a pressure cooker effect. Put the casserole on a low flame for 5–7 minutes until steam starts escaping from the lid, then

remove from the heat. Set the casserole aside to rest for 5 minutes after taking it off the heat.

Serve the biryani with a raita of your choice.

Over the years this has been such a favourite of ours that we couldn't resist the temptation to add it to this book. Small tweaks such as using young chicken (poussin) just make it slightly different from our previous versions.

SERVES 4

OLD DELHI STYLE BUTTER CHICKEN

2 x 750g free-range young chicken (poussin), skinned and each cut in half along the backbone (alternatively use 800g boned chicken thighs cut into two)

For the marinade
120g Greek yoghurt
2 tablespoons Ginger and Garlic Paste (page 18)
1 tablespoon vegetable oil
1½ teaspoons salt
juice of 1 lemon
3 teaspoons red chilli powder
1 teaspoon ground cumin
½ teaspoon Garam Masala (page 20)

For the sauce
1kg tomatoes
125ml water
5cm piece of fresh ginger, peeled, half crushed and half finely chopped
4 garlic cloves, peeled
4 green cardamom pods
1 bay leaf
1 tablespoon red chilli powder
80g butter, diced
2 green chillies, slit lengthways
75 ml single cream
1 teaspoon salt
2 teaspoon dried fenugreek leaves, crushed between your fingertips
½ teaspoon Garam Masala (page 20)
1 tablespoon sugar

First prepare the chicken. Make small cuts all over the chicken pieces with a sharp knife to help the marinade penetrate. To prepare the marinade, mix together the yoghurt with all the other ingredients for the marinade in a deep bowl. Smear the cut chicken with the marinade, cover and set aside in the fridge for 10 minutes.

Cook the chicken in an oven preheated to 220°C/Gas Mark 7 for 13–15 minutes. You may need to turn the pieces after 8–10 minutes or so to ensure they colour evenly on both sides. Cut the cooked chicken into smaller pieces as per your preference. The chicken should not be completely cooked at this point as it will be simmered for a few more minutes in the sauce. Strain off the juices through a fine sieve and set aside.

For the sauce, slice the tomatoes in half and place in a pan with the water, crushed ginger, garlic, cardamom, cloves and bay leaf and simmer until the tomatoes have completely disintegrated. Now blend this tomato broth with a hand-held blender and pass it through a sieve to obtain a smooth purée. Return to a clean pan, add the chilli powder and

simmer for 12–15 minutes. It should slowly begin to thicken. When the sauce turns glossy, add the chicken pieces and the reserved roasting juices. Then add a cup of water and simmer for about 3–5 minutes until the water is absorbed and the sauce returns to its original glossy consistency.

Slowly whisk in the butter, a couple of pieces at a time, and simmer for 6–8 minutes, until the chicken is cooked through and the sauce is beginning to acquire a glaze. Add the chopped ginger, green chillies and cream and simmer for a minute or two longer, taking care that the sauce does not split. Stir in the salt, crushed fenugreek leaves and garam masala, then check the seasoning and add the sugar. Serve with naan bread (page 227) or pilau rice.

This is our version of a deconstructed chicken butter masala, but the spicing and cooking allow for much better appreciation of the quality of chicken being used. All the various elements come together to create layers of flavour, colour and texture.

SERVES 4

SPICE-CRUSTED CHICKEN BREAST WITH FENUGREEK SAUCE

4 x chicken breasts, skinned and bone removed
2 tablespoons Coriander Chutney (page 22)

For the marinade
1 tablespoon vegetable oil
1 tablespoon Ginger and Garlic Paste (page 18)
¼ teaspoon turmeric
1 teaspoon salt
4 peppercorns, crushed coarsely
3 or 4 cloves

For the crust
½ tablespoon vegetable oil
2 cloves of garlic, finely chopped
1 red onion, finely chopped
1 tomato, deseeded and finely chopped
1 tablespoon sprouted fenugreek seeds
2 tablespoons finely chopped coriander leaves and stalks
½ teaspoon salt
½ teaspoon sugar
pinch ground cinnamon

For the sauce
2½ tablespoons vegetable oil
1 bay leaf
2 green cardamom pods
1 teaspoon cumin seeds
3 medium onions, finely chopped
2 teaspoons Ginger and Garlic Paste (page 18)
2 or 3 green chillies, slit lengthways
½ teaspoon turmeric powder
1 teaspoon salt
1 teaspoon red chilli powder
2 tomatoes, finely chopped
75g plain yoghurt
240ml chicken stock or water
50g fresh fenugreek leaves (chopped and washed thoroughly)
1 teaspoon dried fenugreek leaves, crushed between your fingertips
1 teaspoon cinnamon powder
½ teaspoon sugar
2 tablespoons single cream
10g salted butter, chilled and cut into small dice

Flatten the chicken breasts slightly, using a rolling pin or a mallet. Mix together the ingredients for the marinade, spread over the chicken, cover and place in the refrigerator for 10 minutes.

Take a piece of aluminium foil large enough to cover a cutting board and place one chicken breast on it. Spread one tablespoon of coriander chutney across it and cover with the second breast, placed so that the top end of one breast overlaps the tail of the second breast. Wrap tightly with aluminium foil. Crimp the edges to seal the wrap properly. Do the same with the second pair of breasts.

To cook the chicken, heat enough water in a heavy-based pan, bring to a boil and then drop in the foil-wrapped parcels, allowing the chicken to simmer in the liquid for 8–10 minutes.

In the meantime, heat the oil in another heavy-based pan to smoking point on a medium-high heat and add the whole spices (bay leaf, cardamom and cumin seeds. Once they crackle, add the onion and cook on a medium heat for 5–6 minutes until it is translucent. Add the ginger and garlic paste, green chillies, turmeric powder, salt and red chilli powder and sauté for 2 minutes. Now add the tomatoes and cook for 5–8 minutes, until the oil begins to separate. Now gradually add the yoghurt, a spoonful at a time, and cook stirring continuously, for 3–4 minutes, until all the yoghurt is incorporated. Pour in the chicken stock or water, cover and simmer for 5–6 minutes. Remove the lid and add the fresh and dried fenugreek leaves, cinnamon powder, sugar and cream and simmer for another 2 minutes.

Stir in the butter and keep warm.

Having poached the chicken breast pairs, remove them from the foil, pat-dry and, each pair still sandwiched together, sear in a hot ovenproof frying pan for a couple of minutes on each side to get a good golden colour. Then transfer the pan to an oven preheated to 170°C /Gas Mark 3 for 4–5 minutes. Remove from the oven and allow to cool slightly for a couple of minutes.

For the crust, heat the oil in a pan and fry the garlic briefly until it turns golden. Add the onions and sauté over a high heat for two minutes until the onions get slightly coloured outside, but still remain crunchy. Now add the tomato, fenugreek and coriander. On a high heat stir for 1 minute, add the salt and sugar and finish with the cinnamon. Remove from the heat and spread the crust across the top of each chicken breast 'sandwich'. Cut across the breasts to expose the layers of chutney and crust. Each half should be enough for a portion.

To serve, divide the sauce between 4 serving plates and place the chicken on top. Serve with pilau rice and wilted spinach, if you like.

Chilli chicken is one of my favourite things to eat, but sadly I can't find the Indo-Chinese version that I so crave, unless, of course, I make a trek to Dalchini – an Indo-Chinese restaurant in Wimbledon. The use of Indian spices alongside soy sauce is a result of a sizeable Chinese population that has lived in India for centuries. I find this dish works well as a starter and as a main, or just served as a snack with drinks.

SERVES 4

INDO-CHINESE STIR-FRIED CHICKEN WITH DRIED CHILLIES

700g chicken thighs, skinned, boned and cut in half
oil for deep-frying

For the marinade
3 garlic cloves, chopped
4 tablespoons cornflour
I egg, lightly beaten
I tablespoon light soy sauce
I tablespoon dark soy sauce
I tablespoon rice vinegar
½ chicken stock cube
I½ teaspoons salt

For the stir-fry
3 tablespoons vegetable oil
2 dried red chillies, broken into pieces
3 garlic cloves, finely chopped
2 red onions, finely chopped
½ red or green pepper, cut into 2.5cm dice
I teaspoon salt
I½ teaspoons sugar
I teaspoon red chilli powder
I teaspoon ground cumin
2 teaspoons dark soy sauce
½ chicken stock cube
I tablespoon cornflour, mixed to a paste with a little water
juice of ½ lemon
2 tablespoons chopped chives or spring onions

Mix together all the ingredients for the marinade, then rub them all over the chicken thighs, cover and set aside in the fridge to marinate for 30 minutes.

Heat enough oil for deep-frying in a deep-fat fryer or a deep, heavy-based saucepan to 190°C. Add the chicken pieces and deep-fry for about 5 minutes, until they are crisp, golden brown and just cooked through. Drain on kitchen paper and set aside.

For the stir-fry, heat the oil in a wok until smoking point. Add the dried red chillies and move them around quickly. As they darken, add the garlic and stir quickly. As soon as the garlic starts to change colour, add the onions and the red or green pepper and stir-fry until softened, after about 2 minutes. Then add the fried chicken, salt, sugar, red chilli powder and cumin and continue stir-frying, on a high heat, for 1–2 minutes. Finally add the soy sauce and chicken seasoning and mix well.

When all the vegetables are softened and the spices well combined, add the cornflour paste and stir quickly to mix evenly. This gives the dish an attractive glaze and also thickens the sauce. Squeeze in the lemon juice, add the chives or spring onions and serve immediately with steamed rice or noodles.

Vivek's tip
The secret of this dish is that you should never let the heat in the pan reduce. Your burner should be on high throughout and you should add an ingredient to the pan only when you are sure it is hot enough.

This is my variation on a typical Kashmiri-style yakhni, better known as a korma. The addition of mint and green chillies gives this otherwise traditional and mild curry freshness, zing and bite!

SERVES 4

LAMB KORMA WITH GREEN CHILLIES AND MINT

750g boned leg of lamb, trimmed and
    cut into 2.5cm cubes
1 litre water
5 black peppercorns
2 black cardamom pods
2 bay leaves

½ quantity of Spiced Cashew Nut
    Paste (page 20)
200g plain yoghurt

For the sauce
6 tablespoons ghee or vegetable oil
3 green cardamom pods
2 cloves
5cm piece of fresh ginger, peeled and
    ground in a mortar and pestle or
    blender
4 garlic cloves, crushed
1½ teaspoons salt
6–8 green chillies, slit lengthways
750ml water
1 red onion, finely chopped
½ bunch fresh mint, crushed in a
    blender
¼ teaspoon Mace and Cardamom
    Powder (page 20)
1 tablespoon single cream
juice of 1 lemon

Wash the lamb in cold water, then set aside. Put the water, peppercorns, cardamom pods and bay leaves into a large pan and bring to the boil. Add the lamb, bring the water back to the boil and skim the scum from the surface. Drain through a colander and set the lamb aside.

Next make the paste. Combine the prepared cashew nut paste with the yoghurt, blitz until smooth in a food processor and then pass through a sieve.

For the sauce, heat half the ghee in a heavy-based pan to smoking point and add the cardamom pods and cloves. When they crackle, add the ginger and garlic and cook, stirring to prevent sticking, for 2–3 minutes. Add the lamb to the pan and sauté it on a high heat for 5 minutes without letting it colour. Stir in the salt. Add the green chillies and water, cover the pan, reduce the heat and allow the lamb to simmer for 35–40 minutes, until it is tender.

Gradually stir in the cashew and yoghurt paste and continue stirring until the mixture comes to the boil. Stir in the onion, mint, mace and cardamom powder and the remaining ghee and simmer

for 3–4 minutes, until the onions are cooked but still crunchy. Just before serving stir in the cream and lemon juice and serve with hot rice or parathas.

Vivek's tip
Blanching the lamb helps get rid of any blood in the meat, keeping it light in colour.

This is a deconstructed version of the quintessential Punjabi favourite, saag gosht. In many ways, I prefer this dish over the traditional version as it allows for much better appreciation of both fantastic British lamb and the garlic-spiced spinach. If you want something extra to serve with this, roughly chop any vegetables you have in the fridge and sauté with some garlic, cumin seeds and dried red chilli flakes to serve as an accompaniment.

SERVES 4

CHAR-GRILLED RUMP OF LAMB WITH GARLIC AND SPINACH SAUCE

4 x 175–200g rumps of lamb, fat
   trimmed off
2 tablespoons vegetable oil

For the first marinade
1 tablespoon Ginger and Garlic Paste
   (page 18)
1 tablespoon vegetable oil
1/2 teaspoon salt
1/2 teaspoon red chilli powder
juice of 1/2 lemon

For the second marinade
25g Greek yoghurt
1/2 teaspoon salt
a pinch of sugar
1/2 teaspoon red chilli powder
1/2 teaspoon Garam Masala (page 20)

For the sauce
1kg young spinach leaves
4 tablespoons ghee or vegetable oil
1 teaspoon cumin seeds
2 garlic cloves, finely chopped
1 large onion, finely chopped
4 green chillies, finely chopped
2.5cm piece of ginger, peeled and
   finely chopped
1 1/2 teaspoons ground coriander
1 teaspoon salt
1 1/2 teaspoons gram (chickpea) flour
25g butter
75ml single cream
a pinch of sugar
1 teaspoon dried fenugreek leaves,
   crushed between your fingertips
1/4 nutmeg

Mix together all the ingredients for the first marinade, then rub them over the lamb rumps and leave to marinate for 20–30 minutes.

Meanwhile, mix together all the ingredients for the second marinade and set aside.

To begin the sauce, bring a pan of salted water to the boil. Add the spinach leaves and cook until wilted, then immediately drain and cool in a bowl of iced water. Drain the spinach a second time, squeezing to remove all the water and blitz in a blender or food processor to make a very smooth green paste. Set aside.

Heat the oil in a heavy-based ovenproof frying pan on a medium-high heat, add the lamb and sear for 3 minutes on each side. Remove the pan from the heat and set aside in a warm place for 5 minutes. Now apply the second marinade. Transfer to an oven preheated to 180°C/Gas Mark 4 and roast for 6 minutes. Set aside the meat to rest for 6 minutes while you finish the sauce.

Heat the ghee or oil to smoking point and add the cumin seeds. When they crackle, add the garlic and cook until golden. Add the

onion, reduce the heat and continue cooking for 4–6 minutes until it is translucent. Add the chillies and ginger, stir in the ground coriander and salt and sauté for 2 minutes. Gradually add the gram flour, stirring over a low heat for 1–2 minutes to prevent lumps from forming. When it has turned golden, add the spinach paste and mix thoroughly. Now stir in the butter, then fold in the cream slowly, otherwise the mixture may separate. Add the sugar and adjust the seasoning, if necessary. Finish by sprinkling in the fenugreek leaves and grating in the nutmeg. Do not cook for too long after adding the spinach paste as it will discolour and render the dish unappetising in appearance.

When the meat has rested, slice thinly and serve with the sauce, pilau rice and some stir-fried vegetables, if you like.

Vivek's tips
As with cooking any good roast, remember to rest your meat for a good amount of time – for this rump it needs to rest for as long as it cooks. If you slice it as soon as it comes out of the oven, all the juices will 'bleed' on to the plate.

This is a very traditional curry that the nomadic tribes in Rajasthan would probably make with goat rather than lamb. Feel free to try goat if you can find any.

SERVES 4

LAMB AND SWEETCORN CURRY

750g boneless lamb shoulder meat, trimmed and cut into 2.5cm dice
6 tablespoons ghee or vegetable oil
12 cloves
4 black cardamom pods
2 bay leaves
2 onions, finely chopped
6 green chillies, slit lengthways
2 teaspoons salt
I teaspoon ground coriander
I teaspoon ground cumin
I teaspoon ground turmeric
I tablespoon Garlic Paste (page 18)
200g sweetcorn kernels, either frozen or canned is fine
250g plain yoghurt
125ml lamb stock or water, plus extra, if necessary
6cm piece of fresh ginger, peeled and finely chopped
50g fresh coriander leaves and stalks, chopped
juice of I lemon

To start making the curry heat the ghee to smoking point in a heavy-based pan and add the cloves, cardamom pods and bay leaves. When they crackle, add the onions and cook on a medium heat until golden. Add the green chillies, salt, ground coriander, cumin and turmeric and stir for 1 minute. Stir in the garlic paste and continue cooking for 1–2 minutes. Now add the lamb and cook, moving it around on a high heat, for 4–5 minutes, until lightly browned all over. Stir in three-quarters of the sweetcorn kernels and gradually add the yoghurt, stirring well after each spoonful. If you add it too quickly, it will split and make the curry grainy.

Once yoghurt is incorporated, continue stirring and allow the mixture to come to the boil. Add the lamb stock, reduce the heat and simmer, uncovered, for about 30 minutes, stirring occasionally, until the sweetcorn is creamy and soft and the sauce has thickened. Add the ginger, fresh coriander and the remaining sweetcorn kernels, pour in a little more lamb stock or water, if required, and continue simmering over a low heat for 10 minutes. Check the seasoning and finish by squeezing in the lemon juice.

Serve the curry hot with rice or with chickpea breads (see Missi Roti recipe, page 230).

Don't let the picture and cheffy flourishes with sauce put you off; this is a very simple, yet impressive dish to wow your guests with at a dinner party. You can make the sauce and marinate the meat ahead of time, leaving you just to roast, rest, slice and serve!

SERVES 4

ROAST RACK OF LAMB WITH SAFFRON SAUCE

2 x 8-bone racks of lamb, cut in half
1 tablespoon vegetable oil

For the marinade
1 tablespoon Ginger and Garlic Paste
    (page 18)
1 teaspoon red chilli powder
1 tablespoon vegetable oil
1 teaspoon salt
juice of 1 lemon
12g Greek yoghurt
1 tablespoon chopped fresh coriander
    leaves and stalks
½ teaspoon Garam Masala (page 20)
a pinch of sugar

For the sauce
1 tablespoon vegetable oil
4 cloves
2 black cardamom pods
2 bay leaves
400g tomatoes, roughly chopped
2 garlic cloves, crushed
1 large onion, roughly chopped
2.5cm piece of fresh ginger, peeled
    and ground in a mortar and pestle
2 teaspoons red chilli powder
500ml chicken stock or water
1 teaspoon salt
½ teaspoon sugar
¼ teaspoon Garam Masala (page 20)
a small pinch of saffron strands
2 tablespoons single cream
15g cold butter

If the racks of lamb haven't already been prepared, trim off the skin and most of the fat, leaving just a thin layer of fat on the meat. Mix together the ingredients for the marinade, rub them over the lamb and set aside for 30 minutes.

To make the sauce, heat the oil to smoking point in a large saucepan and add the cloves, cardamom pods and the bay leaves. When they crackle, add the tomatoes, garlic, onion and ginger and cook for 4–5 minutes, until the tomatoes and onions are softened. Add the red chilli powder and stock and simmer on a low heat for about 15 minutes, until the tomatoes have completely broken down and the onion is very soft. Purée the sauce in a blender or food processor, then strain it through a fine sieve into a clean pan. Bring the sauce back to the boil, then simmer until thick enough to coat the back of a wooden spoon. Add the salt, sugar and garam masala, then sprinkle in the saffron and simmer for 2–3 minutes. Just before serving stir in the cream and finally finish the sauce by stirring in the cold butter. Do not let the sauce boil after adding the butter or it will separate and become thin. Set aside and keep hot.

To cook the lamb, heat the oil in a large, heavy-based frying pan on a high heat. Add the lamb racks and sear for 2–3 minutes, until browned all over. Transfer them to a roasting tray and place in an oven preheated to 200°C/Gas Mark 6 and roast for up to 15 minutes, depending on how well done you like your meat. Remove from the oven and leave to rest in a warm place for 5 minutes.

Divide the sauce between 4 serving plates, place the lamb on top and serve immediately with Stir-Fried Greens (see page 220).

Vivek's tips
The cream and butter emulsify the sauce, so they are added at the very end of cooking the sauce, after you have checked the seasoning, so the sauce doesn't separate and become thin.

As a rule of thumb, for a very pink and beautiful medium-rare finish, you rest the meat for as long as you cook it. So, if you like your meat really pink in the centre, sear it for a couple minutes, then roast in the oven for 6–8 minutes, remove it and leave it to rest for 10 minutes before slicing. Slice the meat only when it is well rested.

This is a typical example of Malai marinade prepared in northern India. It is traditionally used with chicken, but I find it brilliant with lambs' pencil fillets (the equivalent of fillet of beef). The tender meat greatly benefits from the aromas of mace and cardamom. The addition of finely chopped pickled onions as a garnish lifts the dish immensely, too. Neck fillets can be a substitute if pencil fillets aren't available, although they need cooking for a little longer.

SERVES 4

CHAR-GRILLED LAMB FILLET FLAVOURED WITH MACE AND CARDAMOM

750g lamb pencil fillets, cut into
    4–6 pieces, trimmed
2 tablespoons vegetable oil

For the first marinade
½ teaspoon salt
½ tablespoon Ginger and Garlic Paste
    (page 18)

For the second marinade
2 green chillies, finely chopped
I tablespoon chopped fresh coriander
    leaves and stalks
½ tablespoon Ginger and Garlic Paste
    (page 18)
2.5cm piece of fresh ginger, peeled
    and finely chopped
25g Greek yoghurt
I teaspoon cream cheese
    (Philadelphia will do)
I teaspoon salt
I teaspoon single cream
½ teaspoon Mace and Cardamom
    Powder (page 20)
⅛ nutmeg, grated

Aubergine Crush (page 219)
Pickled Onions, to garnish (page 23)

Rinse and pat dry the lamb fillets. Mix together the ingredients for the first marinade, then rub this over the lamb fillets and set aside for 10 minutes. In the meantime mix together all the ingredients for the second marinade and stir well to combine.

Heat the oil in a large, ovenproof frying pan on a high heat. Remove the fillets from the marinade and sear for 1 minute on each side until lightly coloured. Remove the fillets from the pan and allow to cool slightly before applying half of the second marinade.

Return the lamb fillets to the pan and place in an oven preheated to 180°C/Gas Mark 4 and roast for 8 minutes.

Remove the pan from the oven and leave the lamb to rest for 5 minutes. Spread the remaining marinade over and flash the fillets under a hot grill for 2 minutes, until they lightly crisp.

Slice each fillet into 3 pieces and serve on a bed of the aubergine crush with pickled onions sprinkled over.

Vivek's tips
The lamb can also be chopped and wrapped in naan bread or served with pilau rice and a sauce of your choice. If you want to grill the fillets on a barbecue, you don't have to brown them in the pan first.

This is one of my favourite recipes, perfect for entertaining lots of guests in one go. Although the recipe calls for lamb, feel free to use hogget, mutton, or even goat, so long as you stick with the shoulders.

SERVES 8–10

SPICE-BRAISED SHOULDER OF LAMB

2 shoulders of lamb, weighing about 1.5kg each, trimmed of any surface fat
2 tablespoons red chilli powder
8 tablespoons Ginger and Garlic Paste (page 18)
250ml malt vinegar
500g plain yoghurt
1 quantity Crisp Fried Onions (page 23), crushed
2 teaspoons royal (black) cumin seeds
1 tablespoon chopped green coriander, stalks and leaves.
1 tablespoon dried rose petals
1 tablespoon salt
3 potatoes, peeled and sliced 1cm thick
3 large red onions, sliced 1cm thick
6 bay leaves
3 cinnamon sticks, about 5cm each
5 green cardamom pods
500ml water
2 tablespoons melted butter
2 teaspoons lemon juice
1 teaspoon Chaat Masala (page 21)
4 tablespoons single cream
1 teaspoon Garam Masala (page 20)
1 tablespoon chopped fresh coriander leaves and stalks

With the tip of a sharp knife, cut small incisions in the lamb shoulders at approximately 5cm intervals. Mix together the red chilli powder, ginger and garlic paste, vinegar, yoghurt, fried onions, cumin seeds, coriander, rose petals and salt. Using your hands, massage the spice mixture over the shoulders, rubbing and pressing the spices into the gashes created by the knife. Set aside for 15 minutes.

Arrange the sliced potato and onion on a deep oiled baking tray. Place the shoulders on top of the potato and onion slices, add the bay leaves, cinnamon and cardamom, then pour the water around the shoulders and cover the tray with foil. Place in an oven preheated to 180°C/Gas Mark 4 and braise for 2½ hours, until the meat is very tender and ready to fall off the bone. Remove the shoulders from the liquid and place on a cooling rack. Pass the liquid through a fine sieve and reserve to make the sauce.

Now roast the shoulders on a barbecue or under a very hot grill, basting frequently with the melted butter, until crisp and well browned. Finish with a drizzle of lemon juice, any leftover melted butter and the chaat masala.

For the sauce, bring the cooking juices to the boil in a small pan and simmer until reduced to a coating consistency. Correct the seasoning and gradually stir in the cream, garam masala and fresh coriander. Pour the sauce over the meat and serve with naan bread (see page 227).

Vivek's tip
It's important to drain all the liquid from the shoulders before roasting them, in order to get a crisp finish.

CINNAMON KITCHEN CLASSICS:
STEP BY STEP

1. Cutting incisions into the lamb with the tip of a sharp knife.
2. Rubbing the marinade ingredients into the lamb.
3. The lamb, covered in its wonderfully flavoursome and aromatic spice mixture.
4. The crisped-up finished lamb.

I enjoy combining British dishes with Indian techniques and flavours. This dish combines two of Britain's best culinary loves, curry and a pie!

SERVES 6

ROGAN JOSH SHEPHERD'S PIE

2 tablespoons vegetable oil
4 cloves
2 bay leaves
2 green cardamom pods
2 dried red chillies
I black cardamom pod
I teaspoon cumin seeds
2 garlic cloves, chopped
3 onions, 2 finely chopped and I sliced
I teaspoon salt
500g boned leg of lamb, diced
1½ tablespoons Ginger and Garlic
   Paste (page 18)
2 teaspoons red chilli powder
2 teaspoons ground coriander
2 teaspoons ground cumin
700g lean lamb mince
2 tablespoons tomato purée
25g plain yoghurt
½ sweet potato, finely diced
100g celeriac, finely diced
100g turnip, finely diced
2 teaspoons chopped fresh coriander
   leaves and stalks

For the potato topping
½ teaspoon ground turmeric
a pinch of salt
200g floury potatoes, such as Maris Piper
25g butter
15g Cheddar cheese, grated

For the spice mix
3 green cardamoms
2 star anise
2.5cm piece of cinnamon stick
I teaspoon fennel seeds

To make the potato topping, bring a pan of water with the turmeric and salt to the boil. Peel and quarter the potatoes, then add them to the pan, return the water to the boil and continue cooking until tender. Drain the potatoes well, then return them to the pan and add the butter and Cheddar cheese. Mash the potatoes, then pass through a fine sieve and set aside.

Heat the oil to smoking point in a large, heavy bottomed pan and add the cloves, bay leaves, green cardamom pods, chillies, black cardamom pod and cumin seeds. When the seeds crackle, add the garlic. When the garlic turns golden, add the finely chopped onion and salt and cook, stirring, on a medium heat until for 4–6 minutes, until the onion is translucent. Add the diced lamb and ginger and garlic paste and cook, stirring, on a medium-high heat for 4–5 minutes, until lightly browned all over. Reduce the heat and simmer, uncovered, for 30 minutes.

Meanwhile, to make the spice mix, roast the whole spices and fennel seeds together in a dry frying pan on a medium heat for 1½ minutes, until their aromas are released. Quickly remove them from the pan and grind or pound them to a fine powder in a spice grinder or mortar and pestle. Set aside.

After the lamb has cooked for 30 minutes, add the chilli powder and ground coriander and cumin and stir for 5 minutes on a medium-low heat. Add the minced lamb and tomato purée and gradually stir in the yoghurt. Cook for another 20 minutes, until the meat is tender and cooked through. Stir in the sweet potato, celeriac, turnip, sliced onion and the spice mix and cook for a further 5–8 minutes, until the vegetables are tender. Check the seasoning and stir in the fresh coriander.

Transfer the meat and vegetable mixture to a pie dish and top with the mashed potato. Transfer to an oven preheated to 200°C/Gas Mark 6 and bake for 10–12 minutes, until the potato topping is golden and the filling piping hot.

Remove the pie from the oven and serve with a green salad.

This rich, sweet and sharp beef stew from Kerala is a thing of joy. My best experience of this curry was in a Christian household in the spice gardens near Cochin. The beef gets so tender it just falls off the fork, and the balance of sweet, spice and heat makes it very special. Serve with plain steamed rice or uttapam: rice flour batter pizzas.

SERVES 4

KERALAN BEEF 'ISHTEW' WITH COCONUT AND VINEGAR

1.5 litres water
2 bay leaves
2.5cm piece of cinnamon stick
4 green cardamom pods
I teaspoon salt
700g beef chuck steak, diced

For the sauce
3 tablespoons coconut or vegetable
  oil
5 cm piece of cinnamon stick
6 cloves
4 green cardamom pods
4 garlic cloves, finely sliced
5cm piece of fresh ginger, peeled and
  cut into strips
3 red onions, thinly sliced
8 green chillies, slit lengthways
10 fresh curry leaves
I teaspoon salt
I tablespoon black peppercorns,
  coarsely crushed
500ml blanching liquor
500ml coconut milk
3 tablespoons toddy (palm) vinegar,
  can be substituted with sherry
  vinegar or white wine vinegar
½ teaspoon Garam Masala (page 20)

Heat the water in a deep pan, add the bay leaf, whole spices and salt and bring to the boil. Let the water boil for 5 minutes, then add the beef and blanch for about 5–7 minutes. Drain the meat and reserve the boiling liquid.

To make the sauce, heat the oil in a pan and add the whole spices, followed by the garlic, ginger, onions, green chillies and curry leaves. Cook over a medium heat for 4–6 minutes until the onion is translucent. Add the blanched beef, salt and pepper and the cooking liquid. Bring to a boil, then reduce the heat and simmer for about 20 minutes. Add the coconut milk and toddy vinegar and cook another 20–25 minutes until the beef is cooked. Sprinkle in the garam masala powder, stir well and remove from heat.

Serve hot with Dosa Pancakes (see page 77).

Indian spiced steak and chips, I suppose! A good steak is hard to beat and this recipe does exactly what it says on the tin. It's steak and chips – but with spice!

SCOTTISH ANGUS FILLET WITH MASALA POTATO WEDGES

4 x 200g fillet steaks

For the marinade
1 teaspoon red chilli powder
½ teaspoon salt
1 tablespoon oil

For the topping
2 tablespoons vegetable oil
1 bay leaf
2 green cardamom pods
1 black cardamom pods
2.5cm piece of cinnamon stick
1 large onion, finely chopped
1 teaspoon salt
2.5cm piece of fresh ginger, peeled
   and finely chopped
1 teaspoon red chilli powder
3 tomatoes, finely chopped
1 green chilli, finely chopped
1 teaspoon Kadhai Masala (page 21)
1 teaspoon single cream
½ teaspoon dried fenugreek leaves,
   crushed between your fingertips
1 tablespoon chopped fresh coriander
30g butter

For the Masala Potato Wedges
4 large floury potatoes, such as Maris
   Piper, peeled and cut into wedges
2 teaspoon salt
1 teaspoon turmeric powder
1.5 litres water
oil for deep-frying

For coating the potatoes
2 tablespoons cornflour
½ teaspoon red chilli powder
1 teaspoon crushed cumin seeds
½ teaspoon onion seeds
2 red onions, sliced into thick rings
1 teaspoon salt

To garnish
½ teaspoon Chaat Masala (page 21)
1 tablespoon of chopped fresh
   coriander leaves and stalks

For the topping, heat oil in a heavy pan on medium-high heat until smoking point, add the whole spices and stir to let them crackle, then add onion and reduce the heat. Then add the salt, cover and cook for another 15–20 minutes until the onions are soft and disintegrated. Add ginger, chilli powder and tomatoes and stir for another 3–5 minutes, until the tomatoes are reduced and the mix becomes quite dry. Add the chopped green chilli and kadhai masala, stir to combine, add the cream, dried fenugreek leaves and chopped coriander. Stir well and remove from the heat. When the crust cools down, pick out whatever whole spices you can from the mix and discard – their job is done.

Blanch the potatoes in a pot of salted hot water and boil with the teaspoon of turmeric for 4 minutes. Drain to discard the liquid. Allow the wedges to cool down. Meanwhile, mix together the ingredients for the coating.

Blend together the marinade ingredients and apply to the steaks. Heat a large heavy-based frying pan to a medium-high heat. Reduce the heat to medium and place the steaks in the pan; sear them on each side for 3–4 minutes for medium-well done. Set the pan aside to rest the meat. Ideally, rest the meat in a warm place for almost as long as you cook it. If you like the meat to be cooked more, place it in a preheated oven at 180°C/Gas Mark 4 to obtain the desired doneness.

Spoon the spice crust onto the steak, dot with blobs of cold butter and keep warm. Place under a grill for about a minute to colour up and serve hot when the guests are ready to eat.

Now finish cooking the potatoes. In a bowl mix together the cornflour, chilli powder, crushed cumin seeds, onion seeds, onion rings and salt and a tiny amount of water if needed and use this mixture to coat the potato wedges. Deep-fry the potatoes for 3–4 minutes until crisp and serve sprinkled with chaat masala and coriander if you like. (The rings of onion add extra texture and colour.)

Divide the potatoes between 4 plates and sit the steak on the side and serve immediately.

Vivek's tip
Fry the wedges just before you serve the steak – this will allow them to remain crisp. You can try the spice-coated potato wedges available in supermarkets if you don't wish to make your own.

This is a rather unusual dish using pork, which is quite uncommon in most of India, but it is even more unusual in that it includes dark soy sauce, usually associated with Indo-Chinese street snacks. Still more unusual for me is the double cooking technique of braising first and then stir-frying, which is very sparingly used in India, but gives a great texture and depth of flavour.

SERVES 4

COORGI-STYLE DOUBLE-COOKED PORK SHOULDER

750g boneless pork shoulder, cut into 2.5cm dice
2 tablespoons fresh chopped coriander leaves and stalks
2.5cm piece of fresh ginger, peeled and cut into fine strips

For the marinade
2 tablespoons Ginger and Garlic Paste (page 18)
1 teaspoon ground turmeric
1 teaspoon red chilli powder
2 teaspoons salt
8–10 black peppercorns
3 bay leaves
4 tablespoons clear honey
3 tablespoons dark soy sauce
10 kokum berries, soaked in 100ml hot water for 30 minutes

For the stir-fry
2 tablespoons vegetable oil
4 dried red chillies
10 fresh curry leaves
4 red onions, sliced 5mm thick

Mix together all the ingredients for the marinade, including the soaking water from the kokum berries. Rub over the pork, cover and leave to marinate in the fridge overnight.

The next day, transfer the pork to a heavy-based saucepan and add just enough water to cover. Bring to a simmer and cook, covered, for 1 hour, or until the pork is very tender. Strain the meat, reserving the liquid.

Heat the oil for stir-frying to smoking point in a large wok or frying pan and add the dried red chillies. When they darken, add the curry leaves and stir-fry for 30 seconds or so, until they start to crisp up. Now add the red onions and stir-fry until translucent. Add the strained pork and stir-fry for 6–8 minutes, until browned. Add a tablespoon or two of the reserved cooking liquid and continue to cook until it has evaporated. The meat will acquire a shiny glaze. Correct the seasoning and serve sprinkled with the fresh coriander and sliced fresh ginger.

Vivek's tip
Use as little water as possible to cook the pork first time around. The liquid will have a stronger flavour when you can add it to the stir-fry later.

Here, ground kadhai spices add crunch and texture to the rich duck livers served on caramelised apple slices. You can substitute chicken livers or foie gras for the duck livers. If you like, serve with Coriander Chutney (see page 22) and a salad of your choice.

SERVES 4

DUCK LIVERS WITH KADHAI SPICES AND GRILLED APPLE

3 tablespoons vegetable oil
I green apple
¼ teaspoon ground cinnamon
¼ teaspoon sugar
I teaspoon coriander seeds
250g duck livers, cleaned and trimmed
I red onion, chopped
I small tomato, deseeded and chopped
I teaspoon ground cumin
I teaspoon chopped ginger
I tablespoon Kadhai Masala (page 21)

I tablespoon chopped fresh coriander leaves and stalks, plus extra to garnish
juice of ½ lemon
micro herbs to garnish

Prepare the apple just before you cook the livers, so it doesn't brown. Core the apple, cut four 1cm slices and brush with oil. Heat a ridged grill pan or frying pan over a high heat. Add the apple slices and cook for about 30 seconds on each side. Sprinkle with the cinnamon and sugar and leave on the heat until the sugar melts and caramelises. The apple should retain a crisp texture. Set aside and keep hot.

Heat the remaining oil in a large frying pan on a medium-high heat, add the coriander seeds and, as they pop, add duck livers and sear for about 30 seconds on each side until browned. Add the onion, tomato and cumin and stir-fry until the livers are cooked through. Sprinkle with chopped ginger and the kadhai masala and finish by adding the coriander leaves and lemon juice.

To serve, divide the grilled apple between 4 serving plates, top each with the stir-fried livers and garnish with more coriander and micro herbs.

This is an example of combining different influences into one dish. Here rabbit legs are braised with spices akin to a French-style confit, then sprinkled with roasted spices and baked for extra flavour and texture.

SERVES 4

BAKED LEG OF RABBIT WITH YOGHURT AND CORNMEAL SAUCE

For the rabbit

1 teaspoon ground turmeric
1 teaspoon salt
1 tablespoon Ginger and Garlic Paste (page 18)
4 rabbit legs, cleaned and left whole with bone in
2 tablespoons vegetable oil
3 green chillies, slit lengthways
½ teaspoon black peppercorns
1cm piece of cinnamon stick
1 bay leaf
1 teaspoon ground turmeric
1 teaspoon red chilli powder

For the spice crust

2 teaspoons black peppercorns
6 cloves
2 teaspoons fennel seeds

For the sauce

1 tablespoon Garlic Paste (page 18)
½ teaspoon turmeric powder
1 teaspoon salt
5cm piece of fresh ginger, peeled and chopped
2 tablespoons fine cornmeal
250ml strained braising liquid
80ml ghee or vegetable oil
8 cloves
2 black cardamom pods
1 bay leaf
2 onions, peeled and finely chopped
50g plain yoghurt
2 tablespoons chopped fresh coriander leaves and stalks
juice of 1 lemon

Firstly, prepare the marinade for the rabbit legs. Mix together the turmeric, salt and ginger and garlic paste, spread over the meat, cover and set aside for 10 minutes. In a deep heavy-based pan, heat half the oil and sear the legs for 2–3 minutes on each side until lightly browned and pour in enough water to cover the legs. Add the chillies, peppercorns, cinnamon stick and bay leaf. Bring the liquid to the boil and simmer, covered, over a low heat for about 45 minutes, or until the legs are tender. Remove the rabbit legs from the heat, drain and reserve the stock. Pat dry the rabbit legs and place on a wire rack. Brush with the remaining oil.

Prepare the spice crust by grinding together the spices in a mortar and pestle; you want a fairly coarse texture. Sprinkle over the rabbit and place in a low oven to keep warm.

Now make the sauce. Mix together the garlic paste, turmeric, salt, chopped ginger, cornmeal and braising liquid in a bowl until well combined. Set aside.

Heat the ghee in a heavy-based pan on a medium-high heat until smoking point. Add the cloves, black cardamom and bay leaf, and when they start to crackle, add the onion and cook on a medium heat for 4–6 minutes until it is translucent. Add the garlic, spice and cooking liquor mixture and cook, stirring well, for 3–4 minutes until everything is thoroughly combined. Gradually add the yoghurt, stirring well after each spoonful. Once all the yoghurt has been incorporated, bring the sauce to the boil, reduce the heat and simmer for 6–8 minutes until thickened. Check the seasoning and finish with the coriander and lemon juice.

Finally, put the rabbit legs on a grill rack and place under a hot grill at for 3–4 minutes, until the legs are warm and the crust begins to crisp. Divide the sauce between 4 plates and serve with the rabbit legs on top.

I love this cut of meat. The cheek is obviously a part of the animal that's done a lot of work, so the muscles are well developed. That means the meat's great for long, slow cooking and it handles spices very well. Remember, as with all tough cuts of meat, the slower the better, and the longer the better!

SERVES 4

BRAISED OX CHEEK IN DATE AND APRICOT SAUCE WITH FONDANT POTATOES

850g cheeks, trimmed and cut into
    90g pieces
3 tablespoons vegetable oil

For the marinade
1 teaspoon Garlic Paste (page 18)
1 teaspoon Ginger Paste (page 18)
2 teaspoons red chilli powder
2 teaspoons salt

For the sauce
3 tablespoons vegetable oil
2 large onions, quartered
4 tomatoes, quartered
1½ teaspoons salt
1 teaspoon red chilli powder
500 ml chicken stock or water
2.5cm piece of cinnamon stick
4 star anise
2 bay leaves
1½ teaspoons black peppercorns
3½ tablespoons malt vinegar
8–10 ready-to-eat dried dates, sliced
5–6 ready-to-eat dried apricots,
    sliced
4 tablespoons single cream

For the fondant potatoes
200g butter
4 Desiree or waxy potatoes, peeled
    and cut in half
4 sprigs of thyme
3 star anise
2.5cm piece of cinnamon stick
1 teaspoon salt
250ml water
oil for shallow-frying

Mix together all the ingredients for the marinade, then rub over the ox cheeks, cover and set aside to marinate for 30 minutes.

Meanwhile, make the sauce. Heat the oil in a heavy-based saucepan. Add the onions and sauté on a medium heat for 4–6 minutes, until translucent. Add the tomatoes, salt and chilli powder and cook for 10–15 minutes, stirring frequently, until the tomatoes start losing their juice. Stir in the stock or water.

Once the ox cheeks have marinated, heat the oil in a heavy-based frying pan on a high heat, add the ox cheeks and sear for 2–3 minutes on both sides until browned.

Arrange the ox cheeks in a casserole just large enough to accommodate them all and evenly spread the sauce on top, making sure the ox cheeks are completely covered. Stir the cinnamon, star anise, bay leaves, peppercorns and malt vinegar into the sauce. Cover the casserole and transfer to an oven preheated to 150°C/ Gas Mark 5 for about 2 hours, until the ox cheeks are tender.

Meanwhile, to make the fondant potatoes, slice the cold butter into a heavy-based pan and neatly arrange the potatoes on top, trying to avoid leaving gaps in between. Add the thyme, star anise and cinnamon and pour over just enough water to cover the potatoes. Add the salt and place the pan over the heat. Cover the potatoes with baking parchment or the pan lid to prevent them from drying out and simmer for about 35 minutes, until the potatoes are tender. Turn up the heat, uncover and cook until the base of the potatoes turns brown.

Remove the potatoes from the buttery liquid and allow to cool slightly. Heat enough oil for shallow-frying in a heavy-based frying pan on a medium-high heat. Add the potatoes and fry for about 3 minutes on each side, until crisp and golden. Drain on kitchen paper and keep hot. Do not discard the oil in the pan.

When the ox cheeks are tender, remove them from the casserole and set aside. Strain the sauce though a fine sieve into a saucepan, pressing down to extract as much flavour as possible. Add the dates and apricots and boil, stirring, for 3–4 minutes, until they are soft. Stir in the cream and simmer for an additional minute and check seasoning. Set aside and keep hot.

Warm the oil in the frying pan on a medium-high heat and transfer the ox cheeks to the pan to caramelise for a couple of minutes on each side for extra texture.

Divide the sauce between 4 serving plates, place the ox cheeks and fondant potatoes on top and serve immediately.

I love cooking with game, but never had the opportunity to do so in India. The British game season gives me an opportunity to revisit, recreate and sometimes re-imagine dishes that have been lost over the years. Traditionally, venison in India was thoroughly cooked with pickling spices over several days, the spices essential for preserving the meat. Today, with such better quality meat and storage conditions, it seems a shame to cook the meat for so long. Instead, we cook the venison to medium and cook the sauce separately. This has become one of our signature dishes.

SERVES 4

ROAST SADDLE OF VENISON WITH PICKLING SAUCE

Ikg venison from the saddle, trimmed
    and cut into 4 steaks
I tablespoon vegetable oil

For the first marinade

I teaspoon salt
I teaspoon red chilli powder
I tablespoon mustard oil (or use
    I tablespoon vegetable oil mixed
    with 1/2 teaspoon English mustard)
IO cloves

For the second marinade

I tablespoon Ginger and Garlic Paste
    (page 18)
25g Greek yoghurt
1/2 teaspoon Garam Masala (page 20)

For the pickling sauce

3 tablespoons mustard oil (or use 3
    tablespoons vegetable oil mixed
    with 1 1/2 teaspoons English mustard)
1/2 teaspoon cumin seeds
1/4 teaspoon fennel seeds
1/4 teaspoon black onion seeds
1/4 teaspoon black mustard seeds
a pinch of fenugreek seeds
I onion, finely chopped
1/2 teaspoon ground turmeric
IO0g cashew nut kernels, soaked in
    warm water for IO minutes, then
    boiled and ground to a paste
45g plain yoghurt
250ml chicken stock or water
4 green chillies, slit lengthways
1/2 teaspoon salt
I tablespoon jaggery or molasses sugar

For the stir-fried beetroot

I tablespoon vegetable oil
2 garlic cloves, finely chopped
1/2 teaspoon cumin seeds
2 cooked beetroots, peeled and cut
    into Icm dice
2 green chillies, finely chopped
Icm piece of fresh ginger, peeled and
    finely chopped
1/2 teaspoon ground coriander
1/2 teaspoon ground cumin
1/2 teaspoon salt
juice of 1/2 lime

Mix together the salt and chilli powder for the marinade, then rub over the steaks and place them on a heatproof tray. Heat the oil in a small pan and, when it reaches smoking point, add the cloves. Once they have started to smoke, remove the pan from the heat and pour the entire mixture evenly over the steaks. Set aside to marinate for 30 minutes.

Meanwhile, prepare the pickling sauce. Heat the oil to smoking point in a heavy-based frying pan and add all the seeds. When they begin to crackle, add the onion and sauté for 4–6 minutes until it is translucent. Add the turmeric, followed by the cashew paste and cook, stirring, on a medium heat for 5 minutes. Now gradually stir in the yoghurt and continue stirring on a low heat for another 5 minutes, taking care the yoghurt does not split. Add the stock, green chillies, salt and jaggery or molasses sugar and simmer for about 10 minutes, until the sauce thickens and becomes glossy. Remove and keep warm while you cook the steaks.

Heat the oil in a large, ovenproof
frying pan on a medium-high heat,
add the meat and sear for
2–3 minutes on each side until
browned all over. Transfer to an
oven preheated to 200°C/Gas Mark 6
and roast for 5 minutes if you like
your meat pink, longer if you like
it cooked more. Remove the
steaks from the oven and leave
to rest for 5 minutes.

Meanwhile, stir-fry the beetroot.
Heat the oil in a heavy-based
frying pan or wok until smoking
point and add the cumin seeds
and when they crackle add the
garlic. When the garlic turns golden,
add the beetroot, chillies, ginger,
ground coriander, cumin and salt
and stir-fry on a high heat for
1 minute. Add the lime juice and
remove the pan from the heat.

Divide the stir-fry between 4 serving
plates, place the venison steaks on
top and pour the sauce on the side.

This is a very basic, rustic curry that could be made with any kind of fowl, but works particularly well with free-roaming, older birds. Their meat is slightly tougher than that of young birds, but there is so much more flavour. I'm using guinea fowl, but you could easily replace this with chicken if you prefer. In the past, people cooked this outdoors over a wood fire with very basic implements; the spices would often be added whole and the vegetables roughly cut, hence the name jungle curry.

SERVES 4

JUNGLE CURRY OF GUINEA FOWL WITH FRESH FENUGREEK

5 tablespoons vegetable oil

5 cloves

2.5cm piece of cinnamon stick, broken in half

2 black cardamom pods

1/2 teaspoon black peppercorns

1/4 teaspoon fenugreek seeds

1 bay leaf

4 onions, finely chopped

1 tablespoon chopped garlic

1 x 1.2–1.5kg whole guinea fowl, skinned and cut into 8 pieces

1 tablespoon Ginger and Garlic Paste (page 18)

2 teaspoons salt

1 teaspoon turmeric

1 1/2 teaspoons red chilli powder

1 teaspoon red chilli flakes

1 teaspoon ground cumin

1 teaspoon ground coriander

4 tomatoes, chopped

120g plain yoghurt

2 green chillies, chopped

500ml water

5 tablespoons fresh fenugreek leaves, blanched in boiling water for 1 minute, then drained and chopped

1/4 teaspoon Garam Masala (page 20)

1/2 teaspoon dried fenugreek leaves, crumbled between your fingers

juice of 1/2 lemon

Heat the oil to smoking point in a large, heavy-based pan, add the whole spices and bay leaf and let them splutter. Once the spices change colour, add the onion and garlic and cook for 4–6 minutes, until the onion is translucent. Add the guinea fowl (or chicken) pieces and stir-fry for 6–8 minutes over a high heat, until starting to brown. Add the ginger and garlic paste, salt, turmeric, chilli powder, chilli flakes, cumin and coriander and cook, stirring, on a high heat for 2–4 minutes. Add the tomatoes and cook for 8–10 minutes, stirring constantly to ensure that the spices do not stick to the bottom of the pan.

Once the oil starts to separate from the masala, gradually add the yoghurt, stirring well after each spoonful. Then add the green chillies, reduce the heat and cook, stirring frequently, until the liquid comes to the boil again. Add the water, bring to the boil, then simmer over a low heat for 10 minutes, or until the meat is fully cooked. Stir in the blanched fenugreek leaves, followed by the garam masala, dried fenugreek and lemon juice. Serve with rice or chapattis.

Vivek's tip
To make this dish dairy free, you could easily replace the yoghurt with water.

This is a great alternative to a traditional Christmas roast goose and can easily be adapted to use up any roast goose leftovers the next day.

SERVES 4

STIR-FRIED SOUTH INDIAN GOOSE BREAST

800g boned goose breast
1 teaspoon salt
2 tablespoons vegetable oil
10 fresh curry leaves
2 green chillies, slit lengthways
2.5cm piece of ginger, peeled and cut into fine strips
2 garlic cloves, finely chopped
2 red onions, thickly sliced
2 tablespoons grated coconut, fresh or thawed
1/2 teaspoon sugar
1/2 teaspoon ground turmeric
3 tablespoons coconut milk
juice of 1/2 lime
1 tablespoon chopped fresh coriander leaves and stalks

For the spice mix
2 dried red chillies
1 1/2 teaspoons coriander seeds
1 tablespoon fennel seeds
1/2 teaspoon cumin seeds
1/2 teaspoon black peppercorns
5cm piece of cinnamon stick
3 cloves
2 green cardamom pods

Start with the goose breast. Heat a heavy-based frying pan on a medium-high heat, add the breast, skin-side down, and sear for 3–4 minutes, until the skin crisps. Sprinkle with salt, turn over and sear the other side for a minute or so. Remove from the heat and leave to rest for 5 minutes.

In the meantime, make the spice mix. Roast all the spices in a dry frying pan on a medium heat for a minute or two, until the aromas are released. Quickly remove them from the heat and pound them in a mortar and pestle to a coarse powder. Set aside.

After the goose breast has rested for 5 minutes, the meat should be medium-rare. Cut it into very thin slices (3–5mm) and set aside.

Heat the oil in a heavy-based frying pan or wok and add the curry leaves, chillies, ginger, garlic and onions and sauté on a high heat for 1 minute, until the onions are coloured, but still crunchy. Add the grated coconut, spice mix, sugar and turmeric and continue stirring for another minute. Now stir in the seared meat. Reduce the heat, stir in the coconut milk and continue sautéing until the liquid has evaporated and the meat pieces are evenly coated with the spices. Add the lime juice, sprinkle with the coriander and serve hot with naans or parathas.

Saag Paneer, saag aloo, saag gosht, saag vegetables... you get the drift. This is an entire list of Indian dishes based around a spinach curry. I, too, love these dishes, but feel that most Indian cooks don't treat spinach well enough to fully preserve its nutrients, taste and colour. Here I deconstruct this classic by cooking the sauce separately from the vegetables to better preserve the spinach and its nutrients.

SERVES 4

ROASTED YOUNG VEGETABLES IN SPINACH CURRY

1½ tablespoons vegetable oil
1 teaspoon cumin seeds
4 garlic cloves, finely chopped
200g baby carrots, washed and trimmed
200g baby turnips, washed and cut in half
100g baby fennel, washed and cut in half lengthways
100g young celery stalk, washed and cut lengthways
100g radishes, washed and trimmed
2.5cm piece of fresh ginger, peeled and finely chopped
2 green chillies, finely chopped
½ teaspoon ground turmeric
1 teaspoon salt
½ teaspoon sugar
1 teaspoon Kadhai Masala (page 21)
2 tablespoons chopped fresh coriander leaves and stalks
juice of ½ lemon

For the sauce
1kg young spinach leaves
50ml ghee or vegetable oil
1 teaspoon cumin seeds
2 garlic cloves, finely chopped
1 large onion, finely chopped
4 green chillies, finely chopped
2.5cm piece of ginger, peeled and finely chopped
1½ teaspoons ground coriander
1 teaspoon salt
1½ teaspoons gram (chickpea) flour
25g butter
75ml single cream

a pinch of sugar
1 teaspoon dried fenugreek leaves, crushed between your fingertips
¼ nutmeg

Start by roasting the vegetables. Heat the oil in a heavy-based pan to smoking point and add the cumin seeds. Allow it to crackle, then add the garlic and stir for a minute until it becomes golden. Now add the vegetables, one by one, in the order as they appear in the ingredient list, followed by the turmeric. Cook the vegetables for a good 3–4 minutes on a high heat. Add the salt, sugar, and kadhai masala and transfer the vegetables to an ovenproof tray. Cook in a preheated oven at 180°C/ Gas Mark 4 for 10–12 minutes. Add the coriander and sprinkle with lemon juice before serving with the spinach curry.

For the spinach curry, begin with the sauce. Bring a pan of salted water to the boil. Add the spinach leaves and cook until wilted, then immediately drain and cool in a bowl of iced water. Drain the spinach again, squeeze to remove all the water and blitz in a blender or food processor to make a very smooth green paste. Set aside.

Heat the ghee or oil to smoking point and add the cumin seeds. When they crackle, add the garlic and cook until golden. Add the onion, reduce the heat and continue cooking for 4–6 minutes until it is translucent. Add the chillies and ginger, stir in the ground coriander and salt and sauté for 2 minutes. Gradually add the gram flour, stirring over a low heat for 1–2 minutes to prevent lumps from forming. When it has turned golden, add the spinach paste and mix thoroughly. Now stir in the butter, then gradually add the cream, stirring well after each spoonful. Add the sugar and adjust the seasoning, if necessary. Finish by crumbling in the fenugreek leaves and grating in the nutmeg. Do not cook for too long after adding the spinach paste, as it will discolour and render the dish unappetising in appearance.

Divide the spinach curry equally between 4 plates and sit the cooked vegetables on top. Serve with either rice or chapattis.

This is a very good vegetarian main course, and easy enough to put together – an ideal dish that allows for better appreciation of colours, flavours and textures.

SPINACH DUMPLINGS AND LEMON RICE

For the dumplings
250g grated cottage cheese
2 large boiled potatoes, grated
100g spinach leaves washed, dried and shredded
2.5cm piece of fresh ginger, peeled and finely chopped
3 green chillies, finely chopped
1 teaspoon salt
½ teaspoon ajowan seeds

For the batter coating
50g gram (chickpea) flour
¼ teaspoon ajowan
½ teaspoon salt
70ml water
150g spinach leaves cleaned, dried and shredded
oil for frying dumplings

For the sauce
6 large tomatoes
100ml water
1 garlic clove, crushed
1cm piece of fresh ginger, peeled and crushed
3 lime leaves, torn
½ lemongrass stalk, outer layer removed and bruised
2 green cardamom pods
2 cloves
1 bay leaf
½ teaspoon salt
1 teaspoon red chilli powder
50ml coconut milk
¼ teaspoon Kadhai Masala (page 21)
¼ teaspoon Garam Masala (page 20)

½ tablespoon sugar
1 quantity of Lemon Rice (page 217)

First make the dumplings. Mix in all the ingredients for the dumpling to form a smooth dough. Divide the mixture into 12 individual balls, the size of golf balls.

For the batter coating, make a smooth batter with the gram flour, ajowan, salt and water. Place the shredded spinach in a tray. Dip the balls in the batter and roll them in the spinach to form a good overall coating. The dumplings are now ready for frying. When you are ready to serve, deep-fry the dumplings at 180°C degrees for about 1½ minutes until crisp and golden green.

For the sauce, wash and cut the tomatoes in half, place them in a heavy-based pan on a medium-high heat and, as they soften, pour in water, add the garlic, crushed ginger, lime leaves, lemongrass and the whole spices and boil until the tomatoes have disintegrated. Add the bay leaf, salt and red chilli powder and cook for a couple of minutes, then pass the tomatoes through a sieve to get a fine tomato purée.

Bring the purée back to the boil, add the coconut milk, stirring constantly and, when the sauce turns glossy, add the kadhai masala and sprinkle in the garam masala powder. Check the seasoning and add sugar if required (sugar helps to balance the sourness of the tomatoes).

Divide the rice between 4 serving plates and serve with the spinach dumplings and the sauce poured around.

A Chinese influence is evident in this vegetarian feast, but the most distinguishing feature of the dish is the thin omelettes we make to envelop the stir-fried rice. The mushrooms on their own are also good to pass round as a snack with drinks.

SERVES 4

ASSAMESE STIR-FRIED MUSHROOMS WITH EGG-FRIED-RICE PARCELS

700g shiitake, chestnut or closed-cup
  mushrooms, stems removed, but
  kept whole and washed and dried
oil for deep-frying

For the marinade
4 tablespoons cornflour
3 garlic cloves, finely chopped
I tablespoon light soy sauce
I tablespoon dark soy sauce
I tablespoon rice vinegar
I teaspoon dried red chilli flakes
I teaspoon salt

For the omelettes
4 eggs
2 teaspoons light soy sauce
2 tablespoons vegetable oil

For the egg-fried rice
I tablespoon vegetable oil
50g green beans, finely chopped
2 green chillies finely chopped
2.5cm piece of fresh ginger, peeled
  and finely chopped
50g shelled peas, fresh or thawed,
  preferably petits pois (optional)
$^{1}/_{2}$ carrot, finely chopped (optional)
I tablespoon light soy sauce
I tablespoon tomato ketchup
a pinch of salt
a pinch of ground black pepper
I egg
250g basmati rice, boiled
2 tablespoons sesame oil

For the stir-fry
2 tablespoons vegetable oil
2 dried red chillies, broken into smaller
  pieces
3 garlic cloves, chopped
2 red onions, chopped
100g tender bamboo shoots, sliced
  5mm thick
I$^{1}/_{2}$ teaspoons sugar
I teaspoon red chilli powder
I teaspoon ground cumin
I teaspoon salt
2 teaspoons light soy sauce
2 spring onions, finely chopped
juice of $^{1}/_{2}$ lemon
I tablespoon chopped chives

First make the omelettes. Break the eggs into a bowl and beat them lightly with the soy sauce. Heat a few drops of oil in a large, non-stick frying pan and pour in one-quarter of the egg mixture. Cook, without stirring, on a medium-high heat until the omelette begins to set, then remove the pan from the heat (without turning the omelette over) and leave the omelette to finish cooking in the residual heat. Remove from the pan and make 3 more. Set aside and keep warm.

Mix together all the ingredients for the marinade in a large bowl, add the mushrooms and set aside to marinate for 10 minutes.

Meanwhile, make the egg-fried-rice. Heat the oil in the frying pan, add the beans, chillies, ginger and the peas and carrot, if using, and stir-fry, on a high heat, for 1 minute. Add the soy sauce, ketchup, salt and pepper and stir-fry for another minute. Break the egg into the pan and scramble, on a high heat, for 30 seconds, then fold in the rice and sesame oil and stir until mixed well and heated through. Lay the omelettes on a work surface, divide the egg-fried rice between them and wrap each to make a neat parcel. Set aside and keep hot.

To deep-fry the mushrooms, heat enough oil for deep-frying in a deep-fat fryer or a deep, heavy-based saucepan to 190°C. If necessary shake any excess liquid off the mushrooms before deep-frying for about 3 minutes, until they are crisp and golden. Drain well on kitchen paper.

For the stir-fry, heat the oil in a wok or large frying pan until smoking point. Add the dried red chillies and stir them quickly.

As they start to darken, quickly stir in the garlic. Almost immediately it will start to change colour. Now add the onions and the deep-fried mushrooms and stir-fry for a couple of minutes. Add the bamboo shoots and stir for another couple of minutes. Add the sugar, chilli powder, cumin and salt and stir-fry for another minute. Add the soy sauce and mix well. Finish with the lemon juice and sprinkle with the spring onions and chopped chives.

Serve immediately with the egg-fried-rice parcels.

Vivek's tip
The secret of any stir-fry is that you should never let the heat in the pan go down; the heat of your burner should always be on maximum the whole time. Add an ingredient to the pan only when you think it's hot enough.

This rather unusual trio of vegetarian dishes makes for an impressive main course. It might look like a long list of ingredients and appear daunting, but the result is well worth the effort. This yoghurt sauce is very versatile and can be thinned and used as a soup, too.

SERVES 4

STUFFED POTATOES, STUFFED COURGETTES AND YOGHURT KADHI SAUCE

oil for deep-frying

For the stuffed potatoes
4 Desiree potatoes, peeled and cut in half
125g paneer cheese, grated
25g salted cashew nuts, roasted in a dry frying pan and then crushed
1½ tablespoons raisins
½ teaspoon salt
I green chilli, finely chopped
Icm piece of fresh ginger, peeled and finely chopped

For the stuffed courgettes
2 courgettes
I tablespoon vegetable oil
½ teaspoon cumin seeds
½ onion, chopped
150g cauliflower, cut into small florets
2 tablespoons shelled peas, fresh or thawed (preferably petits pois)
I teaspoon salt
½ teaspoon red chilli powder
½ teaspoon ground cumin
½ teaspoon ground turmeric
I tomato, deseeded and finely chopped
½ teaspoon Garam Masala (page 20)
I tablespoon chopped fresh coriander leaves and stalks
juice of ½ lemon

Yoghurt Kadhi Sauce (page 225), to serve

First prepare the potatoes and courgettes. With an apple corer or a melon baller, carefully scoop out the centre of each potato half to make a hollow shell about 5mm thick, then set aside. Cut each courgette in half lengthways and use a small spoon to scoop out the centres, leaving hollow shells. Reserve the trimmings. Sprinkle the courgette shells with salt and set aside, upside down, to drain.

To fry the potatoes, heat enough oil for deep-frying to 170°C in a deep-fat fryer or a large, heavy-based saucepan. Add the potatoes and deep-fry for 6–8 minutes, until they are softened and cooked through, but not coloured. Remove them from the oil and drain on kitchen paper. Now heat the oil to 190°C and fry the potatoes again for 2–3 minutes, until crisp and golden brown. Drain well on kitchen paper and leave to cool.

Mix together all the remaining ingredients for the stuffed potatoes. When the potatoes are cold, fill them with the stuffing and set aside.

Next, prepare the courgettes. Heat enough oil for deep-frying in a deep-fat fryer or a deep, heavy-based saucepan. Add the courgettes and fry on a high heat for 1 minute or so, until crisp and light golden brown. Drain them on kitchen paper and leave to cool.

Heat the 1 tablespoon oil to smoking point in a heavy-based frying pan and add the cumin seeds. When they crackle, add the onion and sauté for 4–6 minutes until translucent. Add the cauliflower florets and cook for 3 minutes. When they start to soften, add the green peas, the reserved courgette trimmings, salt, chilli powder, cumin and turmeric and sauté for a couple of minutes. Reduce the heat to the minimum and let the vegetables cook uncovered in their own juices for about 5 minutes. Stir in the tomatoes, sprinkle with garam masala and finish with fresh coriander and lemon juice. Use a spoon to divide the vegetables between the courgette shells.

Put the stuffed potatoes and
courgettes on a baking tray and
transfer to an oven preheated to
180°C/Gas Mark 4 for 6–8 minutes,
until the potatoes and the filling
are hot.

Divide the potatoes and
courgettes between 4 serving
plates and serve with pilau rice
and the yoghurt kadhi sauce.

Vivek's tip
Both the stuffed potatoes and
courgettes can be served as
individual main courses and they
work just as well with either the
Yoghurt Kadhai Sauce, or the
Fenugreek Sauce on page 148.

The paneer element of this dish is particularly good grilled on a barbecue. The smokiness of barbecue cooking is reminiscent of the tandoor. I find that vegetarians are especially thankful to see this at a barbecue party as it gives them at least one proper vegetarian option!

SERVES 4

TANDOORI STYLE PANEER, TOMATO FENUGREEK SAUCE

750g paneer cut into discs, 4cm diameter x ½cm thickness

For the marinade

2 tablespoons vegetable oil
2 tablespoons red chilli powder
2 tablespoons Ginger and Garlic Paste (page 18)
1½ teaspoons ground cumin
250g plain yoghurt
1½ teaspoons salt
juice of 1 lemon

For the tomato and fenugreek sauce

12 very ripe tomatoes, roughly chopped
2 bay leaves
3 garlic cloves, peeled
5cm piece of fresh ginger, half crushed and half chopped finely
3 cloves
3 green cardamom pods
250ml water
2 teaspoons red chilli powder
60g unsalted butter
2 green chillies, finely chopped
½ teaspoon Garam Masala (page 20)
1 teaspoon dried fenugreek leaves, crushed between your fingertips
4 tablespoons single cream
1½ teaspoons salt
2 teaspoons sugar
1 tablespoon finely chopped coriander leaves and stalks

Combine all the ingredients for the marinade in a large bowl, add the paneer pieces and mix well. Thread the paneer on to metal or soaked bamboo skewers and place in the fridge for at least 30 minutes.

Meanwhile, make the sauce. Put the tomatoes, bay leaves, garlic, ginger, cloves, cardamom and water in a pan and bring to the boil. Simmer for 20 minutes until the tomatoes have disintegrated, then remove the bay leaves and leave to cool. Purée the mixture in a blender and then pass it through a sieve. Bring the sauce to the boil in a clean pan, add the red chilli powder and simmer on a low heat for 6–8 minutes until it is quite thick and it coats the back of a spoon. Now add the butter and green chillies and cook for 6–7 minutes over a low heat, stirring constantly so the butter does not split. Add the garam masala and fenugreek and cook for 2–3 minutes. Add the chopped ginger and gradually stir in the cream. Simmer, stirring constantly, until the sauce becomes thick and glossy. Adjust the seasoning by adding salt and sugar, then finish with the coriander stalks. Remove from the heat and keep warm.

Place the paneer skewers on a medium-hot barbecue and cook for 4–5 minutes on each side, until coloured on both sides (or you could cook them under a hot grill). Pour the sauce over the barbecued paneer and serve with naan bread (see page 227).

This version of a Hyderabadi biryani is, suitable for entertaining large numbers and the perfect one-pot meal. It would make an excellent alternative to a Christmas roast or could be served as a side dish. Assorted vegetables are cooked with rice and baked inside a pumpkin shell until steaming hot. When the lid is removed at the table, aromas of rose water, saffron and other spices fill the room – so make sure all of your guests are seated around, ready to be impressed!

SERVES 4–6 AS A MAIN COURSE; 8–10 AS VEGETABLE ACCOMPANIMENT

HYDERABADI BIRYANI OF VEGETABLES IN A PUMPKIN SHELL

1 large pumpkin, top removed and reserved, with the inside scraped out to remove all the seeds and fibres

100g tamarind paste

1 tablespoon dried red chilli flakes

250g basmati rice

1/2 teaspoon salt

3 tablespoons warm milk

a pinch of saffron strands

4 tablespoons ghee or vegetable oil

2 tablespoons rose water or screwpine essence

50g snow peas or thin green beans

75g all-butter puff pastry, thawed if frozen, and cut to cover the top of the pumpkin and rolled to 4–5mm thickness (optional)

1 egg, beaten, to glaze

For the vegetable filling

200g chunky meaty mushrooms of your choice, trimmed and sliced

10 thin green beans, cut into 1cm pieces

2 Jerusalem artichokes, cut into 1cm dice and moistened with lemon juice

1 carrot, cut into 1cm dice

1/2 swede, cut into 1cm dice

1/2 turnip, cut into 1cm dice

1/2 orange-fleshed sweet potato, cut into 1cm dice

1/4 celeriac, cut into 1cm dice

For the marinade

150g plain yoghurt

75ml single cream

6 green chillies, slit lengthways

2 onions, sliced and deep-fried until golden

1/2 bunch of fresh coriander, chopped

2 tablespoons Ginger and Garlic Paste (page 18)

2 tablespoons vegetable oil

1 tablespoon red chilli powder

1 teaspoon ground turmeric

1 teaspoon Garam Masala (page 20)

1/8 nutmeg, grated

juice of 1 lemon

1 teaspoon salt

1 teaspoon sugar

leaves from 1 small bunch of mint, chopped

Spices for boiling

3 litres of water

4 cloves

3 green cardamom pods

2 bay leaves

2 blades of mace

1 tablespoon cumin seeds

3 tablespoons salt

Smear the inside of the pumpkin with the tamarind paste, sprinkle with the chilli flakes, place on a rack and roast in an oven preheated to 180°C/Gas Mark 4 for about 25 minutes, until almost tender, but firmly holding its shape.

Meanwhile, soak the rice in cold water for about 10 minutes, then drain.

Mix together all the ingredients for the marinade in a flameproof casserole, but include only half the mint, then stir in the vegetables for the filling and set aside to marinate for 15 minutes.

Meanwhile, put the water and remaining ingredients for the boiling spices in a large saucepan and bring to the boil. Add the drained rice and boil, uncovered, for 6–8 minutes, until the rice is not quite cooked. Drain well.

Put the warm milk and saffron in a bowl and leave for 3–5 minutes to infuse. Stir in the ghee and rose water or screwpine essence and set aside.

After the vegetables have marinated, put the casserole on a low heat and simmer for about 5 minutes, stirring constantly until the vegetable are about half cooked.

Layer the rice over the simmering vegetables, pour over the saffron mixture and sprinkle with the remaining mint. Cover tightly, increase the heat to high and leave to cook for 5–7 minutes to let steam build up. As soon as the steam starts escaping from the pot, reduce the heat to low and cook for another 8–10 minutes. Remove the casserole from the heat and leave to rest for 5 minutes.

Transfer the biryani to the pumpkin shell, sprinkle with snow peas or beans and cover either with the reserved pumpkin top or with puff pastry, brushed with beaten egg. Place on a baking tray and roast in a preheated oven at 200°C/Gas Mark 6 for 15 minutes, or until the pastry (if using) is crisp and golden.

Vivek's tips
If you don't want to bother with the pumpkin shell, prepare the vegetable biryani as described above, leaving it in the casserole and serve it after it has rested for 5 minutes after coming out of the oven.

You can make a dough seal if your casserole lid isn't tight fitting. Mix together 250g plain white flour and 125ml water. Stretch the dough into a thin strip, long enough to cover the edge of the lid all the way round. Stick the dough on the edge of the lid and place it on the casserole, pressing lightly to make sure the gap is well sealed.

This is actually quite a restaurant-style vegetarian dish which you can easily recreate at home with a little bit of planning. The three different elements bring colour, flavour and texture and create a great 'wow!' factor at a dinner party. It's well worth the effort, so do give it a go.

SERVES 4

CHAR-GRILLED BROCCOLI FLORETS, STUFFED BABY PEPPERS AND TANDOORI PANEER

For the broccoli

1 tablespoon grated Cheddar cheese

25g Greek yoghurt

1 tablespoon Ginger and Garlic Paste (page 18)

1 teaspoon salt

1cm piece of fresh ginger, peeled and finely chopped

1 green chilli, finely chopped

1 tablespoon single cream

1 teaspoon dried rose petals

½ teaspoon Mace and Cardamom Powder (page 20)

1 head of broccoli or two stalks of purple sprouting broccoli, cut into florets, blanched in salted water for 30 seconds, drained and refreshed in iced water

2 tablespoons vegetable oil

1 tablespoon flaked almonds

juice of ½ lemon

For the baby peppers

4 baby red peppers

1 tablespoon vegetable oil

½ teaspoon cumin seeds

½ onion, finely chopped

½ teaspoon salt

½ teaspoon ground turmeric

2.5cm piece of fresh ginger, finely chopped

2 green chillies, finely chopped

⅓ cabbage, finely shredded

1 tablespoon sultanas

1 tablespoon chopped fresh coriander leaves and stalks

For the Tandoori Paneer

1 teaspoon oil

1 teaspoon red chilli powder

½ teaspoon turmeric powder

1 teaspoon Ginger and Garlic Paste (page 18)

1 teaspoon salt

juice of ½ lemon

30g Greek yoghurt

1 teaspoon dried fenugreek leaves, crushed between your fingertips

½ teaspoon sugar

250g paneer cheese, cut into 4 x 1cm thick slices

Garlic and Spinach Sauce (page 113)

First prepare the broccoli. In a bowl, rub the cheese with your fingertips to break up any lumps. Add the yoghurt and mix until smooth. Add the ginger and garlic paste, salt, the chopped ginger and chillies and mix well, then fold in the cream carefully, as the mixture might separate if mixed too vigorously. Finally add the rose petals, mace and cardamom powder and then fold in the broccoli florets. Gently drizzle with a tablespoon of oil, mix everything together, cover and set aside for 20 minutes. Meanwhile, put 4 bamboo skewers in water and leave them to soak for 30 minutes.

Meanwhile cut the baby peppers about ½ cm from the stem end, discard the seeds, but leave whole. Heat ½ tablespoon of oil in a small frying pan on a medium-high heat and sear the peppers for a minute until they slightly char on the outside but still firmly hold their shape. Allow them to cool.

Now prepare the stuffing. In the same pan heat the remaining ½ tablespoon of oil to smoking point and add the cumin seeds.

When they start to crackle add the onion and cook on a medium heat for 2–3 minutes until shiny, but still crunchy. Add the salt, ground turmeric, ginger and chillies and cook for another minute. Now add the cabbage, stirring continuously. Reduce the heat and cook for 3–4 minutes, until the cabbage is soft. Finally add the raisins and coriander. Adjust the seasoning and stuff the blanched peppers with the cabbage mixture. Set aside and keep warm in a low oven.

For the tandoori paneer, mix all the ingredients apart from the cheese in a mixing bowl to make a marinade. Fold in the sliced paneer and set aside to marinate for 15 minutes.

To cook the broccoli, thread the florets on to the soaked bamboo skewers, arrange on an oiled baking tray and place under a hot grill for 5–6 minutes, until the broccoli florets are cooked and slightly charred at the edges. Now sprinkle with the almond flakes and return to the grill to toast for another minute or so until golden brown.

To serve, divide the paneer slices between 4 serving plates. Arrange the broccoli and peppers on the paneer and serve with the spinach sauce poured to the side.

A kadhai is a double-eared Indian wok made of iron. It is different from a Chinese wok, as it does not have a handle and is considerably heavier. Kadhais have a variety of uses in Indian homes. They are used to deep-fry breads and sweets, to make 'dry' curries with coating sauces and to stir-fry vegetables and small pieces of poultry, too. Dishes prepared in a kadhai are traditionally finished with a coarsely ground blend of spices, such as coriander, cumin and fennel seeds, dried red chillies and black peppercorns. You will find many references to kadhai spice mixtures throughout this book and a useful basic recipe for kadhai masala on page 21.   SERVES 4–6

KADHAI PANEER

For the kadhai sauce

7 tablespoons ghee or vegetable oil
2 garlic cloves, finely chopped
2 dried red chillies
1 teaspoon coriander seeds
2 onions, finely chopped
750g fresh tomatoes, finely chopped
3 green chillies, finely chopped
5cm piece of fresh ginger, peeled and
    finely chopped
2 teaspoons salt
1½ teaspoons dried fenugreek leaves,
    crushed with your fingertips
1 teaspoon Garam Masala (page 20)
1 teaspoon sugar (optional)

For the stir-fry

1 tablespoon ghee or vegetable oil
2 red and/or green peppers,
    deseeded and cut into 1cm x 3cm
    pieces
1 red onion, thickly sliced
1 teaspoon dried red chilli flakes
600g paneer cheese, cut into 1cm x
    1cm x 3cm pieces
1 tablespoon Kadhai Masala (page 21)
a pinch of salt (optional)
1 tablespoon chopped fresh coriander
    leaves and stalks
½ teaspoon dried fenugreek leaves,
    crushed between your fingertips
juice of 1 lemon

To make the kadhai sauce, heat the ghee or oil in a heavy-based frying pan over a medium-high heat. Add the garlic and stir. When it starts to colour, stir in the dried chillies and coriander seeds. As they start to release their aromas, add the onion and stir on a medium-high heat for 4–6 minutes, until it is translucent. Now add the tomatoes, green chillies and ginger, reduce heat and cook until all the moisture has evaporated and the fat starts to separate. Add the salt, fenugreek leaves and garam masala and stir. Add the sugar if needed.

For the stir-fry, heat the ghee to smoking point in a large kadhai, wok or heavy-based frying pan. Add the peppers, red onion and chilli flakes and stir-fry on a high heat for less than 1 minute. Add the paneer and stir for another minute. Add the sauce and mix well. Once the dish is heated through, add the kadhai masala and check for seasoning; add a pinch of salt, if required. Finish with fresh coriander, dried fenugreek leaves and lemon juice, and serve with naan bread (see page 227).

Vivek's tip
If you want to get ahead, the sauce can be cooled and stored in the fridge for up to a week. It also goes well with sliced chicken, fish or prawns and mixed vegetables.

Kedgeree, or khichri as it is known in India, is a humble dish perfectly suited to cold, rainy days. When it is combined with sharp, crunchy, caramelised, spicy cauliflower, there is a fascinating interaction of textures and flavours.

SERVES 4

KEDGEREE WITH PICKLED CAULIFLOWER AND PEAS

2 tablespoons vegetable oil
I teaspoon cumin seeds
3 green chillies, finely chopped
2.5cm piece of ginger, peeled and finely chopped
½ teaspoon fennel seeds
½ teaspoon black onion seeds
½ cauliflower head, broken into small florets
2 tablespoons of white vinegar or cider vinegar
½ teaspoon salt
¼ teaspoon sugar
a pinch of ground turmeric
50g fresh coriander leaves and stalks, chopped
150g shelled peas, fresh or thawed (preferably petits pois)
juice of I lemon

For the kedgeree
100g split yellow moong lentils, rinsed
400ml water
a pinch of ground turmeric
3 tablespoons ghee or vegetable oil
4 garlic cloves, finely chopped
½ teaspoon cumin seeds
I large onion, chopped
2 green chillies, finely chopped
Icm piece of fresh ginger, peeled and finely chopped
I½ teaspoons salt
75g basmati rice, boiled
I tomato, deseeded and cut into Icm dice
2 tablespoons sprouted green moong lentils

2 tablespoons chopped fresh coriander leaves and stalks
juice of I lemon

To make the kedgeree, wash the yellow moong lentils, put them in a pan with the water and turmeric and bring to the boil. Simmer for about 20 minutes, until the lentils are tender and all the water has evaporated. Remove the pan from the heat and set aside.

Heat 2 tablespoons of the ghee to smoking point in a heavy-based frying pan on a medium-high heat and add the cumin seeds and, when they crackle, add the garlic. When the garlic turns golden, add the onion and sauté for 4–6 minutes until it is translucent, then stir in the chillies and ginger and cook for 1 minute. Stir in the cooked yellow moong lentils and salt, then fold in the cooked rice. Add the tomato, sprouted green moong lentils and fresh coriander and stir, on a low heat, for 3–4 minutes. Finish by adding the remaining tablespoon of ghee and the lemon juice. Remove from the heat and keep warm.

To make the pickled cauliflower and peas, heat the oil until smoking point in a heavy-based frying pan and add the cumin

seeds. When they crackle, add the chillies, ginger and fennel and onion seeds, then add the cauliflower and stir-fry on a high heat, for a couple of minutes, until slightly crisp and brown on the edges, but still crunchy inside. Add the vinegar, salt, sugar and turmeric and stir to mix. Cover with a lid, reduce heat and leave the cauliflower to cook in its own steam for 2–3 minutes. Stir in the coriander and peas and cook, uncovered, for 2–3 minutes. Finish with the lemon juice.

Divide the kedgeree between 4 serving plates and serve with the pickled cauliflower and peas on top.

This dish was inspired by a traditional Karnataka-style stir-fry, also known as 'kempu' in the local dialect. It's usually made with chicken, but this is a great little number for vegetarians. Purple sprouting broccoli and bok choy also make very good additions to this versatile dish.

SERVES 4

CAULIFLOWER AND BROCCOLI STIR-FRY

oil for deep-frying
1 head of broccoli, broken into florets
1 head of cauliflower, broken into florets
2 tablespoons vegetable oil
10 fresh curry leaves
3 garlic cloves, finely chopped
1 red onion, chopped
2 green chillies, slit lengthways
1 red pepper, deseeded and cut into 1cm dice
1 yellow pepper, deseeded and cut into small dice
2.5cm piece of fresh ginger, peeled and finely chopped
½ teaspoon salt
½ teaspoon sugar
juice of ½ lemon
a few fresh coriander leaves

For the batter
300g cornflour
150ml white vinegar
2 teaspoons red chilli powder
1 tablespoon sugar
1 teaspoon cumin seeds, roasted and ground
1 teaspoon salt

Firstly, put the cornflour in a bowl, then stir in the remaining ingredients to make a thick batter. Set aside.

Heat the oil for deep-frying in a deep-fat fryer or a deep, heavy-based saucepan. Dip the broccoli and cauliflower florets in the batter, letting the excess drip off, and deep-fry for about 3 minutes, until crisp and golden brown. Transfer to kitchen paper to drain and keep hot.

Heat the oil in a large kadhai, wok or heavy-based frying pan until smoking point. Add the curry leaves and garlic, onion, chillies and peppers and stir-fry on a high heat for 2 minutes. Add the fried broccoli and cauliflower, ginger, salt and sugar and continue stir-frying for 2 minutes. Squeeze in the lemon juice and sprinkle with the fresh coriander. Serve with steamed rice.

Vivek's tip
If you prefer a non-vegetarian dish, substitute either chicken or any firm white fish for the cauliflower and broccoli.

CRILL

GRILL

These massive prawns have become a signature dish at Cinnamon Kitchen since its opening in 2008. A real head-turner of a dish, this is sure to wow your guests, too. And, if you don't find wild African prawns, you could use langoustines or black tiger king prawns instead – the bigger, the better.

WILD AFRICAN PRAWNS WITH PEANUTS AND COCONUT

8 large wild African prawns (more if the prawns are smaller)
I tablespoon vegetable oil
I quantity of Peanut Chutney (page 237)
50g fresh coriander, finely chopped
juice of I lemon

For the marinade
2 tablespoons vegetable oil
2 green chillies, finely chopped
2 lime leaves, finely chopped
I teaspoon Ginger and Garlic Paste (page 18)
I teaspoon salt
1/2 teaspoon sugar
1/2 teaspoon ground turmeric

Slice each prawn lengthways, with the head and shell still on. With the point of a sharp knife remove the dark intestinal vein that runs down the back, then pat the prawns dry on kitchen paper.

Mix together the ingredients for the marinade, then rub them all over the prawns and set aside to marinate for 10 minutes.

Cook the prawns on a low barbecue, grilling them for 6–8 minutes on each side.

Alternatively, heat the oil in a large frying pan on a high heat and sear for 3 minutes on each side, then transfer them to a baking tray and roast in an oven preheated to 180°C/Gas Mark 4 for 6–8 minutes, until the prawns are done.

Remove from the barbecue or oven, sprinkle with coriander and lemon juice and serve with the peanut chutney.

Fish in an envelope, Kerala style – that is probably the best way to describe this dish, except it uses a banana leaf instead of paper for the envelope. This is easy to prepare and it can be cooked either in a hot frying pan or on a glowing barbecue. If you can't get hold of a banana leaf, wrap the fish in kitchen foil instead.

SERVES 4

SEA BREAM WRAPPED IN BANANA LEAF

4 sea bream fillets, scaled and pin-boned
1 banana leaf, cut into 4 x 30cm squares
1 tablespoon vegetable oil
1 quantity Jerusalem Couscous Upma (page 219)

For the marinade
½ teaspoon salt
½ teaspoon ground turmeric
juice of ½ lime
1 green chilli, finely chopped
½ teaspoon Kadhai Masala (page 21)

For the spice crust
10 fresh curry leaves, finely shredded
6 black peppercorns, crushed coarsely
2 shallots, finely chopped
2 garlic cloves, finely chopped
1 tablespoon vegetable oil
1 tablespoon white vinegar
1 teaspoon red chilli powder
1 teaspoon salt
½ teaspoon sugar

Mix together all the ingredients for the marinade, then rub them over the sea bream fillets and leave to marinate for 10 minutes.

For the spice crust, mix together all the ingredients in a non-metallic bowl to get a sweet, sharp, crunchy mixture.

Heat the banana-leaf squares on a hot heavy-based frying pan, or in the microwave for 30 seconds, until they are soft and pliable. Cover the fish fillets with the spice crust, then wrap them, one by one, with the pieces of banana leaf, taking care that they are well secured so that the marinade and spice crust don't ooze out during cooking.

Rub the wrapped fillets with the oil and cook, firstly with the join side down on a low barbecue for 3-5 minutes on each side. You can open up the parcels to check whether the fish is cooked.

Alternatively, heat the oil in a frying pan. Add the wrapped fillets, cover and cook on a low heat for 3–5 minutes on each side. Serve the fish still wrapped in the banana leaf for your guests to unwrap themselves and appreciate the wonderful aromas. Jerusalem couscous is an ideal accompaniment, but Yoghurt Rice (see page 80), Green Mango and Coconut Chutney (see page 238) or kachumber (a spiced tomato, cucumber and onion salad) are also good for a barbecue lunch.

This method of double cooking ribs - first cooking in liquid and then grilling - gives a fantastic silky, fall-off-the-bone texture and deep rich flavours. Yes, you can argue that the spicing is quite Chinese, but, hey, it's the second most popular cuisine in India! The hot, sharp mustard dressing, with its delightfully big flavours that will leave you licking your sticky fingers for long after the ribs are gone.

SERVES 4

CHARRED PORK RIBS
WITH HOT-AND-SWEET GLAZE

1kg pork back ribs, cut into 3-bone
    portions
50ml clear honey
1 tablespoon soy sauce
25ml malt vinegar
1 teaspoon sesame seeds, toasted, to
    garnish

For the marinade
3 tablespoons red chilli powder
3 tablespoons tomato purée
1 teaspoon Ginger Paste (page 18)
1 teaspoon Garlic Paste (page 18)
1 tablespoon soy sauce
2 teaspoons salt
1 teaspoon sugar
50ml clear honey
25ml malt vinegar
4cm piece of cinnamon stick
1 teaspoon black peppercorns
4-5 garlic cloves, peeled and finely
    chopped
3 star anise
3 bay leaves

For the dressing
1 tablespoon vegetable oil
1 tablespoon wholegrain mustard
1 tablespoon clear honey
juice of ½ lemon

Mix together all the ingredients for the marinade in a large bowl, then rub them on to the pork ribs and leave for an hour (or considerably longer if you can). Put the pork ribs in a roasting tray and add just enough water to cover the ribs. Check the seasoning, as the cooking liquid should be correctly seasoned before the ribs are placed in the oven. Put the ribs in a roasting tray, covered with foil. Transfer the tray to an oven preheated to 190°C/Gas Mark 5. Cook for 60 minutes. Remove the tray from the oven and separate the ribs from the stock. Set aside the ribs to cool and for the meat to firm up.

Meanwhile, make the dressing. Beat the oil, mustard, honey and lemon juice together until a smooth emulsion forms. Set aside.

Strain the stock into a heavy-based saucepan, then boil the stock until it reduces and thickens without tasting too salty. Add the remaining soy sauce, honey and malt vinegar and simmer for about 15 minutes, stirring, until the sauce is a thick glaze. Check the seasoning to make sure it isn't too salty, which it can be if the glaze has reduced too much. If it tastes too salty, add more honey.

Place the pork ribs on a baking sheet on a hot barbecue for 2-3 minutes, brushing with the glaze, until they are coloured. Move the ribs to the edge of the barbecue (where it is cooler) and brush with more glaze. Cook for a couple of minutes, turning continuously to get a deep rich, shiny caramelised gloss on the ribs. Sprinkle with sesame seeds and serve hot with chunky kachumber and spiced cucumber, onion and tomato salad.

Alternatively, the final cooking stages can be done in the oven, reducing the heat for the second stage.

This tender lamb kebab is famed for its melt-in-the-mouth texture, the result of including a small amount of raw papaya or pineapple to tenderise the meat. Once this was essential to mask the poor quality of the meat used, but, today, with good-quality meat, this recipe lets you appreciate the fine texture. When you mince the meat three times you have a really tender version, but if you mince it ten more times, you have a paste so fine you can simply serve it on brioche!

SERVES 4

GALOUTI KEBABS

2 tablespoons ghee or vegetable oil

500g lean boneless leg of lamb, minced at least 3 times

3 tablespoons Ginger and Garlic Paste (page 18)

4 tablespoons dried-fried onions

2 tablespoons Fried Cashew Paste (page 18)

1½ tablespoons red chilli powder

a pinch of saffron, soaked in 2 tablespoons of water

1½ teaspoons salt

1 tablespoon of puréed or pounded pineapple (or 1 tablespoon pineapple juice)

4 drops of rose water or kewra water

1 large banana leaf, cut into 15–20cm long strips

For the spice mix

8 cloves

4 green cardamom pods

seeds of 1 black cardamom pod

1 blade of mace

⅛ nutmeg, pounded

½ teaspoon cumin seeds, roasted

½ teaspoon black peppercorns

To make the spice mix, set aside 6 cloves and transfer the remainder to a spice grinder or mortar and pestle. Add the remaining ingredients and grind into a fine powder, then set aside.

Heat half the ghee or vegetable oil in a small pan, and when it reaches smoking point add the 6 reserved cloves. Once they have started to smoke, after about 30 seconds, remove the pan from the heat and set aside for the ghee to cool.

Put the minced meat in a mixing bowl and add the spice mix and all the remaining ingredients, except the rosewater and banana leaf, and mix together well. Add the clove-infused oil, but not the cloves, and mix together again. Chill the mixture for 10 minutes.

Take the chilled mince out of the fridge, add the remaining tablespoon of ghee and the rosewater and mix together thoroughly. Return the mixture to the fridge for 15 minutes.

Heat the banana leaf strips in a hot heavy-based frying pan, or in the microwave for 30 seconds, until they are soft and pliable.

Shape the minced meat into 12 equal patties, each about 4cm in diameter. Wrap each patty in a piece of banana leaf and brush with oil. Grill over a hot barbecue for 2–3 minutes on each side, starting with the joint side down.

Alternatively, heat 2 tablespoons ghee or vegetable oil in a heavy-based frying pan. Add the patties and cook over a low heat for 1-2 minutes on each side, until they are well cooked. Remove them from the pan and drain well on kitchen paper.

Serve the kebabs hot with Pomegranate Raita (see page 225).

This is the dish the Cinnamon Kitchen team entered in the British Barbecue Championship at Jody Scheckter's Laverstoke Park Farm in 2011. Head Chef Abdul has been our team captain each of the three times we have entered this competition, and we have won twice. This recipe is for barbecue champs everywhere!

SERVES 4

ABDUL YASEEN'S RAJASTHAN ROYAL BARBECUED LAMB

2 x 8-bone lamb racks
500g lamb's liver, cleaned, sinews trimmed and cut into 4cm cubes
1 red onions, 1 finely chopped, 1 thickly sliced and 1 thinly sliced
4 lamb's kidneys, split and trimmed
1 teaspoon turmeric
2 tablespoons malt vinegar
20g butter, chopped
4 green chillies, slit lengthways
8 cloves
1 quantity Calouti Kebabs (page 166)
lemon wedges to garnish

For the marinade for the racks of lamb
2 tablespoons lemon juice
2 tablespoons vegetable oil
25g Greek yoghurt
1 tablespoon Ginger and Garlic Paste (page 18)
1 teaspoon Soola Masala (page 21)
1 teaspoon red chilli powder
1 teaspoon salt
1/2 teaspoon ground turmeric
2 tablespoons chopped coriander stems

For the lamb's liver marinade
1½ tablespoons vegetable oil
1 tablespoon Ginger and Garlic Paste (page 18)
1 tablespoon gram (chickpea) flour, roasted
1 tablespoon red chilli powder
2 garlic cloves, finely chopped
1 teaspoon dried fenugreek leaves, crushed between your fingertips
1 teaspoon salt
1/4 teaspoon ground turmeric
juice of 1/2 lemon
a pinch of sugar

For the spice paste for the lamb's kidneys
2 tablespoons vegetable oil
1/2 onion, finely chopped
3 green chillies
1 garlic clove, finely chopped
2.5cm piece of fresh ginger, peeled and chopped
2.5cm piece of cinnamon stick
1/2 teaspoon black peppercorns
1 teaspoon salt
1/2 teaspoon sugar
1 tablespoon tomato purée
6 ready-to-eat dried apricots, soaked and puréed
1 tablespoon Ginger and Garlic Paste (page 18)
2 tablespoons lemon juice
1 teaspoon red chilli powder
1/2 teaspoon ground turmeric

If the lamb racks haven't already been prepared, trim off the skin and most of the fat, leaving just a thin layer of fat on the meat. Mix together all the ingredients for the marinade for the lamb racks, then rub this over the lamb, cover and refrigerate for 2 hours.

For the marinade for the lamb's liver, mix together all the ingredients, whisking so the flavours are well combined. Add the liver and half the chopped red onions, cover and refrigerate for 2 hours.

To prepare the lamb's kidneys, combine the turmeric and vinegar in a bowl. Thoroughly wash the kidneys, then add them to the bowl and leave for 30 minutes to get rid of any 'off' flavours.

Meanwhile, make the spice paste for the kidneys. Heat the oil in a heavy-based frying pan and add the onion. When it has softened, but not coloured, add the chillies, garlic and ginger and cook for a few minutes. When they start to brown, add the cinnamon stick and peppercorns and stir quickly over a high heat, taking care that the spices do not burn. Stir in the salt and sugar, then add the tomato and apricot purées. Remove the pan from the heat and leave the mixture to cool. Transfer it to a blender and blend to a paste.

Transfer the paste to a bowl and mix together with the garlic and ginger paste, lemon juice, chilli powder and turmeric. Add the kidneys and coat them in the marinade, then leave, covered, to marinate for 30 minutes in the fridge.

Prepare the recipe for the galouti kebabs, shape the mixture into 4 patties and wrap with the banana leaves. Chill until ready to cook.

Remove the galouti kebabs and all the other meat from the fridge 10–15 minutes before cooking. Just before you are ready to cook, thread the liver and thickly sliced red onion on skewers.

Place the racks of lamb skin side down on a hot barbecue and let the fat render for 3 minutes, then move the racks of lamb towards the low heat to crisp the fat and to help the meat maintain a definite shape. Turn over after 6 minutes and allow the rack to cook for a further 3 minutes.

Remove the racks of lamb from the grill and transfer each to a piece of aluminium foil large enough to wrap around it. Divide the butter, chillies, red onion and cloves between the pieces of foil and wrap up securely, so none of the juices will drip out. Transfer the foil parcels to the side of the

grill, away from direct heat, and leave for 8 minutes, by which time they should be perfect to unwrap and serve.

Meanwhile, place the liver skewers on the barbecue and grill for 3 minutes, then rotate and grill for a further 3 minutes, until cooked through. Leave to rest for 3-4 minutes before serving.

Cook the galouti kebabs following the instructions on page 166.

Sear the kidneys on the hot barbecue for 1–2 minutes on each side, then move them to the side, away from the direct heat. Add the lemon juice and serve.

Unwrap the racks of lamb and cut into individual chops. Serve the lamb chops with the liver and kidneys. Garnish with lemon wedges.

This is a good example of how we use tandoori spicing on rather special cuts of meat to create an impressive dish that is actually very simple to prepare.

SERVES 6 OR 10–12 FOR SNACKS

RACK OF LAMB WITH MINT, CHILLI AND BASIL

3 racks of lamb, cut into one-bone chops
2 tablespoons vegetable oil

For the first marinade
4 green chillies, chopped and pounded into a paste
2 tablespoon Ginger and Garlic Paste (page 18)
juice of 1 lemon
1½ teaspoons salt

For the second marinade
20g mild Cheddar cheese
1 teaspoon plain flour
35g Greek yoghurt
2 green chillies, finely chopped
⅓ nutmeg, grated
1cm piece of fresh ginger, peeled and finely chopped
1 teaspoon Mace and Cardamom Powder (page 20)
1 teaspoon salt
½ teaspoon ground white pepper
2 tablespoons single cream
2 tablespoons chopped mint
2 tablespoons finely chopped basil leaves

For the first marinade, mix together all the ingredients, then rub them over the lamb chops. Set aside to marinate for 20 minutes.

Heat the oil in a large, heavy-based frying pan on a high heat, add the lamb chops and sear for about 2 minutes on each side until they are browned. Set aside and leave to cool.

For the second marinade, put the cheese in a bowl with the flour and rub together. The flour prevents lumps from forming. Add the yoghurt and mix into a smooth paste, then mix in the chillies, nutmeg, ginger, mace and cardamom powder, salt and white pepper. Fold in the cream – slowly, otherwise the mixture may separate – then add the mint and basil. Generously rub the marinade over the lamb chops and leave to marinate for a further 10 minutes or so.

Transfer the lamb chops to a hot barbecue and cook for 2–3 minutes on each side. Remove the chops from the heat and leave to rest for another couple of minutes, then serve.

Rabbit and mustard is a classic combination in French cuisine, and here we use a mustard-and-honey marinade, which helps to seal in the rabbit's flavours, as well as highlighting them. Although rabbit isn't commonly cooked in India, this is an ideal barbecue dish, as the smokiness from the charcoal brings out the best of this marinade. The papaya in the marinade has a tenderising effect on the meat, breaking down the meat proteins. This dish also works well served as a canapé with drinks.

SERVES 4

RABBIT TIKKA

500g boned rabbit legs, cut into
    2.5cm chunks

For the first marinade
2.5cm piece of green papaya, grated,
    or 2 tablespoons fresh pineapple
    juice
1½ tablespoons Ginger and Garlic
    Paste (page 18)
1½ teaspoons salt
1 teaspoon red chilli powder
1 teaspoon ground turmeric
juice of 1 lemon

For the second marinade
100g Greek yoghurt
2 tablespoons wholegrain mustard
2 tablespoons mustard oil (or use 2
    tablespoons vegetable oil mixed
    with 1 teaspoon English mustard)
1 tablespoon chopped fresh coriander
    leaves and stalks
1 tablespoon clear honey
1 teaspoon Garam Masala (page 20)

Mix together all the ingredients for the first marinade, then rub them all over the rabbit meat and leave to marinate for 1 hour.

Mix together all the ingredients for the second marinade, then add to the rabbit and leave to marinate for another hour or so.

Thread the rabbit pieces on to skewers and cook on a hot barbecue, turning the skewers regularly, for about 8–10 minutes.

Alternatively, place the rabbit skewers on a baking tray and roast in an oven preheated to 180°C/Gas Mark 4 for 10–12 minutes, turning the pieces regularly.

Vivek's tip
If the rabbit cooks but does not take colour, place it under a very hot grill for a couple of minutes.

This is a goat dish inspired by the Sanskrit classic, *Manasollasa*, with its many verses about food and drink, written by the ancient ruler and scholar Somesvara III in the 12th century. Here I serve the marinated and spiced goat meat with a refreshing lassi. Goats are easy to rear in India and have been useful for both milk and meat for many centuries.

SERVES 4–6

BHADITRAKHA, SERVED WITH MINT LASSI

750g boneless goat leg, trimmed
  (lamb can be used instead)
2 tablespoons mustard oil (or use
  2 tablespoons sunflower oil blended
  with I teaspoon English mustard)
  (optional)

For the Rajastani spice paste
I quantity of Soola Masala (page 21)
25g Greek yoghurt

For the marinade
I tablespoon pineapple juice
2 teaspoons Garlic Paste (page 18)
2 teaspoons salt
I½ teaspoons red chilli powder
I teaspoon Ginger Paste (page 18)
juice of I lemon

For serving
I red onion, thickly sliced
I tablespoon vegetable oil
a pinch of salt
a pinch of sugar

For the mint lassi
200g plain yoghurt
I00ml water
½ teaspoon cumin seeds, roasted and
  crushed
I tablespoon chopped mint
I teaspoon salt
I teaspoon sugar

First make the Rajastani spice paste by mixing the yoghurt with the soola masala. Cover and set aside until required.

Slice the meat thinly (5mm or so would be ideal), ensuring the slices are roughly the same size. Smear the spice paste on to the goat slices and set aside for 10 minutes.

In a separate bowl, mix together all the ingredients for the marinade, then rub them over the slices of goat meat and set aside to marinate for 20 minutes.

Skewer the meat slices on long metal skewers and grill them on a hot barbecue for 5–6 minutes. While the meat is cooking, rub the onion slices with the oil and grill them until softened.

Alternatively, cook the meat in a roasting tray in an oven preheated to 200°C/Gas Mark 6 for 4–5 minutes.

Make the mint lassi by mixing together all the ingredients in a large bowl, blending to a smooth and creamy consistency. Pour the lassi into 4 shot glasses.

Serve the goat kebab garnished with onions scattered over and with the mint lassi on the side.

This is a versatile recipe that can be either cooked in a tandoor oven, as we do here at the restaurant, but which I can assure you tastes every bit as good when cooked on a barbecue.

SERVES 4

DRY-SPICE-CRUSTED GUINEA FOWL

4 guinea fowl breasts, skinned, boned
  and trimmed
1 tablespoon vegetable oil

For the first marinade
1 tablespoon Ginger and Garlic Paste
  (page 18)
1½ teaspoons salt
1 teaspoon red chilli powder
1 teaspoon dried red chilli flakes
½ teaspoon ground allspice
½ teaspoon sugar
juice of 1 lemon

For the second marinade
6 cloves, coarsely ground
2 teaspoons black peppercorns,
  cracked
2 teaspoons fennel seeds, coarsely
  ground
25g plain yoghurt
1 tablespoon finely chopped coriander
  stalks

Mix together all the ingredients for the first marinade, then rub them over the guinea fowl breasts and leave to marinate for 15 minutes.

For the second marinade, mix half the coarsely ground spices with the yoghurt and coriander stalks. Apply this mixture to the breasts and leave for another 20 minutes.

On a hot barbecue sear the guinea fowl breasts for 2 minutes on each side. Sprinkle the rest of the coarsely ground spices over the breasts, then wrap in foil and cook on the barbecue for 4–5 minutes, until cooked through.

Alternatively, cook the guinea fowl breasts in an oven preheated to 200°C/Gas Mark 5 for 10 minutes.

Allow the guinea fowl breasts to rest before serving with a raita and chutney of your choice.

Vivek's tip
You could replace the guinea fowl with boneless chicken breasts or thighs, if you like.

Partridges respond well to any tandoori-style marinade, and I find this Thai-inspired marinade particularly good. It is slightly acidic and has a gentle curing effect on the flesh. The spiced walnuts add an interesting texture.

SERVES 4

CHAR-GRILLED BREAST OF PARTRIDGE WITH CHILLI WALNUTS

4 partridges, breasts only (keep the legs in the freezer for another time)

For the first marinade
1 tablespoon Ginger and Garlic Paste (page 18)
1 teaspoon salt

For the second marinade
1.25cm piece of fresh ginger, peeled and chopped
4 lime leaves
3 Thai bird's-eye chillies
1 lemongrass stalk, outer layer removed and bruised
3 tablespoons vegetable oil
2 tablespoons finely chopped coriander stalks
1 teaspoon ground turmeric
1 teaspoon Garam Masala (page 20)
a pinch of sugar
juice of ½ lemon

For the Chilli Walnuts
100g walnuts
2 tablespoons vegetable oil
1 garlic clove, finely chopped
1cm piece of fresh ginger, peeled and finely chopped
1 teaspoon red chilli powder
1 teaspoon cumin seeds, roasted and roughly crushed
½ teaspoon salt

Rub the partridge breasts with the ginger and garlic paste and salt and leave to marinate for 10 minutes.

Put all the ingredients for the second marinade in a blender or food processor and process until a fine paste forms. Coat the partridge breasts with this green paste and set aside to marinate for a further 30 minutes.

Meanwhile, make the chilli walnuts. Put the walnuts in a baking tray and roast in a preheated oven at 160°C/Gas Mark 3 for 5–7 minutes, until crisp. Transfer to a mortar and roughly crush. Heat the oil in a large frying pan, add the garlic and cook for a few seconds until it starts to colour. Add the remaining ingredients, mix well and cook for about 30 seconds, stirring. When everything is crisp, add the walnuts, remove the pan from the heat and stir around to mix. Drain the walnuts on kitchen paper and set aside.

Alternatively, roast the breasts in an oven preheated to 220°C/Gas Mark 7 for 5–6 minutes.

Now skewer the partridge breasts with long metal skewers and grill on a medium-hot barbecue for 4–5 minutes, turning them over once.

Serve the partridge breasts with the chilli walnuts sprinkled around.

When we first launched The Cinnamon Club, the menu featured a deconstructed version of Hyderabadi duck curry consisting of seared duck breast served with a sesame and tamarind sauce cooked separately. This version that we created for Cinnamon Kitchen's famous Tandoor & Grill Bar, pushes the idea even further. The City slickers love to keep it light, and we managed just that by losing the rice and rich sauce from the original recipe, and, instead, serving a bolder-flavoured chutney to incorporate the same flavour co-ordinates.

SERVES 4

BARBECUED DUCK BREASTS WITH SESAME AND TAMARIND CHUTNEY

4 duck breasts, preferably
    Cressingham duck, skin on
fruit, such as diced papaya, dragon
    fruit and melon balls, to garnish

For the marinade
3 tablespoons vegetable oil
I teaspoon red chilli powder
I teaspoon salt

For the Sesame and Tamarind Chutney
I tablespoon coriander seeds
I tablespoon sesame seeds, plus extra
    for sprinkling
I teaspoon cumin seeds
1/2 teaspoon fenugreek seeds
3 tablespoons desiccated coconut
I tablespoon vegetable oil
2 tablespoons cashew nuts
50g tamarind paste
I tablespoon jaggery or molasses
    sugar
2 teaspoons red chilli powder
I teaspoon salt
up to 150ml water

For tempering
2 tablespoons vegetable oil
I teaspoon black mustard seeds
1/2 teaspoon black onion seeds
10 fresh curry leaves

Mix together all the ingredients for the marinade and rub them over the duck breasts, then set aside to marinate for 30 minutes.

Meanwhile, make the sesame and tamarind chutney. Mix together the coriander, sesame, cumin and fenugreek seeds in a dry frying pan on a medium heat and stir for 1–2 minutes. When they begin to colour, remove from the pan and set aside. Roast the coconut in the same pan until it is golden, then add it to the seeds. Heat 1 teaspoon of the oil in the pan, add the cashew nuts and fry until golden. Set aside half the spice mix. Add the tamarind, jaggery (or molasses sugar), chilli powder and salt to the remaining spice mix and combine well to make the sesame and tamarind chutney. Use a mortar and pestle to grind the other half of the spice mix into a coarse crumble.

Barbecue the duck breasts, skin side down on a medium barbecue, and sear for 6–8 minutes, until the skin crisps. Turn the breasts over and cook for a couple more minutes.

Alternatively, sear the breasts skin side down first in a pan on a high heat for 2–3 minutes on each side, then transfer to the oven preheated to 180°C/Gas Mark 4. Roast for 8–10 minutes; the duck should still be pink inside.

Heat the oil for tempering in a heavy-based pan until smoking. Add the ingredients for tempering, followed by the nut and seed paste. Reduce the heat and cook, stirring, for a couple of minutes to mix well, then remove from the heat.

Once the duck breasts are cooked, leave them to rest for 5 minutes, then slice neatly and divide between 4 plates. Add some chutney to each plate and sprinkle with sesame seeds, then add spiced crumble for extra texture to each plate. Garnish with fruit and fried curry leaves.

This is another great barbecue dish and it cooks especially well if the birds are spatchcocked, which your butcher will do for you. The lentil salad not only makes a good accompaniment for the quail, but is a substantial salad in its own right.

SERVES 4

QUAIL WITH RED SPICES AND PUY LENTIL SALAD

4 large quails, spatchcocked

For the marinade
2 tablespoons vegetable oil
Icm piece of fresh ginger, peeled and finely chopped
I green chilli, chopped
2 tablespoons Ginger and Garlic Paste (page 18)
I tablespoon chopped fresh coriander leaves and stalks
I teaspoon red chilli powder
½ teaspoon dried red chilli flakes
½ teaspoon Garam Masala (page 20)
juice of ½ lemon

For the Puy Lentil Salad
150g Puy lentils, soaked overnight, then cooked in stock for 12–15 minutes until tender but still crunchy
2 green chillies, finely chopped
2 tomatoes, deseeded and diced
I red onion, finely chopped
4 tablespoons chopped fresh coriander
Icm piece of fresh ginger, peeled and finely chopped
I teaspoon salt
½ teaspoon sugar
juice of I lemon

For the Puy lentil salad, drain the cooked lentils and place in a bowl. Add all the remaining ingredients and mix together. Adjust the seasoning. Set aside and keep cool until ready to serve.

In a large bowl, mix together all the marinade ingredients, then rub them all over the quail and leave to marinate for 15–20 minutes.

On a barbecue, sear the quails on a medium heat for 3–4 minutes, until coloured. Then wrap them in tin foil and cook another 10–12 minutes, until the quail are cooked through.

Alternatively, sear the quail in a pan on a high heat for 3–4 minutes on each side, then transfer to an oven preheated to 220°C/ Gas Mark 7 for 10 minutes.

Divide the quail among 4 serving plates and serve with the Puy lentil salad.

This is another one of our very popular grilled dishes at Cinnamon Kitchen. I suppose grilled vegetables simply cooked straight on a hot barbecue must be quite a useful option for vegetarians. Trust me, this is one of those dishes that vegetarians can enjoy without feeling that they're missing out on something!

SERVES 4

MARINATED AND GRILLED PORTOBELLO MUSHROOMS

8 Portobello mushrooms, trimmed
a few salad leaves, to garnish

For the marinade
2 green chillies, finely chopped
2 garlic cloves, finely chopped
1cm piece of fresh ginger, peeled and
    finely chopped
3½ tablespoons clear honey
2 tablespoons chopped fresh
    coriander leaves and stalks
2½ tablespoons malt vinegar
1 tablespoon sesame seeds
2 teaspoons red chilli powder
1 teaspoon Ginger Paste (page 18)
1 teaspoon salt
1 teaspoon sugar
½ teaspoon Garlic Paste (page 18)

Wash the mushrooms and pat dry with a kitchen paper. Mix together all the ingredients for the marinade in a deep bowl, add the mushrooms and leave to marinate for 30 minutes.

Grill the mushrooms on a hot barbecue for 4–5 minutes until caramelised and slightly charred.

Alternatively, heat some oil in a heavy-based frying or ridged grill pan on a medium-high heat, add the mushrooms and sear for a couple of minutes.

Remove the mushrooms from the heat, cut into quarters and serve immediately with a selection of salad leaves.

This is Cinnamon Kitchen's take on the very traditional, very rustic bharwan karela, or stuffed bitter gourds. The only differences are that we cook ours for less time and use a lot less oil than in traditional recipes.

SERVES 4

BITTER GOURD
WITH SPICED MINCED LAMB

4 bitter gourds
½ teaspoon salt, plus extra for
    sprinkling inside the gourds
1 tablespoon vegetable oil for cooking

For the filling
3 tablespoons vegetable oil
2.5cm piece of cinnamon stick
2 green cardamom pods
1 bay leaf
2 cloves
1 teaspoon cumin seeds
1 large onion, chopped
1 green chilli, finely chopped
2.5cm piece of fresh ginger, peeled
    and finely chopped
1 tablespoon Ginger and Garlic Paste
    (page 18)
1 teaspoon salt
1 teaspoon red chilli powder
½ teaspoon ground coriander
½ teaspoon ground cumin
½ teaspoon ground turmeric
2 tomatoes, chopped
350g minced lamb
2 tablespoons chopped fresh
    coriander leaves and stalks
juice of ½ lemon

Prepare the gourds by making a slit in each one and carefully scooping out the seeds and flesh. Season the insides of the gourds with salt, turn them upside down and leave for 10 minutes.

Meanwhile, make the filling. Heat the oil in a heavy-based pan to smoking point and add the cinnamon, cardamom pods, bay leaf, cloves and cumin. When the seeds crackle, add the onion and cook on a medium-low heat for 2–3 minutes. Add the chilli, chopped ginger, ginger and garlic paste, salt and the ground spices. Now add the tomatoes and cook for another minute. Finally, add the minced lamb and continue cooking, stirring, for 15–20 minutes, until the liquid has completely evaporated. Adjust the seasoning and sprinkle over the coriander leaves and lemon juice. Remove the pan from the heat and allow the mixture to cool.

Bring a pan of salted water to boil. Add the bitter gourds and blanch for 2 minutes. Drain the gourds and immediately chill in iced water, then drain again and set aside.

Fill the bitter gourds with cooked lamb mince and wrap butcher's

twine around them to securely enclose the filling.

Brush the gourds with oil and grill on a medium-hot barbecue for 5–6 minutes, turning frequently to colour evenly on all sides.

Alternatively, the gourds could be roasted in an oven preheated to 220°C/Gas Mark 7 for 10 minutes until nicely coloured and tender.

Remove the string and serve the gourds on their own or on a bed of yellow lentils.

Vivek's tip
You can substitute soy mince for the lamb mince to make an impressive vegetarian main course.

Inspired by the ingredients and flavours in a typical Hyderabadi aubergine curry with a sesame, tamarind and peanut sauce, this dish combines those flavours with completely different textures! These types of aubergine are long, thin and virtually seedless – so ideal for grilling.

SERVES 4

GRILLED AUBERGINE WITH PEANUTS

2 firm Japanese or Bengali aubergines, or other long, thin aubergines, cut in half lengthways
4 tablespoons Tamarind Chutney (page 179)

For the first marinade
1 tablespoon vegetable oil
1 teaspoon salt
1/2 teaspoon red chilli powder
1/2 teaspoon turmeric powder
1/4 teaspoon fennel seeds
1/4 teaspoon ajowan seeds
1/4 teaspoon black onion seeds

For the spice crust
1 tablespoon poppy seeds
1 tablespoon sesame seeds
1 tablespoon desiccated coconut
1 tablespoon peanuts
1 tablespoon vegetable oil
2 garlic cloves, finely chopped
1/2 teaspoon red chilli powder
1 teaspoon Chaat Masala (page 21)
1 teaspoon tamarind paste
1 tablespoon chopped fresh coriander leaves and stalks
1 tablespoon jaggery or molasses sugar

Score the aubergines lightly to make criss-cross marks on the flesh side. For the first marinade, sprinkle the flesh side with the salt, chilli powder, turmeric and fennel, ajowan seeds and black onion seeds, drizzle with oil then set aside for 10–15 minutes.

Meanwhile, make the spice crust. Roast the poppy seeds, sesame seeds and desiccated coconut separately in a dry frying pan over a medium heat for 1–2 minutes, until the aromas are released. Quickly tip them into a bowl and set aside.

In a heavy-based pan on a medium-high heat, add the peanuts and dry-fry, stirring. When they are golden, remove them from the pan and set them aside to cool. Coarsely chop the peanuts and add to the roasted seeds and coconut. Heat the oil in the pan. Add the garlic and cook, stirring, over a medium heat. When it is golden, remove it from the pan and drain on kitchen paper and allow to cool before adding to the other ingredients.

Add the remaining ingredients for the spice crust and mix together. Spread them on a baking try to dry in an oven preheated to

150°C/Gas Mark 2 for about 10 minutes.

Place the flat side of the aubergines on a hot barbecue and sear for 2 minutes. Repeat the same on the other side for about 3 minutes, until the aubergine pieces are cooked through.

Alternatively, the aubergines could be roasted in an oven preheated to 220°C/Gas Mark 7 for 10 minutes until nicely coloured and tender.

Place the aubergines on a plate with the flat side facing upwards. Apply a dash of tamarind chutney, sprinkle generously with the spice crust and serve hot with green salad, if you like.

Fat Chilli Paneer – must be one of our most popular and long-standing favourites from the Grill. There was a time I'd got so familiar with the sound of the printer that I didn't need to look at the docket to know there was an order for (yet) another Fat Chilli Paneer. The 'fat chillies' refers to the Romano peppers we use, which are large, mild and long red peppers that make a perfect vehicle in which to serve the spiced paneer.

SERVES 4

FAT CHILLIES WITH SPICED PANEER

2 Romano peppers, halved
    lengthways and deseeded
I teaspoon vegetable oil
¼ teaspoon dried red chilli flakes
½ teaspoon salt
a pinch of sugar
dried fenugreek leaves, crushed
    between your fingertips

For the filling
3 tablespoons vegetable oil
I teaspoon cumin seeds
I large onion, chopped
4 green chillies, finely chopped
Icm piece of fresh ginger, peeled and
    finely chopped
85g mixed red and green peppers,
    deseeded and finely chopped
I teaspoon salt
½ teaspoon ground turmeric
½ teaspoon red chilli powder
½ teaspoon sugar
250g paneer cheese, cut into 5mm
    dice
I tablespoon tamarind paste
2 tablespoons chopped fresh
    coriander leaves and stalks
juice of ½ lemon

Start by making the filling. Heat the oil in a heavy-based pan to smoking point and add the cumin seeds. When they crackle, add the onion and cook on a medium-low heat for 2–3 minutes. Add the chillies and ginger and cook for a further 2 minutes. Throw in the mixed peppers and stir-fry over a high heat. Add the salt, turmeric, chilli powder and sugar, then gently fold in the paneer and cook on a medium heat for 4–5 minutes. Add the tamarind and adjust the seasoning. Sprinkle with the coriander and finish with the lemon juice. Remove from the heat and set aside.

Rub the Romano peppers with the oil and salt. Place on a hot barbecue for about 2–3 minutes on each side, until soft.

Alternatively, place the peppers on a baking tray and roast in an oven preheated to 200°C/Gas Mark 6 for 8–10 minutes, until cooked.

Remove the peppers from the heat and divide the spiced paneer filling between them. Sprinkle over the fenugreek leaves and serve immediately with a salad or dip of your choice.

If you are entertaining and want to get ahead, cook the stuffed peppers in advance and leave to cool and set aside in the fridge until your guests are ready to eat. The peppers can then be quickly reheated.

Often people point out to me that asparagus isn't exactly Indian and wonder why I use it on the menu. I point out that - strictly speaking - even tomatoes and chillies aren't Indian, but can you imagine our cooking without these two mainstays? That aside, I love asparagus - our guests love it, so what more can one ask for? Because the season is so short, we waste absolutely no time and put asparagus on our menu as soon as it arrives in the markets. This recipe will give you an idea for a different take on this annual treat.

SERVES 4

ASPARAGUS IN KADHAI SPICES WITH CURRIED YOGHURT

20–24 asparagus spears, trimmed from the bottom and peeled
2 tablespoons vegetable oil
I teaspoon black onion seeds
I teaspoon fennel seeds
I teaspoon rock salt (for texture)
5g butter
I tablespoon chopped fresh coriander leaves and stalks
juice of 1/2 lemon
2 tablespoons Kadhai Masala (page 21)
I quantity Curried Yoghurt (page 23)

Sprinkle the asparagus with the oil and black onion and fennel seeds. Cook on a hot barbecue for about 1 minute on each side, until just tender. Drizzle the asparagus with oil and sprinkle over the kadhai masala.

Alternatively, add the butter and the kadhai spices to a pan. Place the pan under a grill for one minute, or until the asparagus spears are cooked.

Sprinkle over the coriander leaves and the lemon juice and serve with the curried yoghurt on the side.

Vivek's tip
One good way of judging where to cut an asparagus spear is to hold it at both ends and bend until it snaps; wherever it breaks is the point at which to cut, except you don't need to any more! You can use the more fibrous parts in soups or other recipes.

BAR: S

BAR: SNACKS

This was our entry into the Square Meal Canapé Cup competition when Abdul Yaseen went back in 2011 to defend his 'crown', as he likes to put it. Cinnamon Kitchen had been entering this competition every year since 2009, and Abdul ensured we won the competition every single year! This canape may look a little daunting but, trust me, it's worth every bit of the effort.

MAKES 12

TANDOORI-STYLE MASALA PIGEON WITH GREEN PEA AND YOGHURT SHOT

For the pigeons breasts

2 pigeons, breasts deboned, skin on,
    and the leg, liver and heart minced
    for the fritter
1 tablespoon vegetable oil
2 teaspoons Ginger-Garlic Paste
    (page 18)
½ teaspoon salt
1 teaspoon red chilli powder
juice of ½ lemon
½ teaspoon roasted cumin powder
½ teaspoon allspice powder

For the spiced mince fritters

1 tablespoon vegetable oil
¼ teaspoon cumin seeds
1 medium-sized onion, finely chopped
    minced pigeon meat (see above)
1 small beetroot boiled, peeled and
    finely chopped
¼ teaspoon red chilli powder
¼ teaspoon ground roasted cumin
2cm piece of ginger, peeled and finely
    chopped
2 green chillies, chopped
¼ teaspoon Garam Masala (page 20)
1 sprig of mint, shredded
1 teaspoon salt
1 egg, beaten
50g breadcrumbs
oil for deep-frying

For the pickled vegetables

1 medium-sized carrot, peeled and
    sliced into thin ribbons (ideally using
    a mandoline)
½ cucumber, peeled and sliced into
    thin ribbons (ideally using a
    mandoline)
1 green chilli, deseeded
¼ teaspoon black onion seeds
¼ teaspoon sesame seeds
2 tablespoons vinegar
120ml water

1 tablespoon sugar
1 teaspoon salt

For the green pea and yoghurt shot

90g shelled peas, fresh or thawed
    (preferably petits pois)
100g plain yoghurt
200ml water
1 green chilli, deseeded
2 garlic cloves
1½ teaspoons salt
2 tablespoons sugar
1 tablespoon mustard oil (or use
    1 tablespoon vegetable oil mixed
    with ½ teaspoon English mustard)

First prepare the pigeon breasts by marinating them with the rest of the ingredients for 30 minutes. Place the marinated pigeon breast skin side down for 2 minutes on a medium-hot grill or a non-stick pan. Turn over and cook for another 2 minutes and then allow it to rest. Slice each breast into thin strips.

For the fritters, heat the oil in a pan to smoking point, add the cumin seeds and, when they crackle, add the chopped onion and sauté till golden brown. Add the minced pigeon and beetroot and sauté for three minutes, then add the chilli powder, cumin powder and cook until the mixture is almost dry. Now add the ginger, green chilli, garam masala, the mint and salt. Allow the mixture to cool. Set aside the in the fridge.

Shape the mince into 15g balls. Dip them in the beaten egg, then roll in breadcrumbs and deep-fry in hot oil for 2–3 minutes, until golden brown, and place on a perforated tray ready to serve.

To make the pickled vegetables, prepare the pickling liquid by boiling all the ingredients, except the carrots and cucumber, and allowing it to simmer for a couple of minutes. Pour the hot liquid over the vegetable strips. Allow to cool, and set aside in the fridge.

To prepare the green pea and yoghurt shot, mix all the ingredients together in a blender to obtain a smooth soup consistency. Check the seasoning and pour into shot glasses; refrigerate to keep chilled.

To assemble, take a cocktail stick and skewer first a folded-over slice of the pigeon, followed by one of the fritters and then a folded-over ribbon of the pickled carrot and the a ribbon of the pickled cucumber. The green pea and yoghurt shot is offered as an accompaniment and also forms a base on which the skewered canapé rests.

A traditional seekh kebab made from lamb and rolled in the famous handkerchief bread with spiced onions, mint relish and dips is quite common to see as a snack in parts of India, but it's also possible to serve smaller versions of them as a delicious and attractive cocktail snack. You may not wish to go to the trouble of making large chapattis at home. If so, you can easily pick them up at Asian stores or substitute with tortillas from the supermarket. Alternatively, you can make thin breads at home and coat one side with beaten egg and roll the kebab in it. While slightly uncommon, we think it makes for a stunning variation of this snack.

SERVES 4

LAMB KEBAB IN ROOMALI BREAD

I quantity Lamb Kebab (page 200), cooked

I red onion, sliced
juice of ½ lemon
¼ teaspoon Chaat Masala (page 21)
butter for basting

For the bread
100g plain flour
55ml water
a pinch of salt
a pinch of sugar
2 eggs, lightly beaten
I tablespoon oil
melted butter, for brushing

For serving
Coriander Chutney (page 22)
mango purée (made by blending a ripe mango to a fine purée in a blender or food processor and then passing through a sieve to remove any fibres)
Creek yoghurt
pomegranate seeds
coriander cress

Firstly, mix together the red onion, lemon juice and chaat masala and set aside for 15 minutes.

Now make the bread. Mix together all the ingredients and knead them together to a firm, but smooth dough. Leave covered for 20 minutes to rest. Then divide into four equal parts and roll out, using a rolling pin, into circular pancakes, roughly 20cm in diameter.

Heat a pan and place the rolled dough on it, cook on a dry heat for 2 minutes on each side and then apply oil to baste. As the bread starts getting coloured, flip on to the other side and pour a quarter of the beaten egg on to it. Let the egg mix congeal for a minute or so and then turn it over again to cook the side with the egg on it. Remove from the heat and repeat the same process for all the pancakes.

Once all the breads are cooked, lay on a work surface, brush with melted butter and spread the onion mix on the bread.

Place the cooked lamb kebab in the centre of the bread and drizzle with mint chutney and mango purée. Wrap the bread around to cover the kebab completely and form a roll. Stick toothpicks at the edges to prevent the bread from opening and cut into desired size either for cocktail snacks or for starters.

Serve garnished with yoghurt, pomegranate seeds and coriander cress.

These can be made with either raw mince or cooked, The cooked mince ones are easier. In my parathas I like the dough to be less than the quantity of filling, but they're quite hard to make, so the recipe below suggests using half the quantity of filling for every part of dough. Do experiment with more filling as you gain more practice. The secret to making the very best filled breads is to make sure that the consistency of the dough and the filling remains the same. Try to cook the mince out as much as possible to dry it out, so it is easier and less messy to use.

MAKES 8

LAMB MINCE PARATHAS

For the parathas

550g chapatti flour (look for it in Asian food shops), plus about 50g extra for dusting
275ml water
1 tablespoon vegetable oil
1 teaspoon salt
2 tablespoons ghee or vegetable oil

For the filling

3 tablespoons vegetable oil
1 bay leaf
2 green cardamom pods
2cm piece of cinnamon stick
2 cloves
1 teaspoon cumin seeds
2 large onions, finely chopped
1 tablespoon Ginger and Garlic Paste (page 18)
1 teaspoon salt
1 teaspoon red chilli powder
½ teaspoon turmeric powder
½ teaspoon cumin powder
1 teaspoon coriander powder
2cm piece of ginger, peeled and finely chopped
2 green chillies, finely chopped
300g lean lamb mince
2 tablespoons chopped fresh coriander leaves and stalks
juice of ½ lemon

Start by preparing the mince filling. Heat the oil in a pan to smoking point and add the whole spices, followed by the cumin seeds. When they start to crackle, add the onions and cook on a medium-low heat for 2–3 minutes. Add the ginger and garlic paste, salt, the ground spices, chopped ginger, green chillies and stir for 2–3 minutes to cook out the spices. Now add the minced lamb and cook until dry and the liquid has evaporated. Adjust the seasoning and sprinkle with the chopped coriander and the lemon juice. Remove from the heat and let the mince filling cool down completely. Divide into 8 equal parts and shape them as balls.

To make the parathas, put the flour, water, oil and salt in a bowl, mix together and knead lightly to make a smooth dough. Cover with a damp cloth and leave to rest for 15 minutes, then divide into 8 equal portions. Divide the stuffing into 8 equal portions and roll into balls.

Take a ball of dough, make an indent and keep pressing and rotating the dough in your hand to make the cavity slightly larger than the size of the ball of stuffing. The edges of the cavity should be slightly thinner than the centre (the edges of the dough are brought together to envelop the filling with the dough, if the edges aren't thinner, then it will result in a clumpy doughy centre). Sit the ball of stuffing in the cavity and bring together the edges to cover the stuffing from all sides. Do not leave any cracks or the stuffing will come out while rolling the parathas. Lightly dust with flour, gently flatten, then roll out into a 20cm-diameter disk.

Heat a heavy-based frying pan or flat griddle on a medium-low heat and put a rolled paratha on it. Cook for about 2–3 minutes, until the dough begins to dry out and colours on the bottom. Turn and cook the dough on the other side. Brush the top of the bread with ghee and flip it over again until it is golden and crisp on the outside. You will notice that the bread puffs up as it cooks. The application of ghee and flour between the layers facilitates this, and as the steam inside the bread builds up the layers separate. Cook the remaining breads in the same way, wrapping them loosely in foil to keep warm until they are all cooked.

Serve with Coriander Chutney or with Greek yoghurt that has been lightly salted and thinned with a little water.

These parathas can be made with literally anything: spiced potatoes, cooked mince, chopped cooked chicken, cured radishes, cooked or raw cauliflower or just about anything that catches your fancy!

This is a very basic lamb seekh kebab recipe. It's great if you can thread them on skewers, but not a problem if not. You can try shaping them as sausages and cooking them on a barbecue.

SERVES 4 AS NIBBLES

LAMB SEEKH KEBABS

For the mince kebabs
500g minced lamb, or diced boneless
    lamb
¼ teaspoon cumin seeds
2 green chillies
5–8 fresh coriander stems
3 garlic cloves
2cm piece of ginger, peeled
20g Cheddar cheese, grated
½ teaspoon red chilli powder
1 teaspoon salt

Pomegranate Raita (page 225),
    to serve or yoghurt with cucumber
    (see tip)

If you have a mincer, then you can use diced lamb to make your own mince. Mince the lamb and all the other ingredients, except the salt, coarsely together in the mincer. Finally, add the salt and, using your hands, combine the ingredients well to get an evenly spiced mince.

Alternatively, use minced lamb and make the kebab mix in a food processor. Firstly combine the spices in the food processor before adding the lamb. Do not process for long, as you want to maintain the coarse texture of the meat.

To cook the kebabs you need a barbecue and thick skewers. Divide the mince into 4 equal parts; now take a skewer and, with wet hands, slowly spread the mince on to the skewer, covering it and squeezing it so it sticks. The kebabs need to be about 20–25cm long and quite thick so they stay juicy. Cover and set aside in the fridge for 30 minutes.

Now cook the minced lamb kebabs on a barbecue or under a grill for 6–8 minutes, turning regularly to ensure the meat is cooked evenly.

When done, serve the kebabs garnished with the Pomegranate Raita or yoghurt cucumber dip (below) and naan bread, or simply serve them on their own (they make a great accompaniment to a few drinks – no wonder we sell kilos of these each night at Anise!).

Vivek's tip
For a simple yoghurt cucumber accompaniment, mix 100g Greek yoghurt with ¼ cucumber, peeled, deseeded and cut into 5mm dice. Stir in ½ teaspoon salt, ½ teaspoon roasted cumin and 6 finely shredded leaves of mint.

Drawing inspiration from the ubiquitous hummus and pitta bread, this is an Indian innovation! You can eat soft, fluffy, deep-fried bread and dry chunky chickpeas on the streets of Delhi any time of the day; our version turns this sauce on its head, with crisp dried bread and soft puréed spiced chickpeas.

SERVES 4

CHAAT MASALA HUMMUS WITH AJOWAN SEED STICKS

For the hummus

I tablespoon olive oil

2 or 3 cloves

I black cardamom pod

2 garlic cloves, crushed

I medium onion, finely chopped

200g drained boiled chickpeas

I teaspoon cumin seeds, roasted and crushed

I teaspoon Chaat Masala (page 21)

½ teaspoon red chilli powder

juice of ½ lime

I teaspoon salt

½ teaspoon sugar

100ml tahini (sesame seed paste)

4 tablespoons water

2 tablespoons olive oil

For the ajowan seed sticks

200g plain flour

½ teaspoon ajowan seeds

¼ teaspoon black onion seeds

I tablespoon ghee or butters

a pinch of salt

75ml water

oil for deep-frying

Firstly, make the ajowan seed sticks. Make a stiff dough using all the ingredients, rest for 5 minutes under a damp cloth, then roll out into a 2mm thickness. Cut into sticks 8–10cm long and 1cm wide and deep-fry in medium-hot oil for 5–6 minutes, or until golden and crisp. Drain on kitchen paper and leave to cool.

Now make the hummus. Heat the olive oil in a pan, add the cloves and cardamom and allow the flavours to be released; now add the garlic and onion and cook for 4–6 minutes until soft and just about beginning to change colour. Add the chickpeas, roasted cumin seeds, chaat masala and red chilli powder and cook for another couple of minutes. Season with lime juice, salt and sugar, remove from the heat and allow to cool.

Combine the rest of the ingredients in a food processor and blend to a creamy purée. Check the seasonings and refrigerate. Serve the hummus as a dip along with ajowan seed sticks or vegetable crudités.

Vivek's tip

For a stronger-tasting hummus, use a slug of mustard oil to finish the chickpea purée.

Stored in an airtight container, the ajowan seed sticks will keep for over a week. Cut into other shapes, they make an excellent base for canapés.

CHAAT MASALA
HUMMUS
PAGE 201

There are masala nuts and there are masala nuts. These are my favourite ones. I place particular emphasis on the hand-chopping of nuts as opposed to crushing, which brings out the oils and makes the nuts soft. Chopping nuts ensures that the texture is maintained and the increased surface area of the small, even pieces results in much better distribution of flavour.

MASALA CASHEW NUTS

2 tablespoons vegetable oil
I teaspoon finely chopped garlic
I teaspoon cumin seeds
200g roasted salted cashew nuts, chopped coarsely
1/2 teaspoon red chilli powder
I teaspoon dried fenugreek leaves, crushed between your fingertips
1/2 teaspoon Chaat Masala (page 21)
I teaspoon sugar
I tablespoon chopped green coriander leaves and stalks (optional), to garnish

Heat the oil, add the chopped garlic and cumin and cook until crisp, then add the chopped cashew nuts, stir for 30 seconds or so, add the rest of the ingredients and mix well. Remove from the heat, allow to cool down to room temperature and store in an airtight container.

These are a great as a garnish to finish off dishes or, if you're just plain greedy like me, then enjoy them by the fistful with drinks!

This is really nice spread on your bread or to dip your 'papdi' into. In Anise, we serve it as a small plate, but you could serve it as a starter at your dinner party or as an accompaniment with your barbecues.

SERVES 4

TANDOORI SALMON RILLETTES

500g salmon fillet, scaled, pin-boned and cut into 125g pieces

For the marinade
1 tablespoon Ginger and Garlic paste (page 18)
1 teaspoon Garlic Paste (page 18)
1 teaspoon salt
1 teaspoon red chilli powder
1 teaspoon ground turmeric
juice of ½ lemon
12g Greek yoghurt
1 teaspoon chopped fresh coriander leaves and stalks
½ tablespoon mustard oil (or use ½ tablespoon vegetable oil mixed with ¼ teaspoon English mustard)

To finish the rillettes
1 teaspoon chopped fresh tarragon
½ teaspoon cumin seeds, roasted
2 tablespoons crème fraîche

Pat dry the salmon and combine it with the rest of the ingredients. Set aside for 15–20 minutes to marinate in the fridge.

Thread the salmon pieces on to two skewers. Place the skewered salmon in an oven preheated to 180°C/Gas Mark 4 and bake for about 8–10 minutes. We cook it in the tandoor for about 8 minutes. Remove and let the fish cool down to room temperature. Separate the flesh from the skin and flake it using a fork.

Mix the salmon flakes with the tarragon, cumin and crème fraîche and refrigerate.

Transfer the rillettes to small bowls and serve with biscuits or small pieces of toast along with drinks.

Pao Bhaji is common in much of India and is often enjoyed as a breakfast dish. A pao (or 'pav') is like a fluffy bun that is used to scoop up a tangy purée of vegetables. In Bombay, where the dish originates, you can see it being made by street vendors on huge griddles. If you just reverse the proportions, i.e. concentrate the vegetables down to a thick paste, then fill inside the bun, they make for excellent 'hand-helds' – perfect for a late-evening party, when people start feeling peckish again.

SERVES 8

BOMBAY SPICED VEGETABLES IN CUMIN PAO

For the vegetable filling

1 tablespoon ghee or vegetable oil
1 teaspoon cumin seeds
1 teaspoon finely chopped garlic
1/2 onion, finely chopped
1/2 carrot, finely chopped into 5mm dice
100g cauliflower florets, finely chopped
1/2 green pepper, finely chopped into 5mm dice
50g French beans, finely chopped into 5mm dice
1/2 teaspoon cumin powder
1 teaspoon Kashmiri red chilli powder
3 large ripe tomatoes, blended to a purée
1 teaspoon spice mix (equal parts of cloves, black pepper, ajowan seeds, fennel, cinnamon and black salt)
75g boiled potato, grated
2 tablespoons tamarind paste
1/2 teaspoon chopped ginger
1 green chilli, finely chopped
1 tablespoon chopped fresh coriander leaves and stalks
1 tablespoon butter to finish
juice of 1/2 lemon

For the pao

10g fresh yeast
1½ tablespoons caster sugar
100ml lukewarm water
2 tablespoons milk
1 egg, lightly beaten
15g butter, melted
280g plain white flour
1 teaspoon salt
1 teaspoon cumin seeds, plus extra for sprinkling
15g butter melted for brushing

Heat the ghee in a large, flat pan to smoking point, add the cumin seeds and garlic and allow them to crackle. As the garlic starts to change colour, add the onion and sauté until golden. Add the carrots and sweat for a couple of minutes, then add the cauliflower and do the same, constantly stirring to mix evenly. Now add the green pepper and cook for another couple of minutes. Add the beans and cook another minute and then add the cumin and red chilli powder and sauté for a minute. Next add the tomato purée, reduce the heat and cook for about 15–18 minutes, or until the tomatoes dry out and the vegetables have a coating consistency. The colour of the tomatoes will have intensified by now. Quickly stir in the spice mix powder and add the potato – just enough to bind the vegetables together and make the mixture smooth. Add the tamarind paste and cook for another 3–4 minutes to thicken the vegetable mix. Finally add the chopped ginger and green chillies, sprinkle with the coriander and finish with the remaining butter and lemon juice.

Meanwhile, make the pao. Put the yeast and sugar in a small bowl, add the water and milk and stir until the yeast has dissolved. Set aside in a warm place for 15 minutes, until frothy. Add half the egg and the melted butter to the yeast mixture and whisk well.

Sift 250g of the flour with the salt into a bowl. Add the cumin seeds and pour in the yeast mixture and mix to make a smooth dough. Finally mix in the melted butter. Using the remaining flour, knead the dough for 10 minutes, until it becomes smooth and elastic. Cover the bowl with clingfilm or a damp cloth and leave the dough in a warm place for 30 minutes, or until doubled in size.

When the dough has risen, knock it back and divide it into 8 equal balls. Arrange the dough balls on a well-greased baking tray about 2cm deep, placing them 1cm apart. Press the balls lightly so they just touch each other, then cover again with clingfilm or a damp cloth and leave in a warm place for 30 minutes, or until they have doubled in volume. They will merge together.

When the dough has risen, brush with the remaining beaten egg and sprinkle some more cumin seeds on top. Bake in an oven preheated to 180°C/Gas Mark 4 for 25 minutes, until golden brown. Remove the pao from the oven and brush with melted butter while the buns are still hot and allow to cool.

Cut your pao horizontally in half, toast them lightly, then brush with melted butter and spread with the vegetable purée. Serve warm.

These little cakes are quite easy to make and very good to eat, just remember to add the chopped roasted peanuts at the last minute before cooking, as if you add peanuts in advance, they go soggy and lose their crunch.

MAKES 24 AS CANAPÉS OR 12 AS STARTERS

GREEN PEA AND POTATO CAKES WITH SWEET TOMATO CHUTNEY

125g shelled peas, fresh or thawed (preferably petits pois)
4cm ginger, peeled and roughly chopped
4 green chillies, finely chopped
2 teaspoons roasted cumin seeds
3 tablespoons finely chopped coriander stalk
5 medium-sized potatoes, boiled, peeled and grated
50g cornflour
30g roasted peanuts, chopped coarsely
1½ teaspoons salt
4 tablespoons vegetable oil for frying
1 quantity of Tomato and Onion Seed Chutney (page 22)

To make the green pea and potato cakes, place the green peas, ginger, green chillies, cumin seeds and coriander stalk in a food processor and coarsely grind them.

Place the grated potatoes in a mixing bowl, add the ground green pea mixture and the rest of the ingredients and mix evenly.

Form the mixture into 12 equal sized patties for starters or 24 small patties for canapés and, in a heavy-based pan, sear them in medium-hot oil for 1–2 minutes on each side until golden.

Serve the potato cakes hot with the tomato and onion seed chutney.

Think of these as stuffed spicy pizzas. A really well-made paratha is a thing of beauty. In my parathas I like the dough to be less than the quantity of filling, but they're quite hard to make, so the recipe below suggests using half the quantity of filling for every part of dough. Do experiment with more filling as you gain more practice.

SERVES 4

CHEESE PARATHAS

For the parathas
550g chapatti flour (look for it in Asian food shops), plus about 50g extra for dusting
275ml water
1 tablespoon vegetable oil
1 teaspoon salt
2 tablespoons ghee or vegetable oil

For the filling
3 green chillies, finely chopped
10g finely chopped fresh ginger
50g fresh coriander leaves and stalks, finely chopped
1 red onion, finely chopped
½ tablespoon dried pomegranate seeds, crushed
1 teaspoon chilli powder
1 teaspoon salt
250g paneer cheese, grated
50g Cheddar cheese, grated

Start making the filling by mixing together the chillies, ginger and coriander. Add the onion and season with the crushed pomegranate seeds, chilli powder and salt and mix well with the cheese.

To make the parathas, put the flour, water, oil and salt in a bowl, mix together and knead lightly to make a smooth dough. Cover with a damp cloth and leave to rest for 15 minutes, then divide into 8 equal portions. Divide the stuffing into 8 equal portions and roll into balls.

Take a ball of dough, make an indent and keep pressing and rotating the dough in your hand to make the cavity slightly larger than the size of the ball of stuffing. The edges of the cavity of dough should be slightly thinner than the centre (the edges of the dough are brought together to envelop the filling with the dough, if the edges aren't thinner, then it will result in a clumpy doughy centre). Sit the ball of stuffing in the cavity and bring together the edges to cover the stuffing from all sides. Do not leave any cracks or the stuffing will come out while rolling the parathas. Lightly dust with flour, gently flatten, then roll out into a 20cm-diameter disk.

Heat a heavy-based frying pan or flat griddle on a medium-low heat and put a rolled paratha on it. Cook for about 2–3 minutes, until the dough begins to dry out and colours on the bottom. Turn the dough and cook it on the other side. Brush the top of the bread with ghee and flip it over again until it is golden and crisp on the outside. You will notice the bread puffs up as it cooks. The application of ghee and flour between the layers facilitates this, and as the steam inside the bread builds up, the layers separate. Cook the remaining breads in the same way, wrapping them loosely in foil to keep them warm until they are all cooked.

Serve with pickles and Greek yoghurt that has been lightly salted and thinned with a little water.

These parathas can be made with literally anything: spiced potatoes, cooked mince, chopped cooked chicken, cured radishes, cooked or raw cauliflower or just about anything that takes your fancy!

These chilled lentil dumplings are perfect as an anytime snack and are often sold/served on hot summer afternoons or balmy evenings in India. Feel free to sprinkle some Bombay mix or crushed nuts on top for that extra texture.

SERVES 4

CHILLED LENTIL DUMPLINGS WITH STRAW POTATOES

For the lentil dumplings
200g white urad lentils
1½ teaspoons salt
1 teaspoon black peppercorns, coarsely crushed
2 tablespoons semolina
oil for frying

For the yoghurt mixture
500g plain yoghurt
2.5cm piece of fresh ginger, peeled and finely chopped
2 green chillies, finely chopped
2 tablespoons chopped fresh coriander leaves and stalks
½ teaspoon asafoetida
2 teaspoons cumin seeds, roasted and coarsely crushed
1 teaspoon red chilli powder
1 teaspoon salt

For the straw potatoes
oil for frying
2 medium-sized potatoes, peeled and cut into fine sticks
½ teaspoon salt
¼ teaspoon red chilli powder

For the garnish
Tamarind Chutney (page 179)
Coriander Chutney (page 22)
1 tablespoon pomegranate seeds
cress or mixed greens

Clean, wash and soak the lentils overnight. Drain the lentils and blend to a smooth mixture, using just enough water to blend. Add the salt, black peppercorns and semolina. Whip the batter together with a spoon until it is light and fluffy.

Heat the oil in a pan; divide the batter into round balls of equal size and deep-fry them until golden brown. Next soak the fried dumplings in lukewarm water for 20 minutes until soft. Squeeze the excess water and put them in a deep dish.

Beat the yoghurt to a smooth mixture with a whisk (add some water if required). Add the remaining ingredients and pour over the dumplings, covering them entirely. Place in the fridge for 30 minutes.

Heat the oil in a separate pan and fry the potatoes until golden brown, then place on kitchen paper to remove excess oil. Sprinkle with the salt and red chilli powder.

Put the straw potatoes on top of the soaked lentil dumplings and serve garnished with tamarind chutney, mint chutney and pomegranate seeds.

You will come across this on streets across most north Indian towns. We find it works really well as nibbles in Anise, too. Tiny biscuit discs made out of wheat, topped with spiced potatoes, dressed with yoghurt, tamarind and coriander chutneys make for a great canapé any time of the day.

PAPDI CHAAT

For the ajowan seed biscuits
200g plain flour
½ teaspoon ajowan seeds
¼ teaspoon black onion seeds
1 tablespoon ghee or butter
a pinch of salt
75ml water
oil for deep-frying

For the spiced potatoes
2 potatoes, boiled, peeled and grated
1 red onion, finely chopped
2 green chillies, finely chopped
1cm piece of ginger, peeled and
    chopped
1 tablespoon chopped coriander
    leaves and stalks
1 teaspoon salt
1 teaspoon red chilli powder
1 teaspoon roasted cumin seeds

For the yoghurt dressing
250g plain yoghurt
a pinch of salt
½ teaspoon sugar
½ teaspoon ground cumin

To serve
4 tablespoons Coriander Chutney
    (page 22)
4 tablespoons Tamarind Chutney
    (page 179)

To make the biscuits, put all the ingredients in a bowl and mix together to form a stiff dough, rest for 5 minutes under a damp cloth, then roll out into a 2mm thickness. Cut into 4–5cm squares or circles and deep-fry at 120°C until they are crisp.

To make the spiced potatoes, mix together all the ingredients, taste for seasoning and set aside in the fridge.

To make the yoghurt dressing, mix together all the ingredients and check seasoning. Set aside in the fridge.

To assemble, top each biscuit with a spoonful of spiced potato mix and arrange on a large serving platter. Then spoon the yoghurt dressing on top of the loaded biscuits. Next, drizzle with coriander chutney, tamarind chutney and serve immediately.

A distinct Scottish influence can still be found on the menus of some long-standing Anglo-Indian restaurants in Calcutta, (oops! Kolkata). An old menu at Flury's, for example: '...mutton cutlets, fish chops and Scotch-deem ['deem' meaning egg]. The Bengalis like cakes – they make them with potatoes and with fish and call them 'chops' or 'cutlets'. Here we have given the same treatment to a mixture of vegetables, where the colour of the beetroot gives these a distinctive look. These Scotch eggs are one of our most recent additions to the menu. They can be served with any mustard-based sauce mixed with tomato ketchup.

SERVES 6

BANGLA SCOTCH EGGS

18 quail's eggs
2 tablespoons ghee or vegetable oil
¼ teaspoon black onion seeds
¼ teaspoon cumin seeds
¼ teaspoon fennel seeds
I bay leaf
½ onion, finely chopped
I carrot, peeled and finely chopped
100g cauliflower florets, finely chopped
50g French beans, finely chopped
½ teaspoon red chilli powder
½ teaspoon ground cumin
½ teaspoon salt
½ teaspoon sugar
I beetroot, boiled, peeled and finely chopped
2 teaspoons raisins
I floury potato, boiled, peeled and grated
oil for deep-frying

For the spice mix
2 green cardamom pods
½ teaspoon cumin seeds, roasted
½ teaspoon coriander seeds, roasted

For crumb coating
2 eggs, beaten
150g dried breadcrumbs

Start by cooking the eggs until just over soft-boiled. Place the quail's eggs in a saucepan with just enough salted water to cover and bring to the boil. As soon as the water boils, cook for 45 seconds, then drain. Dip the eggs immediately in cold water, then peel and set aside.

To make the spice mix, use a mortar and pestle to coarsely pound the cardamom pods, cumin and coriander seeds, then set aside.

Heat the ghee in a heavy-based frying pan or wok to smoking point and add the black onion seeds, cumin and fennel seeds and the bay leaf. When they begin to crackle, add the onion and sauté until golden. Now add all the vegetables, except the beetroot and potato, in the order they are listed and sauté on a medium heat for 4 minutes. Add the chilli powder, ground cumin and the spice mix and cook, stirring, for 2–3 minutes.

Add the beetroot and raisins and cook for 1 minute. Add the salt and sugar and stir well, then add the grated potatoes and continue cooking, stirring, until the mixture is evenly combined, the

colour turns reddish and the mixture becomes shiny due to the ghee. This should take 3–4 minutes. Set the mixture aside and leave to cool.

When cold, divide the mixture into 18 equal portions and mould each portion around a boiled egg. One by one, dip a coated quail's egg in the beaten egg, then roll it in the dried breadcrumbs until evenly coated. Transfer each egg to the fridge, once fully coated, and chill for 15 minutes.

Heat enough oil for deep-frying in a deep-fat fryer or a deep, heavy-based saucepan to 180°C. Add the eggs and fry about 2–3 minutes, until they are crisp and golden brown. Drain well on kitchen paper and serve hot with a chutney of your choice.

ACCOM

ACCOMPANIMENTS

BOILED RICE

Plain and simple, this is the easiest way to cook rice. You might be most familiar with the 'draining method' from when you make pasta. The only difference being that addition of salt in the water is optional; some people do and some don't. Ideally you would take around 6–8 times the amount water as the quantity of rice, bring it to a boil and cook as per instructions on the packet. Drain through a colander, and serve hot.

SERVES 4–6

400g basmati rice
I litre water
I teaspoon salt

Thoroughly wash the rice in cold running water. Place the rice in a bowl of cold water and leave to soak for 25 minutes. Drain well.

Bring one litre of water to the boil in a large pan and add the salt. Add the rice and simmer, uncovered, for 8–10 minutes, until the grains are tender, but not mushy. Remove the pan from the heat and drain the rice through a sieve. Serve with a curry or another dish of your choice.

Vivek's tip
The rice is ready to use as soon as it is drained; however, if you want to make it in advance but prevent further cooking, you could pour cold water over the rice, or simply spread it out in a large baking tray and leave to cool. Rice is best reheated quickly in a microwave.

EASY PILAU RICE

This is the easiest pilau rice you'll ever make – but you will need a microwave oven. It's a clever way to use your time effectively: the rice can cook on its own while you prepare the rest of the meal. Ideally, you'd put the rice in 15–20 minutes before you're ready to eat and serve it hot.

SERVES 4–6

250g basmati rice
375ml water
1/2 teaspoon salt
50g ghee or vegetable oil
3 cloves
2 green cardamom pods
5cm piece of cinnamon stick
I teaspoon cumin seeds
I bay leaf
2 tablespoons dried sliced onions, deep fried
10g mint leaves, shredded
10g fresh coriander leaves and stalks, chopped

Thoroughly wash the rice in cold running water. Place the rice in a bowl of cold water and leave to soak for 25 minutes. Drain well.

Place the rice, water and salt in a shallow microwave dish and set aside.

LEMON RICE

Heat the ghee in a heavy-based saucepan to smoking point and add the whole spices and bay leaf. When they crackle, add the onion, mint and coriander and mix briefly, then tip all of the ingredients out of the pan and add into the microwave dish with the rice.

Place the dish in a microwave oven and cook, uncovered, on High for 12–13 minutes, until most of the water is absorbed and you see small holes on the surface of the rice. Stir well, then cover with clingfilm and return to the microwave for another 5 minutes. Remove the dish from the microwave, uncover and fluff it with a fork and allow the rice to cool slightly. Serve hot.

Vivek's tip
Soaking the rice before cooking reduces the cooking time and prevents the grains from breaking while cooking.

One of many dishes made from the humble grain that make you appreciate how versatile rice can be! As simple as this recipe is, it adds colour, flavour and vibrancy to any dish it accompanies.

SERVES 4–6

400g basmati rice
1 litre water
3 tablespoons vegetable oil
1 tablespoon black mustard seeds
1 tablespoon chana dal (split yellow chickpeas)
1 teaspoon white urad lentils (optional)
20 fresh curry leaves
1 teaspoon ground turmeric
1½ teaspoons salt
juice of 3 lemons

Thoroughly wash the rice in cold running water. Place the rice in a bowl of cold water and leave to soak for 25 minutes. Drain well.

Bring the water to the boil in a large saucepan and add the rice. Cook, uncovered, for 8–10 minutes, until the grains are tender, but not mushy. Drain through a sieve and set aside.

Heat the oil in a large pan to smoking point and add the mustard seeds, chana dal and urad lentils, if using, and let them

crackle. When they start to turn almost golden, add the curry leaves and the turmeric and stir for 1 minute (sprinkle in some water to prevent the turmeric from burning). Add the cooked rice, salt and lemon juice and gently toss to mix well without breaking the rice grains.

JERUSALEM COUSCOUS UPMA

AUBERGINE CRUSH

Israeli couscous is similar to tapioca pearls in appearance, except the grains are larger and quite dramatic, imparting a rather nice texture to the upma.

SERVES 4

100g Israeli couscous, boiled as per instructions on the packet and drained
1 red onion, finely chopped
2.5cm piece of fresh ginger, peeled and finely chopped
2 green chillies, finely chopped
1 tablespoon chopped fresh coriander leaves and stalks
1 green mango, peeled, and cut into 5mm dice
½ red pepper, thinly sliced
1 teaspoon salt
juice of ½ lemon

For tempering
2 tablespoons vegetable oil
½ teaspoon black mustard seeds
10 curry leaves

Put the Israeli couscous in a bowl and stir in the remaining ingredients, except the oil, mustard seeds and curry leaves. Mix together and check the seasoning. Heat the oil in a small frying pan to smoking point and add the mustard seeds and curry leaves. As soon as they crackle, pour them into the bowl of couscous and serve immediately.

This simple but very effective aubergine crush is an excellent accompaniment to both grilled meats and fish, and is versatile enough that it can be served as a filling for wraps, too. The aubergines can be either roasted in the oven, char-grilled on a very hot grill or even burnt on an open flame. Much like roasting peppers to remove the skin, the last two options impart a wonderful smokiness to the dish. Unlike a north Indian aubergine crush, where the aubergines are cooked further with onions, tomatoes and spices after being roasted, this version is eastern Indian in influence.

SERVES 4 AS A GENEROUS ACCOMPANIMENT

4 garlic cloves, peeled
2 large aubergines
5 tablespoons mustard oil (or use 5 tablespoons vegetable oil mixed with 2½ tablespoons English mustard), or feel free to substitute olive oil
3 green chillies, finely chopped (depending on how hot the chillies are!)
2 red onions, finely chopped
2 tablespoons chopped fresh coriander leaves and stalks
juice of 2 lemons
1 teaspoon salt

Slice the garlic cloves in half and, using a sharp knife, prick each aubergine 4 times. Insert the garlic pieces into the slits in the aubergines. Smear the aubergines with ½ tablespoon of the oil, place on a baking tray and bake in an oven preheated to 200°C/Gas Mark 6 for 10 minutes. Turn the aubergines over and roast for a further 10–20 minutes, until they are very soft and the skins are wrinkled.

Remove the aubergines from the oven and leave until cool enough to handle, then peel and discard the skins and stems. Finely chop the aubergine pulp, including the garlic, and mix with the remaining oil, green chillies, onions, coriander, lemon juice and salt.

Aubergine crush can be served warm or cold.

STIR-FRIED GREENS WITH GARLIC AND CUMIN

As the name suggests, you can use whatever greens are in season – kale, cabbage, beetroot greens and red chard all work well in this dish. Just remember to add the hard bits first and cook longer, then add the softer leaves last and remove from the heat as soon as they wilt.

SERVES 4

2 tablespoons vegetable oil
2 garlic cloves, finely chopped
1 dried red chilli
1 teaspoon cumin seeds
150g broccoli or purple sprouting broccoli, cut into florets
50g shelled peas, fresh or thawed (preferably petits pois)
1 green chilli, finely chopped
2.5cm piece of fresh ginger, peeled and finely chopped
1 teaspoon salt
200g bok choy leaves, cut diagonally
200g spinach leaves
½ teaspoon Kadhai Masala (page 21)
a pinch of sugar
2 tablespoons salted butter
juice of ½ lemon

Heat the oil in a heavy-based frying pan or wok to smoking point and add the garlic, dried red chilli and cumin seeds. When they crackle, add the broccoli florets and peas and stir-fry on a medium-high heat for 2–3 minutes, until the broccoli is tender. Stir in the green chilli, ginger and salt, then add the bok choy and spinach and continue stir-frying on a medium-high heat until the spinach leaves wilt. Sprinkle with kadhai masala and sugar and add the butter and lemon juice, stirring until the butter melts. Serve immediately.

YELLOW LENTILS

This is how yellow lentils are cooked in Indian homes. There are different varieties of yellow lentils used in different parts of the country, for example: split mung beans, red masoor lentils, toor lentils, split yellow chickpeas (chana lentils), white urad lentils. Each of these can be used individually or as a mix of all five lentils as seen in Rajasthani five-lentil mix.

SERVES 4

120g yellow moong lentils (split yellow mung beans)
750ml water
1 teaspoon ground turmeric
1½ teaspoons salt
1 tablespoon ghee or vegetable oil
1 dried red chilli
1 teaspoon cumin seeds
a pinch of asafoetida
2 garlic cloves, finely chopped
1 onion, finely chopped
1 tomato, finely chopped
1cm piece of fresh ginger, peeled and finely chopped
1 teaspoon chopped fresh coriander leaves and stalks
juice of ½ lemon

Wash the lentils in cold running water and drain well. Place them in a pan with the water, turmeric and salt. Bring to a boil, then reduce the heat and simmer for about 15 minutes, until the lentils are tender and disintegrating.

Heat the ghee or oil in a heavy-based pan to smoking point and add chilli, cumin seeds and asafoetida. When they crackle, add the garlic and stir until it turns golden, then add the onion and cook on a medium heat for 4–6 minutes until it is translucent. Add the tomato and cook for 3 minutes, until it has softened, then pour in the cooked lentils. Stir in the ginger and coriander and bring to the boil. Adjust the seasoning, if necessary, and finish with the lemon juice.

BLACK LENTILS

Each of my books has a recipe for black lentils – they're just so popular! These rich, earthy, creamy, musky, black lentils are a comfort food perfect for lifting your spirits in cold, dark wet winters. Traditionally these are cooked for hours, but in every version we've tried to tweak it to make it a little easier to prepare. This one is perhaps the easiest yet.

SERVES 4

250g black urad lentils, soaked in lukewarm water in a warm place overnight
3 litres water
1 tablespoon Ginger and Garlic Paste (page 18)
1½ teaspoons red chilli powder
1½ teaspoons salt
4 tablespoons tomato purée
150g salted butter
2 teaspoons dried fenugreek leaves, crushed between your fingertips
1 teaspoon Garam Masala (page 20)
1 teaspoon sugar
2 tablespoons single cream

Drain the lentils and put them in a pan with 1 litre of the water. Bring to the boil, then reduce the heat and simmer, skimming the surface, as necessary, for

continued on page 224

MARROW AND
LENTILS

continued from page 223

20–25 minutes, until they are nearly half cooked.

Meanwhile, bring the remaining 2 litres to the boil. After the lentils have cooked for 20–25 minutes and the water is dark, drain the dark water off and add the fresh boiling water to them. Continue cooking the lentils for another hour or so, until they are thoroughly tender, but not broken down. Add the ginger and garlic paste, chilli powder and salt and boil again for 10 minutes. Add the tomato purée and butter and simmer, stirring, for 15 minutes, or until the lentils are thick, but taking care that butter does not separate from the lentils.

Add the fenugreek leaves, garam masala and sugar. Check the seasoning, then carefully stir in the cream.

This dish goes very well with most tandoori-style dishes, especially tandoori chicken and also with layered parathas and naans.

This might be a very different way to serve marrow than you are used to. This often bland vegetable is perked up here through quite an extensive list of ingredients and gets extra texture from the lentils. You can replace the marrow with any other squash or even with bitter gourd. This is a good way of incorporating protein into a vegetarian diet.

SERVES 4

75g split yellow lentils or chana dal (split yellow chickpeas)
1½ teaspoons ground turmeric, plus a pinch for cooking the lentils
½ teaspoon salt, plus extra for boiling the marrow
500g marrow, peeled, deseeded and cut into 2.5cm dice
3 tablespoons vegetable oil
1½ teaspoons cumin seeds
I whole red chilli, broken into 3 pieces
I large onion, finely chopped
I teaspoon red chilli powder
I teaspoon ground coriander
2 large tomatoes, deseeded and chopped
3 green chillies, finely chopped
2.5cm piece of ginger, peeled and finely chopped
I teaspoon salt
40g fresh green coriander leaves and stalks, finely chopped
juice of I lemon

Wash the lentils in cold running water and drain well. Put them in a pan with a pinch of turmeric and enough water to cover and bring to the boil. Simmer for 20–25 minutes, until the lentils are just tender but still hold their shape. Drain and set aside.

Blanch the marrow in boiling salted water with 1 teaspoon of the turmeric for a couple of minutes, then drain. Cool it down quickly by plunging into cold water, drain again and set aside.

Heat the oil in a large pan to smoking point and add the cumin and red chilli. When they crackle, add the onion and cook for 4–6 minutes until it is translucent. Add the chilli powder, coriander and the remaining ½ teaspoon turmeric and cook for another couple of minutes. Now add the tomatoes and cook for 5 minutes, until the moisture from the tomatoes has evaporated. Add the drained lentils and cook for another 4 minutes. Add the green chillies, ginger and salt, followed by the blanched marrow, and cook, stirring constantly, for 2 minutes: the lentils should be tender but still firm to bite. Check the seasoning and finish with the coriander and lemon juice.

POMEGRANATE RAITA

YOGHURT KADHI SAUCE

Raita is a common accompaniment to Indian meals. It helps take the heat off certain dishes, keeps the body cool in hot months and aids digestion.

SERVES 4

1 pomegranate
500g Greek yoghurt
1 spring onion, finely chopped
2.5cm piece of fresh ginger, peeled and finely chopped
2 green chillies, finely chopped
1 teaspoon cumin, roasted in a dry frying pan and ground
1 teaspoon salt
1/2 teaspoon sugar
1 tablespoon chopped fresh coriander leaves and stalks

Cut the pomegranate in half and remove the seeds, gently tapping the halves with a rolling pin or the back of a heavy knife to loosen them. Reserve a few pomegranate seeds for garnishing.

Combine the remaining seeds with the rest of the ingredients, except the coriander, and mix well. Transfer the raita into 4 bowls, sprinkle with the coriander and reserved pomegranate seeds and refrigerate until required.

This is a very versatile sauce, commonly seen and served in Gujarat, Rajasthan, Delhi and most of north India. The sauce is cooked a little bit like a custard, but without eggs. Chickpea flour is used to thicken the yoghurt, and the resulting base is a perfect canvas on which to paint a variety of flavours. In the southern part of the country, they make a similar sauce using rice flour to thicken yoghurt, leaving out the turmeric, so resulting in a hot yoghurt soup.

SERVES 4–6

For the yoghurt sauce
150g plain yoghurt
1 tablespoon gram (chickpea) flour
250ml water
1/2 teaspoon salt
a small pinch of ground turmeric

For tempering
1 tablespoon ghee
1 dried red chilli
1/2 teaspoon cumin seeds
a sprig of fresh curry leaves
juice of 1/2 lemon

Start with the yoghurt kadhi. Whisk together the yoghurt, gram flour, water, salt and turmeric and pass through a fine sieve to get rid of any lumps.

Place in a saucepan on a medium heat and bring to the boil, whisking constantly. Reduce the heat and simmer for 5–8 minutes, until the sauce turns glossy and thickens enough to lightly coat the back of a wooden spoon. Skim off any scum or impurities from the surface.

In a small pan, heat the ghee to smoking point. Add the red chilli, cumin seeds and curry leaves and leave on the heat for a few seconds until they splutter and crackle. Tip the contents of the pan over the sauce, pour over the lemon juice and set aside.

Serve immediately if everything else is ready. If not, allow to cool and reheat when ready to serve. Once cooled, the sauce can be stored in a refrigerator for a couple of days and reheated when needed.

CITRUS MASHED POTATOES

This version of spiced mashed potatoes is particularly good with any seafood main course. The addition of lemon juice towards the end has a refreshing effect and the acidity livens up the dish.

SERVES 4

500g floury potatoes, such as Desiree, peeled and cut into chunks
I teaspoon salt
I teaspoon ground turmeric
75g butter
I tablespoon ghee or vegetable oil
½ teaspoon cumin seeds, roasted and crushed
½ teaspoon red chilli flakes
2 green chillies, chopped
2.5cm piece of fresh ginger, peeled and finely chopped
4 tablespoons single cream
2 tablespoons chopped fresh coriander leaves and stalks
juice of I lemon

Cook the potatoes in boiling water with salt and turmeric until tender. Drain and push through a fine sieve or potato ricer into a bowl. Mix in the butter while the potatoes are still warm and set aside.

Heat the ghee or oil in a heavy-based frying pan to smoking point and add the cumin seeds and red chilli flakes. When they crackle, add the green chillies and ginger. Add the mashed potatoes and mix well on a low heat combining the ingredients and reheating the potatoes if necessary. Gradually stir in the cream and continue stirring on a low heat until the potato mixture absorbs all the cream and leaves the sides of the pan. Finish with the coriander and lemon juice.

NAANS

The humble, common naan from Delhi and Punjab is one of the best gifts from tandoor ovens to mankind. It is widely available and popular the world over, and light and fluffy naans can be served with any main course of your choice. Use your imagination and you could soon be using this bread for sandwiches, making rolls or even using it as a base for canapés.

MAKES 16

750g plain white flour
1½ teaspoons baking powder
1 tablespoon salt
400ml whole milk
2 eggs
35g sugar
50ml vegetable oil

Mix the flour, baking powder and salt together in a bowl. Whisk together the milk, eggs and sugar, then add this to the flour mixture and knead lightly to make a soft dough (take care not to overwork the dough or it will become too stretchy). Cover with a damp cloth and leave to rest for 15 minutes.

Pour the oil over the dough and turn it a few times so it is evenly coated. Divide the dough into 16 equal pieces, roll out each one into a circle about 9cm in diameter, then gently stretch out one side to form the traditional teardrop shape. Alternatively just roll them into 10cm circles.

Although naans are traditionally cooked on the side of a hot tandoor oven, they also cook well in an ordinary domestic oven. Preheat the oven to 220°C/Gas Mark 7, putting a baking tray in it to heat up. Place the naan breads on the hot tray and bake for 4–5 minutes, until they are starting to brown on both sides. You might need to turn the bread to make sure it colours on both sides.

Alternatively, heat several heavy-based flameproof frying pans on the hob until they are very hot. Place one naan bread on each pan and cook for a couple of minutes, until it starts to get slightly coloured. Turn the naans over and transfer the pans to a hot grill for a minute or so, until the bread puffs up and gets lightly coloured. Voila! Your naan bread is ready and you didn't even need a tandoor oven!

Serve the naans hot, or wrap in a tea towel to keep warm.

Vivek's tip
You can get as creative as you like with the toppings – try turmeric, crushed red chillies, fresh coriander, garlic, grated cheese, pesto, sun-dried tomatoes, olives – quite simply anything you fancy!

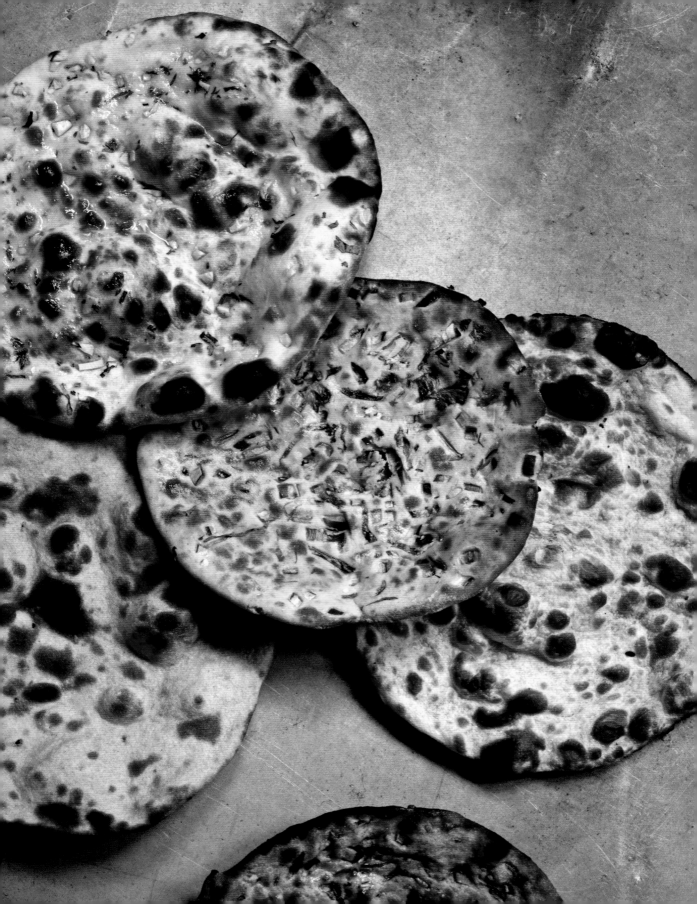

MISSI ROTI

This simple, rustic chickpea bread from Rajasthan is so robustly spiced, it can be eaten on its own or with a simple pickle or chutney. It makes for an excellent canapé, too.

MAKES 8

300g gram (chickpea) flour
200g plain white flour
2cm piece of fresh ginger, peeled and finely chopped
2 green chillies, finely chopped
1 red onion, finely chopped
1 spring onion, finely chopped
1 tablespoon finely chopped fresh coriander leaves and stalks
2 teaspoons salt
1 teaspoon ajowan seeds
½ teaspoon ground turmeric
150ml water
2 tablespoons vegetable oil
3 tablespoons ghee or vegetable oil

Mix the chickpea flour and plain flour together. Remove 3–4 tablespoons of the flour mix and set aside for dusting. Add the ginger, chillies, red onion, spring onion, fresh coriander, salt, ajowan seeds and turmeric and mix well. Add the water and 2 tablespoons of vegetable oil and knead until the mixture is combined and a stiff dough forms. Cover with a damp cloth and leave to rest for 15–20 minutes.

Divide the dough into 8 equal pieces and shape into balls. Roll out each ball on a lightly floured surface, into a circle 15cm in diameter.

Heat a large, heavy-based non-stick frying pan or flat griddle on a high heat and place a circle of dough on it. Cook for 3–4 minutes, until the dough starts to dry out and is lightly coloured underneath; turn over. Reduce the heat, brush the top of the bread with some ghee or vegetable oil and turn it over and cook until the colour has deepened. Brush the top again and remove from the pan. The breads need to be turned twice. Cook the remaining breads in the same way.

SHEERMALS

This rich and flavoursome bread is a speciality from Lucknow, and had its origins in the Mughal courts all over India. Originally made in iron tandoors, which are now rarely seen in India, this version comes out just as well in a Western domestic oven.

MAKES 12

500g plain flour
400ml milk
40g sugar
1 tablespoon chironji (also known as charoli)
2 pinches of saffron, soaked in 1 tablespoon warm milk
1 teaspoon salt
150g ghee or clarified butter, melted, plus an extra 1 tablespoon for brushing

Put the milk in a pan with the sugar and bring to the boil, stirring to dissolve the sugar. Add the chironji and half of the saffron, reduce the heat to low and simmer for 5 minutes. Remove the pan from the heat and, when the milk is cool, stir in the salt.

Mix together the flour and ground cardamom in a large bowl. Gradually add the milk and knead until it comes together as a smooth, soft dough. Cover with a damp tea towel and leave to rest for 15 minutes.

Turn out the dough and knead it again, then slowly add the ghee, little by little, using your fingers to incorporate it. Roll into a ball, cover with a damp tea towel and leave to rest again for 15 minutes.

Divide the dough into 12 equal pieces and roll into balls. Cover the dough balls with a damp tea towel and set aside for 10 minutes.

Roll out each ball into a circle about 10cm in diameter. Arrange the dough circles on 2 greased baking sheets and bake in an oven preheated to 180°C/Gas Mark 4 for 10 minutes. Remove the baking sheets from the oven, brush the circles with ghee and the remaining saffron, return them to the oven to bake for 5 minutes more, until shiny and crisp on the surface. Serve immediately, brushed with more ghee.

Vivek's tip
The secret of perfection with this bread is to incorporate the ghee into the dough slowly by adding a little at a time. This way the fat is dispersed evenly through the entire dough. Chironji is available in good Asian delicatessens or online.

These circular layered parathas are the type traditionally served daily for lunch and dinner in north Indian homes. This is an example of home cooking and a fine one at that. More and more supermarkets sell ready-made frozen parathas, but, when you make your own you can add different spices, chillies, masalas or pesto – almost whatever you fancy. I've numbered the steps in the recipe text below to correspond with the instructional images on the following two pages.

MAKES 8

LAYERED PARATHAS

550g chapatti flour (look for it in Asian food shops), plus about 50g extra for dusting
275ml water
1 tablespoon vegetable oil
1 teaspoon salt
1 tablespoon ajowan seeds
2 tablespoons ghee or vegetable oil
1 tablespoon dried fenugreek leaves
2 tablespoons chopped mint leaves

Put the flour, water, oil, salt and ajowan seeds in a bowl and mix together, kneading lightly to make a smooth dough.[1] Cover with a damp cloth and leave to rest for 15 minutes.

Divide the dough into 8 equal pieces and roll each into a smooth, round ball.[2] Flatten one ball at a time with the palm of your hand. Sprinkle over a little of the reserved flour and roll it into a circle, 6–8cm in diameter.[3] Brush the top with ghee and sprinkle with a little more flour and some of the fenugreek leaves and mint.[4] Lift the disc from one side and fold the dough a few times like a concertina to obtain a thin strip approximately 2.5cm wide.[5] Roll the strip loosely into a coil and let it rest for 5 minutes.[6]

Flatten each coil, one at a time, using your hands or a rolling pin to obtain a disc about 1.5cm in diameter. Take care not to roll it too thinly or you will lose the layers.[7]

Heat a heavy-based frying pan or flat griddle on a high heat and add one of the flattened coils[8] and cook for 2–3 minutes, until the dough begins to dry out and colours on the bottom. Turn the dough over and cook it on the other side, then reduce the heat to medium. Brush the top of the bread with ghee and flip it over again until it is golden and crisp on the outside. You will notice that the layers separate as it cooks. The application of ghee and flour between the layers facilitates this, and as the steam inside the bread builds up the layers separate.[9] Cook the remaining breads in the same way, wrapping them loosely in foil to keep warm until they are all cooked.

CINNAMON KITCHEN CLASSICS:
STEP BY STEP

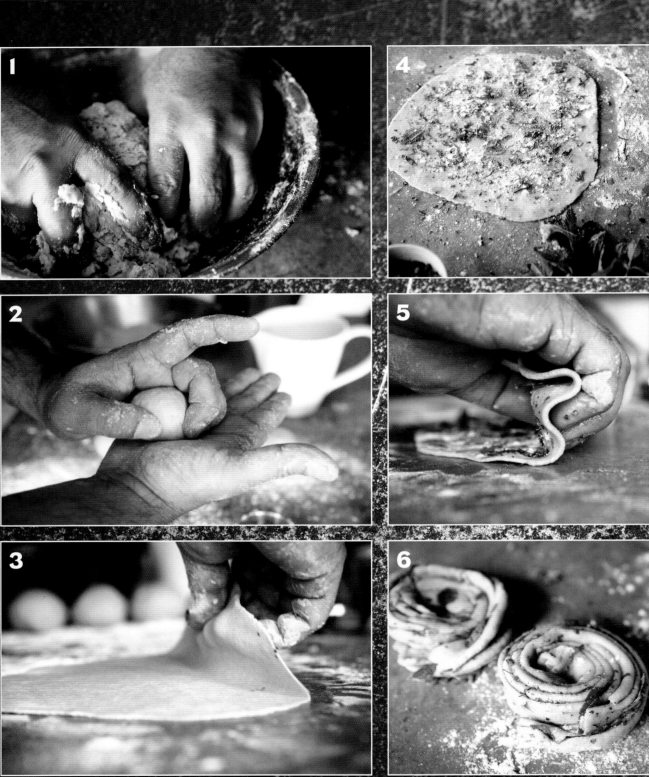

JERUSALEM ARTICHOKE PODIMAS

These are much like the filling you find inside dosa pancakes in the Subcontinent, but the Jerusalem artichokes give it a wonderful smokiness and deep earthy flavour, which I absolutely adore. I hope you like it as much!

SERVES 6–8

1kg Jerusalem artichokes, unpeeled, but thoroughly washed
1 green chilli, slit lengthways
1 red onion, sliced
2cm piece of fresh ginger, peeled and finely chopped
1 teaspoon ground turmeric
salt, to taste
2 tablespoons chopped fresh coriander leaves and stalks
juice of 1 lemon

For tempering
1 tablespoon vegetable oil
10 fresh curry leaves
1 dried red chilli
1 teaspoon urad dhal
1 teaspoon black mustard seeds
a pinch of asafoetida

Bring a pan of salted water to the boil. Add the Jerusalem artichokes and simmer for about 20 minutes, until they are tender. Drain well and set aside.

When the Jerusalem artichokes are cool enough to handle, peel them and return them to the pan. Mash them coarsely, then set aside.

For the tempering, heat the oil in a large, heavy-based frying pan to smoking point and add all the tempering ingredients. When the seeds crackle and the curry leaves wilt, add the chilli, red onion, ginger, turmeric and salt and fry, stirring, on a high heat for 30 seconds. Add the mashed artichokes and the salt to the pan and mix together. Finish off with the coriander and lemon juice and combine well.

GARLIC CHUTNEY

This is a fine example of the very hot chutneys and pickles that are consumed in the region of Rajasthan, where fruit and vegetables are preserved for later use. The heavy-handed spicing is what gives this group of preserves a better keeping quality. In the old days, travellers would simply set off on long journeys with some of these chutneys, which they consumed with bread. Kachri is a tomato-like fruit, sour and with lots of seeds inside a hard shell; it's consumed mostly in dried form. For this recipe, it's pounded coarsely and its addition to the chutney adds texture as well as acidity and sharpness to the chutney. Look for kachri in Asian food shops, but if you can't find any substitute with finely chopped sun-dried tomatoes and reduce the cooking time by half (5–6 minutes instead of 12–15 minutes). Alternatively, replace it with 250g extra garlic cloves, which will make a much hotter chutney.

MAKES ABOUT 500G

75g dried whole red chillies, soaked in 250ml hot water overnight or for at least 2 hours
250ml vegetable oil
1 teaspoon cumin seeds
125g garlic cloves, coarsely chopped

75ml malt vinegar
I tablespoon red chilli powder
2 teaspoons salt
250g kachri (see above) or sun-dried
    tomatoes, coarsely pounded
3 tablespoons sugar (optional)
I tablespoon chopped fresh
    coriander leaves and stalks
    (optional)

Drain the chillies, reserving the water, and put in a blender or food processor. Blitz into a smooth paste – you can use some of the soaking water if it looks a bit dry. Set aside.

Heat the oil in a large heavy-based frying pan to smoking point and add the cumin seeds. When they crackle, add the garlic and fry, stirring, until it begins to turn golden. Add the chilli paste, vinegar, chilli powder and the salt and cook on a low heat, constantly stirring, for 5–6 minutes. Now add the kachri and continue cooking for another 12–15 minutes, until the chutney is reduced and thickened and the fat begins to separate from it. Check the seasoning and add sugar, if required.

Remove from the heat and leave to cool. If you cover the surface with a layer of oil, the chutney can be stored at room temperature for 2 weeks, or in the fridge for a month.

Vivek's tip
Balance the chutney with a tablespoon of ketchup if it's too hot for your liking.

PEANUT CHUTNEY

This simple chutney works very well with any Oriental-style dish or curries from southern India. This is a versatile dip reminiscent of Asian satay sauce and works well even as a dip with bread.

MAKES ABOUT 160G

$\frac{1}{2}$ tablespoon vegetable oil
150g skinned peanuts
$\frac{1}{2}$ teaspoon red chilli powder
3 garlic cloves, chopped
Icm piece of fresh ginger, peeled and
    roughly chopped
2 red chillies, roughly chopped
I teaspoon salt
I teaspoon sugar
4 tablespoons coconut milk
juice from I lemon

Heat the oil in a frying pan, add the peanuts and fry until golden. Remove from the heat and leave to cool. Put the peanuts and remaining ingredients in a blender or food processor and blend into a paste. Check the seasoning and serve at room temperature.
It can be stored in an airtight jar for up to a week if refrigerated.

Vivek's tip
Cashew nuts work just as well. You can also thin the chutney with additional coconut milk and water to make a peanut sauce.

TOMATO AND COCONUT CHUTNEY

This is an example of a twice-tempered chutney from southern India. It is tempered once before blending and then again briefly to finish with the hot oil and spices.

MAKES ABOUT 550G

1 tablespoon vegetable oil
10 fresh curry leaves
½ teaspoon fennel seeds
1 onion, chopped
3 tomatoes, chopped
1 teaspoon red chilli powder
1 coconut, grated
30g chana dal (split yellow
    chickpeas), roasted
1 teaspoon salt

For tempering
2 tablespoons vegetable oil
5–10 fresh curry leaves
1 dried red chilli
1 teaspoon black mustard seeds

Heat the oil in a large heavy-based pan to smoking point and add the curry leaves and fennel seeds. When the seeds crackle, add the onion and cook for 4–6 minutes until it is translucent. Now add the tomatoes and chilli powder and cook, stirring occasionally, until the tomatoes have softened. Stir in the coconut and continue cooking until all the liquid has evaporated.

Remove the chutney from the heat and leave to cool. Transfer to a blender or food processor with the roasted chana dal and a little water and blend until smooth. Mix in the salt.

To temper the chutney, heat the oil to smoking point and add the curry leaves, red chilli and mustard seeds. When the seeds crackle, pour over the chutney.

Remove from the heat and leave to cool. If you cover the surface with a layer of oil the chutney can be stored at room temperature for 2 weeks, or in the fridge for a month.

GREEN COCONUT CHUTNEY

This is a simple, yet versatile chutney to accompany any south Indian dish. The mint leaves are our little addition, but you can interpret this recipe in many different ways – add tomatoes and red chillies for a red colour, or even green mangoes in season to make a fresh, sharper-tasting chutney.

MAKES ABOUT 400G

1 coconut, grated
50g fresh coriander leaves and stalks
20g fresh mint leaves
4 green chillies, chopped
2 tablespoons chana dal (split yellow
    chickpeas), roasted
1 teaspoon salt

For tempering
1 tablespoon vegetable oil
10 fresh curry leaves
¼ teaspoon black mustard seeds

Put the coconut, coriander, mint, chillies, chana dal and salt in a blender or food processor and blend to a soft, spoonable consistency. To temper the chutney, heat the oil to smoking point and add the curry leaves and mustard seeds. As soon as they start to crackle, pour over the chutney.

TAMARIND CHUTNEY

Remove from the heat and leave to cool. If you cover the surface with a layer of oil the chutney can be stored at room temperature for 2 weeks, or in the fridge for a month.

We use this all-round chutney in quite a few recipes: as a marinade, as a glaze, as an accompaniment and also as a garnish. The sweet spice, earthy, deep liquorice flavours and rich, glossy texture make this an attractive garnish. Once cooked, tamarind chutney stores well and can keep for up to 2 weeks in the fridge.

MAKES ABOUT 225G

150g tamarind paste
1 bay leaf
1 black cardamom pod
75g jaggery or molasses sugar
1½ teaspoons ground ginger
1 teaspoon red chilli powder
¼ teaspoon salt

Place the tamarind paste, bay leaf and cardamom pod in a heavy-based pan and bring to the boil. Add the jaggery or molasses sugar and cook, stirring, on a medium-low heat for 15 minutes, until glossy. Stir in the ground ginger, chilli powder and salt.

Remove the chutney from the heat and strain through a sieve, then leave to cool and serve as a dip.

MARINATED
TOMATO SALAD

Summer is a great time for something like this, when it's easy to find numerous varieties of tomatoes, all different colours, sizes, flavours and textures.

SERVES 4 AS A STARTER, OR 6–8 AS AN ACCOMPANIMENT

800g mixed tomatoes, various types and colours – whatever you're able to find – sliced or quartered, depending on their size
2 green chillies, finely chopped
2 garlic cloves, finely chopped
3–4 tablespoons extra-virgin olive oil
2 tablespoons finely chopped fresh coriander leaves and stalks
1 tablespoon chopped dill
1 tablespoon pomegranate seeds
1/2 teaspoon salt
juice of 2 limes
a few twists of freshly milled black pepper
a pinch of sugar (optional)

Arrange the tomatoes on individual plates or a large serving platter or in a bowl.

Whisk together all the remaining ingredients, including sugar to taste, then pour over the tomatoes. Transfer to the fridge and chill for 20–30 minutes, by which time, the dressing will have macerated the tomatoes and they will be ready to serve.

BAR: DRINKS

DRINKS

AGNI COOLER

A perfect summer patio sipper with an added chilli infused kick, Anise style! This sensational summer treat is sure to be a barbecue hit!

1 lemongrass stalk, outer layer removed and cut into 4 or 5 slices
45ml chilli-infused tequila (see below)
5ml Cointreau
5ml agave syrup
10ml orange juice
10ml mandarin purée (or fresh mandarin, satsuma or tangerine pulp)
20ml ginger beer
1 lemongrass stalk and 1 green chilli, slit, to garnish

For the infusion, deseed a green chilli and add it to a bottle of tequila. Leave it for about a week before using.

Muddle the lemongrass and chilli in a cocktail shaker. Add all the ingredients except the ginger beer and shake together with plenty of ice. Double-strain it into a tall glass filled with ice and top it up with ginger beer. Garnish the drink with lemongrass and a big chilli.

ANISE MARGARITA

Our smooth, fruity twist on a classic margarita served with silver tequila and a zest of fresh orange juice – perfect for a sunny afternoon.

10ml agave syrup
50ml silver tequila
20ml Cointreau
20ml orange juice
10ml crème de cassis
a slice of orange to garnish

Pour agave syrup in the centre of the pre-chilled martini glass. Then, in a cocktail shaker, add all the remaining ingredients except the cassis and shake well with ice. Strain the cocktail slowly into the martini glass on top of the agave syrup. Now you have two layers. Next slowly pour the cassis liqueur in to the centre of the cocktail so that the cassis sits in between the agave syrup and the orange margarita, giving the third layer.

Garnish the drink with a slice of orange and always serve the drink with a straw or a stirrer so that the person can mix the cocktail before drinking.

ASIAN ICED TEA

Ideal for those with a sweet tooth, this drink will give you a definite burst of energy! Just to mix it up, we have subsitututed the traditional cola mixture. Cheers!

10ml Stolichnaya vodka
10ml mescal
30ml Midori
20ml lime juice
100ml lemonade

Combine all the ingredients in a mixing glass except for the lemonade. Fill a sling glass with ice, and then add the lemonade. Top it up with the shaken drink, poured carefully so that it floats on top.

MANGO MOJITO
PAGE 249

BALADEVA
PAGE 246

ASIAN TEMPEST

Perfect for those who like a kick in their cocktail, the Asian Tempest has a delicious combination of watermelon and chilli that is sure to make your taste buds cheer.

2 slices of watermelon
10ml passion fruit syrup
50ml chilli-infused Grey Goose citron (see below)
30ml pineapple juice
1 chilli to garnish

For the infusion, deseed a green chilli and add it to the bottle of vodka. Leave it for about a week before using.

Muddle a slice of watermelon in a cocktail shaker. Add all the ingredients and shake well with ice. Double-strain the cocktail into a chilled martini glass. Garnish with a slice of watermelon and chilli.

BALADEVA

A tantalising burst of flavours combining Zubrowka and apple, Anise style! The perfect drink to kick back and relax with after a hard day's work!

50ml Zubrowka vodka
10ml lime juice
10ml cinnamon syrup (see Vivek's tip, below)
15ml pear purée (or 1 pear, cored and blitzed in a blender, or 2 fresh slices of pear, muddled)
20ml apple juice
50ml ginger ale
3 slices of green apple to garnish

Add all the ingredients except for the ginger ale to a cocktail shaker and shake well with ice. Strain the cocktail into a chilled sling glass. Top it up with ginger ale and garnish with 3 slices of green apple.

Vivek's tip
Cinnamon syrup is available from good off-licences. To make your own, bring 400ml of water and 4 cinnamon sticks to the boil and then simmer for 10 minutes. Remove the cinnamon sticks, bring the water back to the boil, add 340g of sugar and stir until it is fully dissolved. Pour into a bottle and store in a refrigerator for up to 2 weeks.

CINNAMON BELLINI

A magnificent mix of Assam tea, Goldschläger cinnamon schnapps, a few drops of cinnamon syrup and a few cinnamon sticks, topped with a splash of fizz. Our signature cocktail is breathtakingly refreshing and boozily seductive.

20ml cinnamon tea (made with Assam tea infused with cinnamon sticks, then allowed to cool)
5ml Goldschläger cinnamon schnapps
2ml cinnamon syrup (see Vivek's tip, below)
125ml Prosecco

Mix together the cinnamon tea, Goldschläger and cinnamon syrup in a Champagne flute and top it up with sparkling wine.

DUTCH COURAGE

You don't need courage to enjoy this drink, just some adventurous taste buds! The aromatic smell combined with the sweetness of the orange is sure to be a party hit.

2 slices of orange
1 green cardamom pod
50ml Bols Genever
10ml Cointreau
3ml cinnamon syrup (see Vivek's tip, opposite page)
15ml freshly squeezed orange juice

Muddle the cardamom and a slice of orange in a shaker. Add the rest of the ingredients and shake with plenty of ice. Double strain the cocktail into a chilled martini glass. Garnish the cocktail with a slice of orange.

ENGLAND 66

A commemorative drink that celebrates our country's love of football; the year we won the World Cup. The red-coloured martini commemorates the jerseys worn by our players. Top it off with a gold leaf and cheer your team to victory!

3 or 4 black peppercorns
50ml 42 Below manuka honey vodka
10ml strawberry purée (or fresh strawberries blitzed in a blender, or muddle one fresh strawberry)
5ml strawberry syrup
5ml cranberry juice
a strawberry and an optional gold leaf to garnish

Crush the black peppercorns in the shaker. Add the remaining ingredients and ice to the shaker and shake well. Strain into a chilled martini glass and garnish with the strawberry, and the gold leaf if using.

ENGLAND 2010

2010 may have not brought England victory, but fans will always stick by their team! This drink commemorates the jerseys worn by England in the 2010 World Cup. This vodka and fruit-infused drink is the perfect way to kick-start the sporting season!

8–10 red peppercorns
50ml Grey Goose pear vodka
20ml pear purée (or 1 pear, cored and blitzed in a blender, or 2 fresh slices of pear, muddled)
10ml apple juice
5ml orgeat syrup

Muddle the red peppercorns. Add the rest of the ingredients and shake with ice. Strain the mixture into a chilled martini glass.

SAFFRON MARTINI
PAGE 251

SPICED MARTINI
PAGE 252

KACHUMBER LEMONADE

A zesty, refreshing drink that will quench any thirst. The subtle taste of elderflower combined with the fresh cucumbers enhances the cool taste of the sparkling lemonade.

3 or 4 cucumber slices
1 cantaloupe melon slice
8–10 coriander leaves
50ml Bulldog gin
5ml elderflower cordial
5ml melon syrup
150ml lemonade
coriander leaves, cucumber or melon slices to garnish

Muddle the cucumber and the melon in a shaker and add the rest of the ingredients except the lemonade. Shake with plenty of ice. Double-strain the drink in a tall glass filled with ice and top up with lemonade. Garnish the drink with either a sprig of coriander or a slice of cucumber or melon.

KAMASUTRA MARTINI

A modern twist on the classic porn star martini. The fragrant aroma and sweetness of the cinnamon makes this drink incredibly desirable!

50ml Stolichnaya vodka
20ml passion fruit purée or 1 fresh passion fruit
5ml cinnamon syrup (see Vivek's tip, page 246)
10ml orange juice
30ml Prosecco

Mix everything in a cocktail shaker except for the Prosecco and strain into a chilled martini glass. Pour the Prosecco into a shot glass and place the shot glass inside the martini glass. Serve.

MANGO MOJITO

A new take on the classic mojito that combines delicious puréed mango and Bacardi rum. This lusciously fruity cocktail has become a staple summer cocktail – delicious and easy to make!

1 whole lime
8 or 9 mint leaves
1 teaspoon caster sugar
60ml mango purée (or the flesh of a fresh mango blitzed in a blender, or chunks of fresh mango, muddled)
50ml Bacardi rum
20ml Perrier water

Cut the lime into 6 wedges and add them to a tall glass. Add the mint leaves and sugar. Now slowly muddle the limes, making sure to just bruise the mint leaves and to get the juice out of the lime. Now add the mango purée and fill the glass with crushed ice. Add the Bacardi and then mix everything thoroughly with the help of a long spoon. Add more crushed ice, if required, and splash some Perrier on top.

PASSION FRUIT AND PINEAPPLE BLOSSOM

RASPBERRY AND THYME MARGARITA

RED DRAGON

Don't let the gentle name fool you; the sour passion fruit in this drink packs a bite! It's perfect with the sweet pineapple and smooth accent of a premium gin.

50ml Bloom gin
10ml passion fruit syrup
20ml passion fruit purée or
    1 fresh passion fruit
20ml pineapple juice
20ml elderflower cordial
a passion fruit sliced in half to garnish

Add all the ingredients to a cocktail shaker and shake with ice until you get a nice froth. Strain the cocktail into a sling glass filled with ice. Garnish the cocktail with fresh passion fruit.

A truly invigorating cocktail made with fresh fruits and herbs that will make your mouth water. This refreshingly delicious cocktail can be served either straight up or on the rocks.

50ml thyme-infused tequila (see below)
20ml raspberry purée (or a handful
    of fresh raspberries blitzed in a
    blender, or 4 fresh raspberries,
    muddled)
5ml Chambord
10ml lime juice
5ml agave syrup
10ml cranberry juice
a fresh raspberry and sprig of thyme
    to garnish

For the infusion, put 4 sprigs of thyme in a tequila bottle and let it infuse for a week.

Mix all the ingredients together in a cocktail shaker with ice. Shake well and then strain into a chilled martini glass. Garnish with a fresh raspberry and a sprig of thyme.

Fancy dancing the night away, samba style? This showstopper is based on the classic Brazilian drink with Anise's signature hot and sweet twist.

1 lime
50ml lemon-infused cachaça
    (see below)
8–10 red peppercorns
20ml pear purée (or 1 pear, cored
    and blitzed in a blender, or 2 fresh
    slices of pear, muddled)
5ml orgeat syrup
10ml apple juice
a slice of pear and crushed red
    peppercorns to garnish

For the infusion, remove the peel from half a lemon and cut into slices thin enough to slide into a bottle of cachaça. Leave it in a cool, dark place for a week to infuse, shake the bottle after a week and taste. By now it should be ready to use.

Cut the lime into 6 wedges and add them to a whisky tumbler. Muddle them with the red peppercorns in the bottom of the glass. Add the rest of the ingredients except for the apple juice and mix well. Fill the glass with crushed ice and top it up with apple juice. Stir before drinking, so the flavours mingle.

ROYAL BLOOM

SAFFRON MARTINI

Garnish the drink with a big slice of pear sprinkled with crushed red peppercorns and serve with 2 short straws.

Have a toast with this fragrantly charming cocktail. The fresh lychees combined with gin give a powerful, yet seductive punch.

3 fresh lychees, plus another for
    garnish
5ml violette syrup
50ml Bloom gin
3 or 4 fresh rosemary sprigs
10ml lime cordial
20ml cranberry juice
10ml blue curaçao
a sprig of rosemary to garnish

Muddle the lychees in a cocktail shaker, then add the rest of the ingredients and fill the shaker with ice. Shake well, then double strain into a chilled Champagne saucer. Garnish the drink with a fresh lychee and a rosemary sprig.

This daring new cocktail is dominated by the bold taste of saffron, which is infused for at least three days for maximum flavour. This innovative cocktail is given a sweet and nutty kick with the apple and orgeat.

50ml saffron-infused Bulldog gin
5ml orgeat syrup
15ml pear purée (or I pear, cored and
    blitzed in a blender, or 2 fresh slices
    of pear, muddled)
30ml apple juice
a few saffron strands to garnish

For the infusion, add a pinch of saffron to a full bottle of gin and leave it for about 3 days. Make sure you shake the bottle at least once a day.

Add all the ingredients to a cocktail shaker, fill with plenty of ice and shake well. Double-strain the cocktail into a chilled martini glass. Garnish the cocktail with few strands of saffron.

SPICED KIR ROYALE

SPICED MARTINI

This delicious mix takes a week to infuse, but we think it's worth every minute of the wait. Be warned: this spicy twist on a classic kir royale will make your taste buds tremor. Once you have your chilli-infused mix, top up with some champers and enjoy!

20ml chilli-infused crème de cassis
  (see below)
125ml Champagne
a fresh blackberry to garnish

For the infusion, deseed a green chilli and add it to a bottle of crème de cassis. Leave it for about a week before using.

Add the chilli-infused cassis to a Champagne flute and slowly top it up with Champagne. Garnish the drink with a fresh blackberry.

Cinnamon, spice and everything nice is the only way to describe this signature Martini. This sweet and fruity blend combined with the brave flavours of cinnamon and cardamom will make you the life and soul of the party.

50ml cinnamon- and cardamom-
  infused Stolichnaya vodka
  (see below)
10ml Chambord
20ml pineapple juice
30ml cranberry juice
2ml cinnamon syrup (see Vivek's tip,
  page 246)
1 star anise or a few strands of saffron,
  to garnish

For the infusion, add 2 sticks of cinnamon and 4 green cardamom pods to the vodka and leave the bottle for about 1 week. Make sure you shake the bottle once every day.

Put all the ingredients into a cocktail shaker and shake well for about 20 seconds. Strain the cocktail into a chilled martini glass, which will leave a nice foam layer on top. Place a full star anise in the centre of the foam to garnish.

CINNAMON BELLINI
PAGE 246

SPICED KIR ROYALE
PAGE 252

DESSERTS

This is an example of combining European dessert techniques with the exotic fruit and spices of India to create something new, light and healthy.

SERVES 4

COCONUT AND PEPPER MOUSSE WITH GUAVA SOUP

For the pineapple jelly
200ml pineapple juice
1 teaspoon vegetable gel powder or
    agar-agar

For the coconut and pepper mousse
2 leaves of gelatine
1 egg white
20g caster sugar
300g thick coconut purée
½ teaspoon black peppercorns, finely
    ground

For the guava soup
250ml guava juice
1 sprig of mint leaves, finely chopped
2cm piece of fresh ginger, peeled and
    finely chopped
juice of ½ lemon

various exotic fruit, such as melons,
    papaya, dragon fruit and pineapple,
    cut into 1cm dice, to decorate
coriander cress to garnish

To make the pineapple jelly, put the pineapple juice in a saucepan and bring to the boil. Whisk in the vegetable gel or agar-agar, then pour into a shallow tray and leave to cool and set. Cover and chill until required.

To make the coconut and pepper mousse, put the leaves of gelatine in a bowl with water to cover and leave to soak for 10 minutes. Meanwhile, beat the egg white until soft peaks form, then add the sugar and continue beating until a stiff, glossy meringue forms. After the gelatine has soaked, lift the leaves out of the water and squeeze to remove any water. Place the squeezed gelatine in a small pan over a low heat to melt, or microwave on Low. Add the melted gelatine to the meringue and stir in. Add the coconut purée and black pepper and fold them in, then divide the mixture between 4 moulds and chill until set.

To make the guava soup, mix all the ingredients together and chill until required.

When ready to serve, gently dip the moulds containing the mousse in hot water, then invert them and unmould into 4 soup bowls.

Unmould the pineapple jelly and cut it into small decorative shapes or into discs equal in size to the mousse. Divide the soup between the bowls, then garnish with the pineapple jelly and exotic fruit and serve quickly.

Kala khatta is one of my favourite flavours of the ice-lollies I used to enjoy as a child in India. In the days before ice cream was easily available, the ice lolly vendor's arrival was eagerly awaited on hot, balmy afternoons during the long summer holidays. Here at Cinnamon Kitchen, we've tried to re-create the memories of those hot summers with this sharp, acidic dessert. A hint of lemongrass adds an Indian flavour to the otherwise traditionally French lemon pots.

SERVES 6

LEMON POTS WITH KALA KHATTA SORBET AND INDIAN SPICED CHOCOLATE BISCUITS

For the lemon pots

300ml double cream
100g sugar
1 stick of lemongrass, outer layer removed and bruised
grated zest of 3 lemons
6 egg yolks
juice of 2 lemons
fresh redcurrants, to decorate
fresh mint leaves, to decorate
lemon slices, to decorate

For the kala khatta sorbet

500ml water
150g sugar
50g glucose powder
340g kala khatta syrup (or use 680ml blackberry juice boiled until reduced by half and left to cool, or 340ml crème de mûre)
25 ml lemon juice

For the Indian-spiced chocolate biscuits

85g butter, softened
70g soft brown sugar
185g caster sugar
1 egg white
1 teaspoon vanilla essence
150g plain white flour
60g cocoa powder
4 pinches of ground black pepper
4 pinches of red chilli powder or cayenne
1 teaspoon ground cinnamon
¼ teaspoon salt
¼ teaspoon bicarbonate of soda

1 teaspoon ajowan seeds
white chocolate, melted, to decorate

Firstly, make the sorbet. Pour the water, sugar and glucose into a pan and gently bring to a boil, reduce the heat and allow to simmer for 3–4 minutes. Remove the sorbet syrup from the heat, set aside and cool to room temperature. In a separate bowl combine the kala khatta syrup or blackberry purée and lemon juice and mix with the sorbet syrup. Depending on the size of the ice cream machine, pour the mixture in batches and allow 25 minutes of churning before transferring the mixture into containers for freezing.

Now make the lemon pots. Put the cream, sugar, lemongrass and lemon zest in a heavy-based saucepan and bring to the boil, stirring. Beat the egg yolks in a heatproof bowl and stir in the lemon juice, then whisk in the cream mixture, whisking constantly. Strain the mixture into 6 ramekins or other ovenproof containers, (more or fewer, depending on their size).

Place the ramekins in a roasting tray half full of hot water. Bake in an oven preheated to 150°C/Gas Mark 2 for 30 minutes, or until just set on the outside edge, but still wobbly in the centre. Remove from the tray and leave to cool, then chill until required.

To make the biscuits, using an electric mixer, cream the butter until smooth. Add both sugars and continue beating, on high speed, for one minute until fully incorporated. Add the egg white and vanilla and beat until smooth, scraping down the side of the bowl, as necessary. Sift over the flour, cocoa powder, ground spices, salt and bicarbonate of soda and beat, on a low speed, until a soft dough forms. Stir in the ajowan seeds.

Divide the dough into 2 equal portions, then use your hands to roll into 'logs' 2.5cm thick. Wrap tightly in clingfilm and chill for at least 10 minutes.

To bake, cut off slices 2–3mm thick and arrange on an oiled baking sheet. Transfer to an oven preheated to 180°C/Gas Mark 4 and bake for 11 minutes. Remove the biscuits from the oven and allow them to cool on wire racks. When cool, drizzle with white chocolate and place in the fridge to set, then put in an airtight container and store at room temperature.

Holy basil, also know as tulsi, is a much revered plant in India. It is not commonly used in cooking, although it's sometimes included in teas. It has a wonderful fragrance and a beautiful calming and purifying effect. I think it works particularly well in this dessert.

HOLY BASIL CRÈME BRÛLÉES WITH RED FRUIT COMPOTE

For the crème brûlées
1 litre double cream
50g holy basil
6 eggs
4 egg yolks
200g caster sugar
100g demerara sugar

For the red fruit compote
50g strawberries, hulled and
    quartered
50g raspberries, halved
50g redcurrants
50g blueberries, halved
100g caster sugar
10 lemon balm leaves, finely sliced

Put the cream and holy basil in a pan and bring to boiling point, then remove from the heat and leave to infuse for 20 minutes. Strain the cream, then return it to the pan and bring it to just below boiling point. Whisk the egg, egg yolks and sugar together in a bowl, then slowly pour in the cream, whisking constantly. Pour the mixture into 12 ramekins and place in a roasting tin half full of hot water. Bake in an oven preheated to 110°C/Gas Mark 1/4 for 30 minutes, or until just set. Remove the ramekins from the roasting tin and leave to cool, then chill.

To make the red fruit compote, gently mix together all the ingredients in a bowl, cover with clingfilm and leave to macerate for 2 hours.

To serve, sprinkle the demerara sugar over the holy basil brûlées and caramelise with a blowtorch or under a very hot grill. Leave until the top becomes crisp, then serve with the berry compote alongside.

This is a very fresh and light take on the ever-popular cheesecake, and it works particularly well with cherries when they are in season. When cherries aren't available, I like to serve it with the Red Fruit Compote (see page 259).

SERVES 4

HONEY AND LIME CHEESECAKE WITH MARINATED CHERRIES

120g thick strained Greek yoghurt (250g yoghurt that is left to drain overnight)
110g mascarpone cheese
60g clear honey
50g caster sugar
juice of 1 lime
finely grated zest of ½ lime
90g double cream, whipped

For the marinated cherries
200g cherries, some stoned and some left whole with the stalks still on
40g icing sugar
juice of 1 lime
2 mint leaves, finely chopped

4 Brandy Snap Tuiles, to serve (see page 280)

Mix together the Greek yoghurt and mascarpone cheese. Beat in the honey, sugar and lime juice and zest, then quickly and lightly fold in the whipped cream. Divide the mixture between 4 ring moulds lined with greaseproof paper, then cover with clingfilm and chill for at least 20 minutes, until set.

For the marinated cherries, mix all the ingredients together and refrigerate until required.

When ready to serve, unmould the cheesecakes by lifting out the ring moulds and peeling away the greaseproof paper and place on 4 plates, then surround with the cherries and serve with a brandy snap tuile on each plate (you can sit the cheesecakes inside the tuiles if you wish).

Kulfi is India's answer to ice cream, and there is little that beats mango kulfi when this luscious fruit is in season.

MANGO AND CHILLI SOUP WITH MANGO AND PISTACHIO KULFI

For the Mango and Chilli Soup

2 large ripe mangoes, peeled with flesh removed from the stone and puréed in a blender or liquidiser with 100ml of water
1 green chilli, finely chopped
2 mint leaves, finely shredded
juice of 2 limes
sugar, to taste (optional)
salt, to taste (optional)
1 fresh ripe mango, peeled and flesh cut into 5mm dice to garnish

For the Mango and Pistachio Kulfi

480ml evaporated milk
100g caster sugar
¼ teaspoon ground cardamom
¼ teaspoon ground fennel
a pinch of saffron strands
3 large ripe mangoes, peeled with flesh removed from the stone and puréed in a blender or liquidiser with 150ml of water
100g shelled pistachios, chopped

Start by making the kulfi. Put the evaporated milk and sugar in a pan and bring slowly to the boil, stirring to dissolve the sugar. Remove the pan from the heat, stir in the ground cardamom and fennel and the saffron. Set aside and cool to room temperature, then stir in the mango purée, mix together and transfer to the fridge to chill.

Place the mixture in an ice-cream machine and process towards freezing, according to the manufacturer's instructions, but you want to ensure it's not quite frozen. Transfer to a bowl, fold in the pistachio nuts, then divide between 10 kulfi moulds and freeze.

To make the soup, in a bowl beat together the mango purée, chilli, mint and lime juice and add sugar or salt, if required. Transfer the soup to the fridge to chill.

To serve, turn out the kulfi into 4 bowls, add the soup and sprinkle with the diced mango at the last moment.

Vivek's tip

Look for kulfi moulds in Asian food shops and cookware shops and from online suppliers. If you can't find any, you can use small yoghurt pots. To unmould, take the kulfi straight from the freezer and dip them up to the rim in hot water for a few seconds. Place one top down in a bowl, invert the mould and bowl and give a good shake - you should hear it drop out. Gently remove the mould and unmould the remainder.

I developed this dessert as an Indian take on a quintessential British favourite: treacle tart. It was created as part of the London Restaurant Festival celebrations in 2011. To my mind, this combines the best of both countries.

SERVES 12

CARROT-GINGER HALWA TART WITH BLACK CARDAMOM ICED DOUBLE CREAM

100g ghee or clarified butter
500g carrots, grated
100g caster sugar
1 tablespoon raisins
250ml evaporated milk
50g piece of fresh ginger, peeled and finely chopped
3 green cardamom pods, ground

For the tart base
150g plain white flour, plus extra for rolling
40g icing sugar
80g cold unsalted butter, diced
1 egg, beaten

For the tart filling
4 eggs
2 egg yolks
250g treacle

For the iced double cream
50g caster sugar
1 tablespoon milk powder
175ml whole milk
50ml double cream
4 pods black cardamom, seeds removed and crushed

First make the tart base. Mix together the flour and icing sugar in a mixing bowl. Rub in the butter to get a breadcrumb texture, then add the egg and mix until a soft dough forms. Wrap in clingfilm and chill for 20 minutes.

Meanwhile, make the halwa. Heat the ghee in a heavy-based saucepan, add the carrots and cook gently, stirring, for 10 minutes, until the juice from the carrots has evaporated. Add the sugar and raisins and cook until the sugar melts. Add the evaporated milk and cook on a medium heat, stirring constantly, until the mixture looks like orange fudge. Stir in the ginger and cardamom, then spread the mixture on a baking tray and leave to cool.

Roll the dough out thinly on a lightly floured surface and use to line a 23cm loose-bottomed tart tin. Prick the base all over with a fork, then place in the fridge for about 20 minutes.

To make the iced double cream, mix together the sugar and milk powder in a heavy-based saucepan. Add the whole milk and cream and bring to the boil. Pour into a blender or food processor and quickly blitz. Strain into an ice cream maker, and when it is almost frozen, fold in the black cardamom pods and finish churning. Transfer to the freezer.

Alternatively, pour into a shallow container and place in the freezer, until semi-frozen. Then transfer to a chilled bowl and whisk well to break down the ice crystals. Return to the container and place in the freezer again. Repeat the process 3 or 4 times. Leave until frozen.

Remove the tart case from the fridge and cover with baking parchment or clingfilm and weigh down with rice or baking beans. Bake in an oven preheated to 140°C/Gas Mark 1 for 40 minutes.

Meanwhile, to make the filling, put 500g of the carrot halwa in a bowl and mix in the eggs, egg yolks and treacle. Remove the paper and rice or beans from the pastry case and pour in the filling carefully. Return the tart to the oven preheated to 120°C/Gas Mark ½ and bake for 40 minutes, until the filling is just set.

Leave the tart to cool on a wire rack for a few minutes, then carefully remove it from the tin. Cut into slices and serve with a scoop of the iced double cream.

MANDARIN AND CHILLI SORBET

GREEN MANGO SORBET

I love this sorbet for its fresh, clean taste. It pairs very well with most chocolate desserts and I particularly love the way that the heat from the chillies comes through later.

SERVES 4

200ml mandarin purée (often available in frozen form)
200ml water
50g caster sugar
grated zest of I lemon
½ teaspoon finely chopped green chilli
1½ tablespoons liquid glucose

Put the mandarin purée, water and sugar in a heavy-based pan and heat gently, stirring occasionally, until the sugar has dissolved. Increase the heat and simmer gently for 20 minutes, skimming off the scum that has gathered on the surface. Add the lemon zest, chilli and liquid glucose and leave to cool.
Place in an ice-cream machine and freeze according to the manufacturer's instructions. Alternatively, pour into a shallow container and place in the freezer until semi-frozen, then remove and stir briskly with a fork to break down the ice crystals. Return to the freezer and repeat these processes 3 or 4 times, then freeze until the sorbet is firm.

This draws inspiration from the quintessential favourite summer drink made with cooked, green mangoes and cumin. Well, ours has just had a makeover and turned into a sorbet – how cool!

SERVES 4

4 green mangoes
finely grated zest and juice of I lime
60g caster sugar
300ml water
50g liquid glucose
I teaspoon cumin seeds, roasted
I tablespoon finely chopped mint leaves

Put the green mangoes in a baking tray and roast in an oven preheated to 190°C/Gas Mark 5 for 25–30 minutes, until they are softened. Set aside and leave to cool completely, then peel, de-seed and strain the pulp, which should amount to about 200ml.

Mix together the green mango pulp with lime zest and juice, sugar, water, liquid glucose and cumin seeds. Place in an ice cream machine and freeze according to the manufacturer's instructions, adding the mint leaves just before the sorbet finishes churning. Transfer to the freezer until required.

Alternatively, pour into a shallow container and place in the freezer, until semi-frozen. Then transfer to a chilled bowl and whisk well to break down the ice crystals. Return to the container and place in the freezer again. Repeat the process 3 or 4 times. Leave until frozen.

Tapioca kheer is something Hindus eat when they are fasting during religious festivals. Tapioca is one of the few starches allowed during these religious festivals and, therefore, used a lot at those times, but not often otherwise. Even though it's not very traditional to team tapioca and citrus, I like the zingy effect of orange zest and the acidity works well with the clean taste of tapioca. This pineapple carpaccio is very simple, clean and salad-like, and works well as a light dessert option.

SERVES 6

PINEAPPLE CARPACCIO WITH TAPIOCA KHEER

½ pineapple, peeled, cored and sliced finely, ideally using a mandoline or a thin knife
1 teaspoon pink peppercorns, crushed
2cm piece of fresh ginger, peeled and finely chopped
1 teaspoon clear honey
juice of ½ lime
coriander cress to garnish

For the Tapioca Kheer
2 tablespoons ghee or vegetable oil
120g tapioca
750ml milk
2 green cardamom pods
grated zest of 1 orange
2 teaspoons sultanas
50g granulated sugar

Heat the ghee in a heavy-based saucepan, add the tapioca and fry, stirring, for 2–3 minutes. Add the milk and cardamom pods and bring to the boil. Reduce the heat and simmer for 20 minutes, stirring occasionally, until the tapioca has softened. Add the orange zest and raisins and stir for 3–4 minutes. Add the sugar and stir until it has completely dissolved. Remove the pan from the heat and leave the tapioca to cool.

Meanwhile, make the pineapple carpaccio. Put the pineapple, pink peppercorns, ginger, honey and lime juice in a non-metallic bowl and gently mix together. Place in the fridge until required.

Just before serving, gently stir the carpaccio again, then sprinkle with coriander cress leaves and serve with the tapioca kheer.

I love the beautiful green colour and the incredibly deep flavour of pistachio in this cake and it works wonderfully with the slight hint of background flavour of long peppers in the ice-cream. We use both butter and olive oil for this recipe, but you can make the cake with just olive oil if you prefer. The long pepper we use here is 'piper longum', the Indian long pepper. It has a mild pepperiness, and deep, haunting woody notes that help to make this dessert unique. You should be able to buy it from specialist suppliers online.

SERVES 4-6

SPICED PISTACHIO CAKE WITH LONG PEPPER ICE-CREAM AND SATSUMA CHUTNEY

100g ground pistachios
25g plain white flour
25g coarse semolina
1/2 teaspoon baking powder
a pinch of ground cardamom
a pinch of ground black pepper
50g butter, melted
3 tablespoons olive oil
1 tablespoon vegetable oil
100g caster sugar
2 eggs
juice and grated zest of 1/2 lemon
juice of 1/2 orange

For the long pepper ice cream
200ml milk
200ml double cream
4 tablespoons liquid glucose
50g granulated sugar
7 long peppers
3 egg yolks

For the satsuma chutney
2 tablespoons vegetable oil
2.5cm piece of cinnamon stick
1 bay leaf
1 dried red chilli
8 satsumas, peeled, separated into segments and deseeded
50g granulated sugar

First make the ice cream. Put the milk, cream, liquid glucose, sugar and long peppers in a pan and slowly bring to the boil, stirring occasionally to dissolve the sugar. Remove from the heat and strain into a bowl to remove the peppers. Lightly whisk the egg yolks, then gradually whisk into the milk mixture. Pour into an ice-cream machine and freeze. Alternatively, pour into a shallow container and place in the freezer, until semi-frozen. Then transfer to a chilled bowl and whisk well to break down the ice crystals. Return to the container and place in the freezer again. Repeat the process 3 or 4 times. Leave until frozen.

For the pistachio cake, combine all the dry ingredients in a bowl, apart from the sugar. Mix the butter and the oils together. Whisk the sugar and the eggs together, gradually adding the butter and the oil mixture. Gently fold in the flour mix, followed by the zest and the juices. Pour the mixture into a greased 15cm springform cake tin and bake in an oven preheated to 160°C/Gas Mark 3 for 30 minutes, or until a cocktail stick inserted in the centre comes out clean. Leave to cool completely on a wire rack. Meanwhile, make the satsuma

chutney. Heat the oil in a heavy-based pan to smoking point and add the cinnamon stick, bay leaf and chilli. When they give off their aromas, add the satsumas and stir on a medium-low heat for 3–4 minutes, until they have softened. Add the sugar, stirring until it dissolves, then reduce the heat and cook on a low heat, stirring, for 15–20 minutes, until the mixture thickens. Remove from the heat and leave to cool.

To serve, place slices of the pistachio cake on plates with the satsuma chutney and serve the long pepper ice cream alongside.

Possibly the longest-serving dessert at The Cinnamon Club, Cinnamon Kitchen and now at Cinnamon Soho, this dish has had so many makeovers that I've lost count. Our latest version includes caramelised pear halves, served on a yoghurt and raisin mix with pieces of saffron jelly and coriander cress.

SERVES 4

SAFFRON-POACHED PEAR

2 William pears (not too ripe)
600ml water
250g caster sugar
a generous pinch of saffron strands
5cm piece of cinnamon stick
5 green cardamom pods
2 star anise
50g demerara sugar
I quantity of Saffron Jelly (page 281), to decorate
IO sprigs of coriander cress, to decorate

For the raisin raita
200g Greek yoghurt
2 tablespoons raisins
I tablespoon chopped fresh coriander leaves and stalks

Peel the pears, leaving the stems on, and put them in a bowl of water to prevent discolouration. Put the water, sugar, saffron, cinnamon, cardamom and star anise in a saucepan in which the pears will just fit upright. Slowly bring to the boil, stirring to dissolve the sugar. Add the pears, reduce the heat and poach for 15–20 minutes, until the pears are tender, but still slightly firm. Remove from the poaching liquid and leave the pears to cool. Increase the heat, bring the poaching liquid to the boil and allow it to reduce by half. Once you have a syrupy liquid, remove from the heat and set aside.

When the pears are cool, cut them in half lengthways and remove the cores and any pips. (You may wish not to core them so as to present them as we have opposite – in which case be sure to warn your guests!)

Mix together all the ingredients for the raisin raita and spoon on to 4 plates. Place the pear halves upright on a baking sheet, sprinkle the demerara sugar over the halves and caramelise with a blowtorch or under a very hot grill. Leave until the glaze becomes crisp, then add to the plates, decorate with saffron jelly, spoon over the poaching liquid, sprinkle with coriander cress and serve.

Lots of chefs pair strawberries with good aged balsamic, and I once tried Heston Blumenthal's strawberries with coriander at The Fat Duck. At the time our menu included cardamom shrikhand which was paired with fresh strawberries, and I thought it would work with tamarind chutney. We tried, and it works very well, so here it is.

SERVES 4-6

SHRIKHAND CHEESECAKE WITH FENNEL- AND CORIANDER-FLAVOURED STRAWBERRIES

For the cheesecake
250g strained Greek yoghurt (500g yoghurt that is left to drain overnight)
100g mascarpone cheese
100ml double cream, whipped to soft peaks
50g caster sugar
½ teaspoon ground cardamom

For the crumble base
250g plain white flour
250g caster sugar
180g ground almonds
250g cold salted butter, diced

For the fennel- and coriander-flavoured strawberries
250g strawberries, hulled and some sliced and some left whole (or use any other berries in season)
grated zest and juice of ½ lime
2 mint leaves, finely shredded
I teaspoon fennel seeds, roasted and crushed
I teaspoon coriander seeds, roasted and crushed
a pinch of salt
a pinch of sugar

To make the crumble base, mix together the flour, sugar and ground almonds, then rub in the butter until the mixture resembles coarse crumbs. Spread on a baking tray lined with greaseproof paper and bake in an oven preheated to 180°C/Gas Mark 4 for 10–12 minutes, until golden brown. Remove from the pan and leave to cool, then use your fingertips to break into fine crumbles.

For the cheesecake, gently fold together all the ingredients and chill for 20 minutes.

To assemble the cheesecake, press a layer of the crumble about 1.5cm thick in a 15cm springform cake tin. Add the cheesecake mixture, smooth the surface and place in the fridge to chill for at least 2 hours.

Meanwhile, prepare the strawberries. Put the strawberries in a non-metallic bowl, add the remaining ingredients and toss gently. Leave to macerate for 10–15 minutes.

Slice or scoop the cheesecake onto serving plates and serve with the strawberries dotted around. In the restaurant we add a strawberry caramel tuile. The Saffron Caramel Tuiles on page 280 would also work well.

I recently discovered how well this traditional south Indian-style kheer, sweetened with jaggery, tastes with fresh mangoes when they're in season. Give it a go! The kheer is so versatile it can be served hot or chilled, either on its own or as a substitute for custard with Christmas pudding!

SERVES 6

SOUTH INDIAN MOONG LENTIL KHEER WITH FRESH MANGO

50g yellow moong lentils
35g basmati rice
1 tablespoon ghee or vegetable oil
500ml water
1 litre whole milk
100g jaggery, molasses sugar or
    unrefined muscovado sugar
pinch of ground cinnamon
50ml made up coconut cream
2 ripe mangoes, peeled and sliced, to
    serve

For tempering
1 tablespoon ghee or vegetable oil
20g cashew nuts
10g raisins

Wash the lentils and rice separately under cold running water, then leave to soak separately for 15 minutes.

Heat the ghee in a heavy-based saucepan to smoking point. Add the lentils and stir until they turn golden brown. Add the water and let the lentils simmer on a low heat for 20–25 minutes, until they are almost half cooked. Stir in the rice and milk and cook, stirring, for 20 minutes, or until the rice is just cooked.

Stir in the jaggery or sugar and cook for another 10–15 minutes, until the mixture coats the back of a wooden spoon. Stir constantly and take care that the lentils and rice do not catch on the bottom of the pan. Add the cinnamon powder and coconut cream and cook for another 5 minutes, until the mixture has a custard-like consistency. Remove the pan from the heat.

For tempering, heat the ghee in a heavy-based frying pan to smoking point and add the cashew nuts and raisins. When the cashew nuts turn golden brown, immediately pour this mixture on to the kheer. Serve the pudding hot or chilled with the slices of fresh mango.

We had realised pretty early on during the opening of Cinnamon Kitchen that, if we were to stand any chance of getting people to have three courses, we could not have just traditional Indian desserts like halwa, gulab jamuns or ras malai. We decided to either lighten up Indian desserts or spice up Western desserts. This is an example of how we gave a popular European dessert the spice treatment. When I can get them, I like to use the small Indian bananas that have a nice acidity and sharpness to them; but feel free to substitute with regular bananas, if you prefer. The tart is also enhanced by the delicate aromatic spice and bite of the pink peppercorns.   SERVES 4-6

SPICED BANANA TARTE TATIN

4 bananas
½ teaspoon pink peppercorns,
    coarsely crushed
150g puff pastry

For the caramel
150g granulated sugar
50ml water
15g butter, plus extra for greasing the
    tin

To make the caramel, put the granulated sugar and water in a small, heavy-based pan and heat gently, stirring occasionally, until the sugar has melted. Increase the heat and cook, without stirring, until it forms a dark golden caramel. Add the butter, standing well back in case it splutters, then simmer for 8 minutes. Remove the pan from the heat and pour into a greased 20cm cake tin to coat the base. Leave until cool and set.

Peel and slice the bananas and arrange them in overlapping circles on top of the set caramel. Sprinkle the pink peppercorns over. Now roll out the puff pastry to about 3mm thick and cut out a 23cm round. Cover the bananas with the pastry, tucking the edge down inside the tin. Bake in an oven preheated to 190°C/Gas Mark 5 for about 15 minutes, until the pastry puffs up and turns golden. Remove the tart from the oven and invert it on to a plate so the bananas are on top. Alternatively, you could make individual tarts, as we do in the restaurant (see picture), using 12cm discs of pastry and smaller tins. The larger tart is an easier one to make and share at home.

Serve hot with ice cream such as Black Cardamom Iced Double Cream (see page 264).

This is a selection of desserts inspired by the religious offerings made in temples across different parts of India. Some of my most memorable dessert experiences while growing up in India are linked to visits to different temples and the different offerings being prepared and distributed at these festivals. Following are three of the most distinct memories.

PRASAD

PANCHAMRUTH OR CHARAN AMRUTH

Amruth literally means 'immortal nectar', and this is a combination of five (panch) immortal nectars (amruths), or ingredients.

⅓ banana
50ml milk
50ml Greek yoghurt
30g granulated sugar
2 teaspoons clear honey

Blend all the ingredients and chill for 30 minutes. Serve as a lassi in a small cup or bowl.

SOOJI HULWA OR KESARI

A typical semolina pudding served in Sikh temples every Sunday.

2 teaspoons ghee or vegetable oil
10 raisins
5 cashew nuts
50g coarse semolina
50g sugar
4 strands of saffron (optional)
150ml milk or water

Melt the ghee in a heavy-based saucepan and add the raisins and the cashew nuts. When the raisins puff up, add the semolina and stir until the grains are golden. Add the sugar and saffron and slowly pour in the milk or water, stirring constantly to prevent lumps from forming. Cook on a low heat for 2–3 minutes, until the pudding leaves the sides of the pan. Divide between 4 bowls and serve hot.

PANJIRI

This is an Indian style-crumble, served as an offering in temples all over northern and eastern India.

2 tablespoons ghee or vegetable oil
4 tablespoons wholemeal flour
2 tablespoons granulated sugar
20g jaggery or molasses sugar
1 green cardamom pod, pounded to a powder in a mortar and pestle

Heat the ghee in a heavy-based pan, add the flour and stir on a low heat until it turns golden brown. Add the granulated sugar and jaggery or molasses sugar and continue stirring until the mixture becomes crumbly. Stir in the cardamom.

To serve, arrange a little of each mixture on 4 plates, and serve the panchamrut chilled, the sooji hulwa hot and the panjiri at room temperature.

No matter what kind of a restaurant you run, you need at least one good chocolate dessert, and this is one of the most popular desserts at Cinnamon Kitchen. Ever.

SERVES 4-6

VALRHONA CHOCOLATE FONDANT AND COFFEE PARFAIT

For the coffee parfait
175ml double cream
3 leaves of gelatine
100ml water
50g caster sugar
3 egg yolks
2 tablespoons instant coffee granules, dissolved in 3 tablespoons boiling water

For the chocolate fondant
125g Valrhona chocolate (we use 55% cocoa)
100g unsalted butter, chopped
2 eggs
80g caster sugar
50g plain white flour
2 teaspoons cocoa powder
½ teaspoon baking powder

To make the coffee parfait, whisk the cream until stiff peaks form, then set aside in the fridge. Soak the gelatine in cold water to cover for 10 minutes.

Put the water and sugar in a large saucepan and stir to dissolve the sugar, then boil, without stirring, until it reaches 118°C on a sugar thermometer. Remove the pan from the heat.

Squeeze out excess water from the soaked gelatine and whisk it into the syrup. Add the egg yolks and dissolved coffee. Fold in the whipped cream. Pour into a deep baking tray lined with clingfilm and use a wet palette knife to spread to a thickness of 1cm. Leave to cool, then transfer to the fridge to set.

For the chocolate fondant, melt the chocolate with the butter in bowl placed over simmering water (take care to ensure the bowl isn't touching the water), then remove from the heat and leave to cool.

Meanwhile, whisk the eggs and sugar together until thick and creamy. Mix together the flour, cocoa powder and baking powder. Fold the cooled chocolate mixture into the eggs, then fold in the flour mixture. Spoon the mixture into 4 greased 4cm metal ring moulds on a baking sheet lined with a silicone mat or a baking tray lined with greaseproof paper. Transfer to an oven preheated to 180°C/Gas Mark 4 and bake for 8-9 minutes, until the mixture starts to rise up and shrinks back from the moulds.

Meanwhile, invert the coffee parfait on to a cutting board, peel off the clingfilm and cut to whatever shape you wish.

Remove the fondants from the oven to rest for a minute or so, then carefully unmould with a small knife and transfer to 4 plates. Serve immediately with coffee parfait pieces.

BRANDY SNAP TUILES

SAFFRON CARAMEL TUILES

Perfect for desserts such as Honey and Lime Cheesecake with Marinated Cherries (page 261).

MAKES 10 TUILES

25g icing sugar
25g butter
25g liquid glucose
25g plain flour

Whisk the sugar and butter until light and fluffy. Add the flour and liquid glucose and mix until well combined. Wrap the dough in clingfilm, rolling it to form a fat sausage, and set aside in the fridge for 30 minutes to chill. Unwrap the dough and slice into 10 and place on a baking sheet. Flatten each slice into thin discs either using a rolling pin or pressing with your fingers to spread evenly.

Bake the tuiles in an oven preheated to 180°C/Gas Mark 4 for 5–6 minutes, until golden brown. Remove from the oven, allow to cool just enough to be able to handle them and, while still warm and pliable, shape them around a rolling pin or jam jar. Cool and store the tuiles in a cool, dry air-tight container for 2–3 days away from moisture. Should they go soft, they can be reheated slightly and become crisp again once cooled.

This is a useful garnish to adorn the fruits of your labour.

600g caster sugar
400g liquid glucose
a pinch of saffron, soaked in
    3 tablespoons hot water for
    10 minutes

Combine the sugar and liquid glucose in a heavy-based pan and stir until the sugar dissolves. Strain in the saffron-infused water and cook, without stirring, on a high heat until the mixture reaches 150°C on a sugar thermometer. Pour out onto a silicone baking mat on a baking sheet or onto a baking tray lined with greaseproof paper, and use a wet palette knife to spread into an even layer. Once cool, break the caramel and transfer to a food processor and quickly blitz until a fine powder forms. Store in an air-tight container until required.

When ready to bake, sprinkle the ground caramel thinly on to a silicone baking mat or baking tray lined with greaseproof paper and place in an oven preheated to 180°C/Gas Mark 4 and bake for about 4–5 minutes, until the sugar melts and forms a thin film. Remove from the oven and let cool, then break into smaller pieces to use as a garnish for any of your desserts.

CHOCOLATE CUMIN SAUCE

SAFFRON JELLY

This is a good recipe for a spiced chocolate sauce that works well to decorate a plate or simply to dunk your biscuits into. Feel free to replace the cumin with chilli flakes for that extra kick!

250ml milk
75g caster sugar
20g cocoa powder
½ teaspoon cumin seeds, roasted and
    lightly crushed
225g dark chocolate with at least
    70% cocoa, chopped
2 drops of vanilla extract

Mix together the milk, sugar, cocoa powder and cumin seeds in a heavy-based saucepan and bring to the boil, stirring to dissolve the sugar. Put the chocolate and vanilla in a heatproof bowl and pour the boiling mixture over them, stirring until the chocolate melts. Transfer to a jug to cool, then seal for later use. The sauce can be kept for up to a week in the fridge.

A by-product of the saffron poached pears we make at the restaurant (see page 271). The poaching liquor is reduced a little, then turned into a jelly, either to add a new texture on the plate as a garnish, or to be served on its own rolled in caster sugar as a petit four.

100ml water
75g caster sugar
a pinch of saffron strands
1 green cardamom pod
1 star anise
1g vegetable gel or 2g agar-agar

Bring the water to the boil in a heavy-based saucepan and stir in the sugar until it dissolves. Remove the pan from the heat, add the saffron strands and leave for about 30 minutes to infuse. Add the cardamom and star anise, return the pan to a low heat and simmer for 5 minutes.

Whisk in the vegetable gel, stirring to dissolve. Pour into a shallow tray or any other mould and leave to cool and then chill for about 30 minutes, until set. Unmould and cut into cubes or any desired shape to use as a decoration on any dessert, for an extra dimension.

INDEX

tadka 27
tandoori:
    tandoori dishes 25
    chicken with fennel and coriander 51
    king prawns with kedgeree 97
    paneer with broccoli and peppers
        152
    paneer with tomato fenugreek
        sauce 148
    pigeon with green pea and yoghurt
        194
    potato wedges 92
    prawns with kedgeree 97
    salmon rillettes 205
    spiced oysters 41
tapioca: kheer with pineapple 267
tenderising 25
terrines: rabbit and pistachio 56
tilapia: spice-crusted with kokum
    curry 101
tomatoes:
    broth with curry leaf 46
    chilled soup with green mango 58
    chutney 208
    chutney with coconut 238
    chutney with onion seed 22
    rasam with lentil fritters 61
    salad 241
    sauce with fenugreek 148
    seared scallops with mushrooms
        and lime leaf 36
    tuiles 280
tuna: ceviche with scallop and
    salmon 32

Valrhona chocolate fondant and
    coffee parfait 279
vegetables:
    asparagus with spices and
        yoghurt 191
    beetroot stir-fried with saddle of
        venison 136
    biryani in a pumpkin shell 150
    Bombay spiced in cumin pao 206
    gourd with spiced minced lamb 184
    Jerusalem artichoke podimas 236
    marrow and lentils 224
    minced kebab with dried figs 68
    petits pois stir fried with sea bass 102
    red chard with stir-fried shrimp 42
    roasted in spinach curry 141
    stir-fried greens with garlic and
        cumin 220
    stuffed courgettes with potatoes
        and yoghurt 146
    see also aubergine; broccoli;
        carrots; cauliflower; fennel;
        mushrooms; onions; peas;
        potatoes; spinach; sweetcorn

venison: roast saddle with stir-fried
    beetroot 136

walnuts: chilli with partridge 178
Wild African prawns with peanuts
    and coconut 161

yoghurt:
    curried 23, 191
    kadhi sauce 225
    and pea shot 194
    rice 80
    sauce with cornmeal 132
    sauce with potatoes and
        courgettes 146

THANKS

Abdul Yaseen, without whom there wouldn't have been a Cinnamon Kitchen, let alone a Cinnamon Kitchen cookbook.

The team at Cinnamon Kitchen and Anise, who've made light of the worst recession known to our generation and established CK as the City's favourite Indian.

Awanish Roy, Mor Singh Jakhi, Narendra Yadav, Palash Mitra and Rakesh Nair for help with recipes.

All of you who've attended our cooking masterclasses over the years and helped me collect and correct recipes.

Jon Croft, for believing in a Cinnamon Kitchen cookbook. Lara Holmes, Lucy Bridgers and Matt Inwood, for your patience.

Shanna Manross for keeping it together.

Maya, Eshaan and Archana for all the weekends you lost while I worked on this book. Thank you.